GRAHAM BOWER

secondomics

how coming second can be a winning strategy

Polymath Books, London

Polymath Books
9a Rupert House
Nevern Square
London
SW5 9PL

www.secondomics.com

First published in the UK in 2009 by Polymath Books
This edition 2009

© Graham Bower 2009

Graham Bower asserts the moral right to be
identified as the author of this work

Designed by Graham Bower

Printed by Lulu.com

All rights reserved. No part of this book may be reprinted
or reproduced or utilized in any form or by any electronic,
mechanical, or other means, now known or hereafter
invented, including photocopying and recording, or in
any information storage or retrieval system, without
permission in writing from the publishers.

ISBN 978-0-9561599-0-8 (Trade Paperback)

To the team at the Royal Marsden Hospital in London, who treated my cancer and gave me a second chance in life, and to my partner, Martin, who had been through it himself and showed me that second chances can happen.

Graham Bower, 2009

SECONDOMICS

Contents

Introduction
The winner doesn't always take it all 7
How secondomics works 8
Sharing second place 10

Part 1 - The advantages of leadership
Chapter 1: First Place - what is it, and why do we want it? 13

Part 2 - The disadvantages of leadership
Chapter 2: It can be tough at the top 21

Part 3 - The advantages of second
Chapter 3: Disproportionate share of payoff 40
Chapter 4: Coasting in the slipstream 46
Chapter 5: Cover from threats ahead 52
Chapter 6: Enemy in your sights 59
Chapter 7: Learning from the leader 61
Chapter 8: Room for growth 73
Chapter 9: Total cost of ownership 77
Chapter 10: Supporting the underdog 84

Part 4 - The disadvantages of second
Chapter 11: Sometimes the winner does take it all 90
Chapter 12: Tripping over a fallen leader 93
Chapter 13: Decoys & fall guys 96
Chapter 14: Punishing losers 101
Chapter 15: Becoming predictable and learning the wrong lessons 104
Chapter 16: Punishing cheats 109
Chapter 17: Leadership anxiety 115

CONTENTS

Chapter 18: When two is one too many 116

Part 5 - Secondomics over time
Chapter 19: Anticipating competitor behavior 131
Chapter 20: Anticipating change 133
Chapter 21: What's the frequency? 135
Chapter 22: Resource depletion 145

Part 6 - Leadership bias
Chapter 23: Dualism and zero-sum fallacy .151
Chapter 24: Leadership bias in groups 157

Part 7 - Secondomics in practice
Chapter 25: Secondomics at work 166
Chapter 26: Secondomics in life 186

Conclusion
Attitudes to risk - America vs Britain 197
Second class - a word by any other name .199
The undercover seconomist 200

End notes
Appendix I 202
Appendix II 206
Appendix III 209
Glossary 212
Bibliography 218
Aknowledgements 220

Introduction

"The Winner Takes It All" was an international smash hit for the Swedish pop group ABBA. It epitomizes the popularly held belief that dating, like so many things in life, is a win-lose game, where the amorous victor claims his true love, leaving other unsuccessful suitors with nothing more than melancholy lyrics. If we allow that society is entirely monogamous, and that the popular truism "there are plenty more fish in the sea" is in fact a fallacy, then perhaps we can accept that the winner does indeed take it all. But few things in life are really this clear cut. The winner in a mating ritual may claim the fittest mate, but it is unlikely that he could claim *all* of the available mates - "taking it all" as ABBA would have it. In other words, if you don't get your number one choice, you needn't go without. Ironically, the song "The Winner Takes It All" perfectly illustrates this very point - whilst it only reached number two in the charts in ABBA's native Sweden, it went on to top the charts elsewhere.

Winners rarely "take all" in practice, but they do have a tendency to take more than their fair share of the credit. Consider John Adams, the oft-forgotten second president of the United States. He played a major role in the American Revolution, helping Benjamin Franklin to negotiate peace with Britain and establishing essential financing for the fledgling nation. And yet we have a tendency to focus almost exclusively on his predecessor, the tree-chopping first president, George Washington. Whilst there's no doubting Washington's impressive credentials as a national hero, the revolution, like any popular movement, was more than the work of one man. Adams' contribution was significant, and yet he receives less credit for his efforts than perhaps he deserves.

So why do we focus on those who come first, at the expense of those who follow? As human beings, we have a tendency to perceive life as a series of win-lose encounters, where there is always a clear winner and a loser, and the winner's spoils always come at the loser's expense. But in practice, this is rarely the case. For every win-lose situation, there are at least as many examples of win-win scenarios, where opposing sides could both benefit from cooperation. And yet our language, culture and even our brains themselves seem biased in favor of win-lose scenarios. This flawed view of the world can lead us to make mistakes. Some of these mistakes may be big ones - like refusing to negotiate with an enemy. Whilst others may be smaller, like paying over the odds to dine in the most fashionable restaurant, when a more pleasant evening could be had at a quieter, less pricey establishment. In both cases, our tendency to blindly focus on leadership (winning the war, or dining in the most popular restaurant) precludes the possibility of our exploring alternatives that may prove to be preferable. This kind of behavior is evidence of what I call "leadership bias".

Of course we admire winners. That's only human nature. But the benefits of winning are often so evident that they can distract us from the significant advantages that second place affords. Sometimes, those advantages are so great that they may in fact outweigh the benefits of coming first. For example, have you ever watched someone at a news stand put the magazine that they were browsing back on the shelf and instead purchase the one from behind, even though it seems to be an identical copy? Have you ever ordered the second cheapest bottle of wine on the menu? Or have you ever puzzled over why birds flock in a v-shaped formation? Curiously enough, these are all different aspects of the same phenomenon. A phenomenon so seemingly inconsequential that we're often unaware of it, and yet it exerts such a powerful influence that it has helped to steer the very course of evolution, and continues to influence our behavior to this day. It's the relative utility of second place, or "Secondomics" for short.

How secondomics works

How can the benefits of coming second ever outweigh the benefits of coming first? A few years ago, my parents moved up North, which means that now, in order to visit them, I must drive all the way from London to Carlisle. That's a long drive. Imagine that I was on my way home from my parents, I was in a hurry, and I was prepared to exceed the speed limit. (Of course I would never actually do such a thing, this is just a thought experiment!) How much should I exceed the speed limit by? Supposing that the shortest possible journey time was my only criteria for consideration, then I should drive as fast as my car can travel. In practice, however, I would need to factor in the risk of getting caught by the police for speeding. I must therefore moderate my speed intelligently to minimize this risk. So how much should I reduce my speed by? The answer is simple, and it lies at the heart of secondomics: I should reduce my speed to ensure at all times that another motorist within close proximity to me

INTRODUCTION

is traveling faster, or if no other speed violators are around, I should stick to the speed limit. In doing so, I maximize my potential speed whilst minimizing my risk of getting stopped by the police, since whenever I am speeding, there is always a more serious speeding violation taking place in my vicinity, to divert the police officer's attention.

So what is happening here? Can we infer a generalized principle of secondomics? In this case, a shorter journey time is the *advantage* of being first. But we've also said that a greater risk of getting caught by the police is a unique *disadvantage* of being first. For the driver in second place, the journey time is almost as good as the driver in front, but the risk of being caught by the police is substantially lowered. Where a specific disadvantage applies to being in first place, and this disadvantage outweighs the difference in advantages between first and second place, we discover a window of secondomic opportunity. (There's a formula for this in Appendix II.)

To take another example, did you know that the most popular street name in America is "2nd"? The unimaginative convention of naming streets after numbers is common in America, (whilst in Britain, we prefer to name streets after arcane aristocrats, or forgotten battles). The more streets that a city has, the higher the numbers will go. Therefore, we may expect lower numbers to be more common as street names, since a city must have at least one street, but the probability of it having additional streets becomes progressively less likely. On this basis, you might expect "1st" to be the most common street name, but it is not. The reason for this is simple. 1st Street is often considered to be such an important street that it is frequently given a special name: "Main Street" being the typical choice. Whilst, unlike our motoring example, streets may not be competing with each other for their ranking, the secondomics principle still applies. Just as the fastest motorist gets singled out by the police, so the lowest street number gets singled out by the municipal authorities for a special name. And as a consequence, second place is afforded a unique position.

In this book, I will provide many different illustrations of secondomics in practice. We'll explore secondomics in business, psychology, economics and evolutionary biology. But let's start with an aperitif. Savvy sommeliers know that wine ignoramuses have a tendency to choose the second cheapest bottle on the menu. Since these diners don't know much about wine, they quite reasonably doubt that they'll taste the difference between the cheapest and most expensive bottle. Naturally, therefore they favor the cheaper bottle. But they do not want to be perceived as cheap by their dinner date, and so instead they chose the second from cheapest. This small act of pretension plays right into the

SECONDOMICS

hands of our savvy sommelier, who may select an especially bad wine for the second cheapest - one that in fact may be worth less than the cheapest bottle, since they know that the customer who selects this bottle is unlikely to notice the difference.

The practice of exploiting the wine novice with an especially bad second cheapest bottle is know by economists as decoy pricing, and we'll be exploring it greater detail in Part Four. For now, let's simply note that this is a rare example of where secondomic strategies can fail, because someone (in this case, the sommelier) notices what we're doing, and begins to take advantage of it.

Sharing second place

Of course, we can't all come second, all the time. Imagine how my journey back from my parent's house will change once this book has become a best seller. Suddenly, everyone will want to be the second fastest motorist on the road, and my strategy will no longer work. I may have no option but to stick to the speed limit, since no other car will be willing to go faster than me. Here, game theory provides us with a solution than enables me and my fellow motorist to share the benefits of secondomics. And for discovering this solution, we must thank American mathematician, John Forbes Nash, (who was the subject of the Oscar winning movie, *A Beautiful Mind*, starring Russell Crowe).

Nash provides us a way to solves these *"non-zero sum games"*. Zero-sum is how a game theorist would describe one of our win-lose scenarios, where one player's gain always comes as an equivalent loss to the other player. Superficial, our motoring example may seem to be a zero-sum situation, since only one driver can be the second fastest. Nash introduces the concept of *mixed-strategy equilibria*, which, for our purposes, means taking it in turns to be in second place. By sharing second place, my fellow motorist and I can maximize our potential speed whilst minimize our risk of getting caught. And as a result, the overall benefit, (or *payoff*,) of this strategy to both of us is greater than if either of us pursued a pure strategy of always targeting second. We will return to this example in Part 5, to explore how Nash's equilibriums apply to secondomics in more detail.

Examples of sharing second place can also be found in the natural world. Imagine a crowd of Adelie Penguins, standing on an ice ledge together, thinking about how nice it would be to leap into the ocean and grab a tasty fish-snack. The trouble is that they know that there are a finite number of fish in the sea (there's that plenty more fish fallacy again), and there are leopard seals lurking,

INTRODUCTION

who would like nothing better than to pick up a penguin for lunch. Just as the early bird catches the worm, so the first penguin in the sea may have the best chance of catching a fish (sorry for the mixed metaphor there!) However, the first penguin in the sea is also the most likely to get caught by a leopard seal. The lucky second penguin to jump will have a better chance of catching a fish than those who follow, and is less likely to get caught by the seal because the first penguin has already caught the seal's attention. So who should go first? Of course, a smart group of penguins would follow Nash's advice, but then, penguins don't tend to hold mathematicians in high regard - most of them can't even add up, let alone understand game theory. Fortunately, this is where evolution kicks in to lend a hand.

As the speeding example illustrates, the best solution is to share second place. Even though penguins don't consciously understand game theory, they inherit their behavior from their parents, who in turn inherit their behavior from their parents, and so on. Over thousands of years, the penguins who take it in turns to go first will do slightly better than those who do not, and as a consequence, cooperative penguins should form the majority.

And that seems to be what happens in practice, albeit the penguins are not necessarily acting out of altruism. As Dr G Murray Levick, zoologist to the British Antarctic Survey wrote in 1914:

> "The object of every bird in the party seemed to be to get one of the others to enter the water first. They would crowd up to the very edge of the ice, dodging about and trying to push one another in."

The fact that the first penguin does not voluntarily jump does not negate the game theory interpretation, since we know that the penguins are not capable of premeditated behavior anyway. The point is that in practice, successful penguins tend to jostle, and sometimes "allow" themselves to get pushed off first.

But what about cheats? What if there's a family of sneaky penguins who always go second. They've learned to stay at the front of the group, but to avoid tripping or getting pushed off the ledge. In effect, they play a perpetual game of "after you... no, after you... no really, after you..." Of course, this could happen, and those naughty penguins would get more fish, and avoid more seals. However, a community of penguins can only support so many naughty penguins - after all, if no penguins were ever willing to go first, then no penguins would ever dive into the sea for a fish-snack, and then all penguins would die out.

So in penguin societies, we might expect to find a small group of smart alecks who have unconsciously learned the much misunderstood benefits of second place. They might look just the same as the other penguins, and in every other respect seem completely normal, but somehow they always manage to get a little bit more than the average hungry penguin. Smart birds!

But could the same principle apply in human societies? People are not like penguins. We have much bigger brains, capable of abstract thought. You can't teach an old bird new tricks - successful behavior in penguins may take many generations to evolve. Humans, however, frequently learn new ways of behaving within a single lifetime. Wouldn't we spot people who consistently behave like naughty penguins, taking the benefits of being out in front whilst avoiding the limelight of first place?

The answer is no, we probably wouldn't notice them. These people are successful precisely because they have mastered the art of achieving success without being noticed. They've learned to exploit our leadership bias to their own advantage. They're masters of the art of keeping their head down.

Welcome to the world of secondomics - your journey starts here.

Part 1 - The advantages of leadership

Chapter 1: First Place. What is it, and why do we want it?

What does it mean to come first? And for that matter, what does it mean to come second? Whilst the answers to these questions may seem obvious, it's worth pausing to reflect on them before we explore the benefits of coming second in greater detail.

The concepts of first and second place tend to imply competition. We encounter examples of competitive behavior all around us. Sometimes competitions are consciously organized, with rules, a referee and a prize. But competitive behavior may also be unconscious - an individual may deliberately act to their own advantage without considering that in so doing they are depriving others. Indeed, competition is by no means an activity limited to humans. Animals and even plants compete as well. Trees in a forest may compete to be the tallest, in order to maximize their access to sunlight, at the expense of their competitors. Obviously, these trees have no ability to consciously attempt to grow taller than their peers - this kind of strategy is something that evolves as a result of natural selection over millions of years. Trees that are good at growing tall may have a better chance of reproducing than trees that are not, and so the genes for growing tall become more prevalent over time.

Why do we compete at all? And where did it all begin? Commentators the world over bemoan the relentlessly competitive nature of our society. Reticence towards the forces of competition are prevalent throughout our culture - in the Declaration of Independence, Thomas Jefferson held it to be "self evident" that "all men are created equal", and thinkers throughout time, from Jesus Christ to Karl Marx would have agreed. And yet, Jefferson was hardly a poster child for equality. As a wealthy Virginian planter, he owned countless slaves, and freed almost none of them. Whilst he was writing fine words about what was self evident, his slaves were forced to labor without pay on his plantations. Jefferson was part of a wealthy land owning elite who had, over generations, successfully re-ordered the world around them to their own advantage. Such people must surely have competed as hard as possible, taking full advantage of their innate strengths in order to better their lot - quite possibly, at the expense of others around them. Where had the relentless ambitions of Jefferson and his ancestors originated? To answer that question we must go back several million years to the primordial goo from which all life on earth emerged.

In "The Selfish Gene," Richard Dawkins provides an insightful account of the origins of life from simple self-replicating chemicals into complex organisms. Consistent throughout his narrative is the principle that once chemicals in the goo began to self replicate, competition became inevitable, and has continued ever since. Competition was inevitable because there was a finite amount of natural resources which the replicating chemicals could use in order to make copies of themselves. When these resources became constrained, the chemicals began to "feed" off each other in order to continue replicating - and the rest is history. This competition never stopped. Self replicating chemicals that built protective shells around themselves were able to compete more effectively. And steadily, these simple chemicals became more complex - building arms and legs to fight and run, building mouths in order to eat their competitors, and so on. Eventually, some of these chemicals became so successful that they were able to build Thomas Jefferson, who went on to write that "all men were created equal".

At this stage, it's important to make a distinction between observations that we make relating to how the world appears to work, as opposed to how we think that people should behave. The fact that people are not equal in practice does not mean that they shouldn't be treated as such. The principle that all people should be treated equally is an excellent founding principle for any nation. This doesn't change the fact that Jefferson himself did not treat people equally - in particular his slaves. And even when we do manage to stick to our principles, at a more fundamental level, the competition between those self-replicating chemicals, (our genes,) is ongoing, and we are simply playing bit-parts in a competition that has been ongoing for millions of years.

Evolutionary biology then, has a lot to tell us about the origins and meaning of competition. It's a fascinating area, but not one that I have the space nor qualifications to explore in greater detail here. Another area of study that has something to tell us about competition is economics. Whilst economists sometimes struggle to define their field, a classical definition would be that it concerns human behavior as it pertains to the allocation of limited resources. Of course, in practice resources may not always be limited, but in such cases, it's not so interesting to study how they are allocated, since there needn't been any conflicting interests to resolve.

Ironically, in the same year that founding father Thomas Jefferson was penning the Declaration of Independence, on the other side of the Atlantic, Adam Smith, the founding father of classical economics, was publishing "*An Enquiry into the Nature and Causes of the Wealth of Nations*". It has to be said that the *Wealth of Nations* is a very long, rather dry tome. These days, very few people actually bother to read it (honestly), but somehow, that doesn't stop people, like myself, quoting from it anyway. For a shorter, more entertaining read, I recommend James Buchan's biography of Adam Smith, "*Adam Smith and the Pursuit of Perfect Liberty*". ...Anyway, I digress. In the *Wealth of Nations*, Smith provided some important insights into how individual competition operates to deliver greater benefits for society as a whole:

> "It is not from the benevolence of the butcher, the brewer, or the baker that we expect our dinner, but from their regard to their own interest. We address ourselves, not to their humanity but to their self-love, and never talk to them of our own necessities but of their advantages."

In other words, Adam Smith assumes that people will always put themselves first, but in so doing, they help others. The butcher, the brewer or the baker may compete ruthlessly with each other for customers, but they serve their customers in the process. A society filled with individuals competing solely for their own competitive advantage my inadvertently be improving the lot of society as a whole as a result. According to Smith, we shouldn't expect to see acts of selfless altruism, but we should expect to find acts of enlightened self interest which benefit others in the process. These days, economists would say that "rational actors act to maximize their utility". Simply put, people do what suits them best. And in the course of pursuing their own self interest, it is inevitable that people become involved in competitive behavior as they encounter others looking to consume the same limited resources. This is complicated by the fact that people don't always know what's good for them, as evidenced by the fact that people so often compete to be first, when in fact it may sometimes suit them far better to come second - if they only knew.

But competition is not the only context in which we find a first and second place. Humans have a predilection for order - we love to categorize, sort and rank things - building taxonomies to provide us with common points of reference for observing the world around us. We've been doing it since ancient times, when Plato proposed his *theory of forms* - arguing that the physical world in which our bodies exist is filled with imperfect approximations of ideal forms. So, for example, beds may come in many shapes and sizes, but they all share a common bed-ness, because they all resemble, in some way, a more perfect notion of bed that we have in our heads (or in Plato's view, an ideal form that exists in a more perfect universe). And this implies that beds may be ranked, in accordance with how closely they approximate the ideal bed. In philosophical terms, Plato's ideal forms are *universals*, and any kind of thing that exists in our universe in many instances, sharing sufficient properties as to be recognized as sharing a certain "thing-ness," may be regarded as a *universal*.

In order to rank items resembling a certain universal, we must look for both their similarities and differences. First we must define a category of things that have similar properties. This is often harder than it seems. Whilst oranges may superficially appear to be similar, they can vary enormously in terms of color, size and flavor. At what point does an an orange cease being an orange, and instead is better described as a satsuma or a tangerine? When we have determined how similar things must be in order to belong in our category, we must switch from focusing on their similarities to exploring their differences in order to determine how to rank them. Done right, the process of categorization and sorting can be immensely pleasing, and has occupied music fans with their record collections for generations.

As with our competition examples, we can look at the intrinsic properties of the things we categorize in order to rank them. So for example, we may define "skyscrapers" as our universal, and determine "height" as our method of ranking. Height is an intrinsic property of a skyscraper in the sense that it is something fundamentally to do with the skyscraper itself. Skyscrapers may not grown in the same way that trees do, but their height can be measured in just the same way. But where competition is always concerned with the intrinsic properties of the competitors, ranking more generally may also focus on extrinsic properties. For example, our perpetual appetite for something new drives us to favor different colors in fashion each season. So one year "brown is the new black" and the next year, perhaps "black is back". We can rank the popularity of different colors in fashion by measuring garment sales by color. These data may tell us which colors are most popular, but they don't tell us anything about the colors themselves. So black may be back, but that doesn't mean that black has changed in any way - we're in fact measuring the behavior of fashion shoppers, rather than the behavior of colors. The colors are not competing - they're merely being ranked as indicators of something else. The same might be said of pop songs. The songs themselves are not changing as they rise and fall on the hit parade, but rather the behavior of music fans is changing as reflected in the sales figures of the songs. The difference here, however, is that

THE ADVANTAGES OF LEADERSHIP

whilst we realize that colors do not actually compete with each other, we might think of pop songs as competing in the music charts in the sense that the performers, song writers and record labels who produce the songs are competing with each other, and the song itself is in fact the vehicle for that competition.

So rankings may be a result of competition, but they may not. Competitors may be aware that they are competing, but they may not. And rankings may be concerned with the intrinsic properties of the things being ranked, but they may not. Suddenly what comes first and second doesn't look quite so clear cut! Since ranking appears to be such an inexact science, we might reasonably ask, why does it matter? What does it really mean to come first and second? Are these just abstract concepts that we use to arbitrarily describe the world around us? Perhaps our human obsession with order is driving us to find rankings where in fact this concept is meaningless, more reflecting our mental state than the world around us. Maybe it's time to stop relentlessly competing with each other for a better ranking in life, and settle for being happy. It's a beguiling thought, and it would make a lot of sense if it wasn't for the simple fact that it is wrong!

Rankings matter because they have a material impact upon payoffs. In a simplified world where rankings didn't matter, then the harder you work, the greater your returns. If you work twice as hard, you make twice as much. Isn't this the American dream? Armed with nothing more than brains, pluck and determination, you could be the next John D Rockerfeller or Bill Gates. But it just isn't as simple as that. In the real world, if you work in a factory, you can work as hard as you like, but you won't end up owning the factory.

Take the example of Bill Gates, (Microsoft's chairman). If you worked really hard to make a great operating system that was even better than Windows, could you become richer than Bill Gates? Probably not. Why? Because Windows is the world's leading operating system - even if your product is better, most people will continue to buy Windows. The number one ranking of the product gives it a big advantage in the market. Ask Steve Jobs, (Apple's CEO). So why isn't this book called "firstomics"? Well in fact it could have been. There are any number of advantages to coming first - they're just so obvious that they're hardly worth writing a book about. What's interesting is that for all the advantages that first place affords Windows, it also comes with many disadvantages, which put the operating system's longer term viability in real doubt. Window users are deluged with viruses and security exploits; it is subjected to onerous anti-trust legislation which is not applied to its competitors; and providing support for its enormous, heterogeneous userbase limits the product's potential to change and evolve... But we're getting ahead of ourselves. We will explore the disadvantages of leadership in greater depth later.

Rankings, can be both ambiguous and arbitrary; so much so that they can sometimes seem to be entirely artificial, rather than part of the natural makeup of the world around us. And yet rankings can and do have a material impact on what happens in the real world. Come first in a competition, and you may win a prize. Come second, and you may get a runners up prize. But what's the difference between the two? Answering that question will be our focus for the rest of this chapter.

For my sins, I used to work in sales promotion. If people who work in advertising are pond life (as many of my friends assure me they are), then people who work in sales promotion are right at the bottom of the pond, feeding on the detritus left behind by the others. Why? Well sales promotion just isn't glamorous - it's the art of driving short term sales by means of tactical incentivization. Whereas traditional advertising may try to sell products by making them seem sexy or cool, sales promotion is more likely to tell you to bogof (buy one get one free) or receive a free teddy with every purchase (always popular). A perennial favorite of the sales promotion industry is competitions. And in planning a competition, one important factor to consider is the prize structure. How big will the prize fund be, and how should it be allocated? Ideally, you'd want the overall prize fund to have an eye-catchingly large figure attached to it - "Win a million". But in practice, you'd be wise not to put all of your prize fund into a single first prize, since then people may be put off entering because they'd doubt their chances of winning. Instead, you want to be able to add an encouraging secondary proposition, along the lines of "hundreds of prizes to be won," or better still "every one's a winner". However, if you spread your prize fund too evenly, the individual value of each prize may seem so small that no one is going to be interested in entering. Somehow "a hundred million chances to win a penny" is not going to sound exciting, however you put it.

So with all this in mind, we sales promotion pond life go about planning our competitions, and over time we've found that the best way to divide a prize fund is in some kind of pyramid structure, with the largest prize allocated to the winner, and then tiered prizes of progressively smaller values for runners' up. Almost all competition prize funds are divvied up in this way, although the proportional allocations may vary substantially. But these are arbitrarily allocated payoffs for an artificially constructed competition. How does this compare to competition in the natural world?

THE ADVANTAGES OF LEADERSHIP

To answer that question, let's go on safari. It's a beautifully sunny day, and we're on some fancy reservation in the Serengeti watching wildebeest approach a watering hole. As herd animals, the wildebeest are approaching the watering hole in a group. There are doubtless numerous reasons why they move around in this way, but one major one is presumably safety in numbers. The reservation is filled with predators who will hungrily pick off any lone wildebeest that strays too far from the herd.

So our safety conscious creatures are sensibly approaching the watering hole in a herd. They are so good at doing this that it is as if they move as one single entity, rather than many separate organisms - they match each other's speed and direction perfectly. But however effective they are at moving as a group (and we will studying this phenomenon of flocking in more detail later,) they remain fundamentally separate organisms that gain some benefit for themselves as individuals by moving together as a group. Moving in this way does not imply any sense of group altruism on the part of the wildebeest. In fact, as soon as their interests as individuals are no longer aligned, they are quick to start behaving as individuals again. Some of those individuals find themselves towards the front of the group, and others towards the back.

The position of the wildebeest within the group will have a material impact upon how much water they get to drink at the watering hole. The wildebeest at the front will have unrestricted access to the water's edge, and will be able to drink as much as it likes. The wildebeest at the back may not reach the water's edge at all, because it is entirely obstructed by the wildebeest in front. In fact, since there is a fixed stretch of waters edge from which wildebeest may drink, there are a finite number that may drink at any one time, and this number is less than the total wildebeest in the group. So, whilst the first wildebeest can be certain of getting a drink, the odds of drinking progressively lengthen for each subsequent animal. In other words, after the first wildebeest, the second has the best chance of getting a drink. Looking at it from the perspective of payoff distribution is not smooth - it has a sharp ledge to it - either you drink or you don't. You don't know where the ledge will be, but the closer you are to first place, the greater your chance of not falling off it.

In reality, the payoff for our wildebeest at the water hole would certainly be more complex. For example, it's not a polarized matter of getting to drink or not getting to drink - the last to drink probably get less drinking time than the first, since they will need to move on when the rest of the pack herd becomes restless. The key variables are the size of the herd, the size of the watering hole and the length of time that the herd can afford to stay before moving on.

By adjusting these three variables, we can have a massive impact on what proportion of wildebeest who get to drink. We needn't get too bogged down in modeling the payoffs of wildebeest and watering holes. The example should serve to demonstrate that the structure of payoffs for ranking in the natural world can be every bit as complex and varied a they may be in a promotional competition contrived by a talented sales promotion consultant. In some cases, second place will get exactly the same payoff as first. In other cases first may get substantially more, whilst second place may get the same as most of the rest. The possibilities are endless.

Some of the arguments that we will explore in Secondomics apply to second place in the sense of getting the second highest ranking after first place - in which may encompass one or several participants in a competition. In other cases, we may look at a specific individual actor who ranks second - where this is the case, I'll make that clear, otherwise you can assume that second refers to the second best payoff, rather than the second ranking individual competitor.

So finally, in answer to our question, we have established that for something to come first or second, it must be ranked - often as the outcome of a competition. The significance of that ranking will be determined by the payoff, and we can expect to find any number of different payoff structures, each with distinct implications for the influence that we should expect them to exert upon the participants.

Part 2 - The disadvantages of leadership

Chapter 2: It can be tough at the top

Is it always chivalrous to let the lady go first? Whilst the women's rights movement has effectively put an end to the notion, it's interesting to consider the origins and significance of this gesture. The unspoken corollary to "ladies first" is "men second," and as we know, coming second can have it's own innate advantages. When a man insists upon a woman passing through a door first, he may, inadvertently or unconsciously, be exposing that woman to greater risk, if there are any dangers concealed beyond the doorway. So it's uncertain where the chivalry of "ladies first" has arisen from. Far from being considerate to a girl's needs, such acts of chivalry may be more akin to the use of canaries in mining. Miners (mostly male) would put caged canaries (of either gender) in the tunnel that they were about to enter, in order to test for noxious gasses. "Canaries first," the miners might have said. If the bird lived, the tunnel was safe, if the bird died, the miners knew it wasn't safe, and that they needed a new bird.

Leadership has it benefits. Whether you're the wildebeest who gets the longest drink, the president who calls the shots, or the motorist who has the shortest journey time. But leaders also come in for more than their fair share of flack. Leaders inevitably stand out from the pack - it's in their nature. And as a consequence of standing out, they tend to get singled out for the harshest treatment. This may be as a result of someone or something deliberately targeting the leader (such as our leopard seal picking off the first penguin,) or it may be a simple consequence of their context within the group. For example, imagine that you are part of a group exploring a jungle. There's dense undergrowth that must be cut down in order for the group to establish a trail. The responsibility for this naturally rests with whoever is at the front of the group. Those behind may simply follow in the trail left by the leader - a task requiring substantially less exertion. So, whilst being at the front has its usual benefits (choosing the direction and getting there first), it has its drawbacks (greater exertion required in order to cut through undergrowth). In practice, for a group

SECONDOMICS

to be effective, it will inevitably arrive at a strategy of taking it in turns to be at the front, which merely illustrates that rankings can and do change over time - no one can remain in first place for ever. (We'll explore the implications that time has over Secondomics in greater detail in chapter six).

In 1997, Wired magazine published Kevin Kelly's "New Rules for the New Economy". Kelly argued that the internet turned traditional wisdom on its head. Productivity was a myth, services should be free, the industrial revolution was over and customization was king. In retrospect, it's no wonder that the dotcom bubble collapsed. And as if all of these counterintuitive rules were not enough, it was considered necessary to rush at every opportunity at breakneck speed in order to gain "first mover" advantage. The thinking here was that the networked nature of the "new economy" resulted in rapid feedback loops, meaning that through word of mouth alone, a business could rapidly grow from a standing start to a monopoly, providing it was first to market with a new product or service. The old rules for the new economy insisted that there were no prizes for second place. As Kelly put it:

> *"doing exactly the right next thing is far more fruitful than doing the same thing better"*

Really? Tell that to Apple, who arrived late in the MP3 player market with their iPod offering, which was essentially a finessed version of competitor products that were already on sale, such as Creative's Zen music player. Apple did not invent the MP3 player. They sat on the sidelines, watched the first movers, and worked out how they could do it better. People chose to buy iPods because they were the best, not because they were the first. And the rest is history.

Or consider the remarkable success of Facebook, which launched in 2004, and only allowed the general public to register in 2006. That's a full four years after Friendster, three years after MySpace, and two years after Orkut. Facebook's late arrival on the social networking scene hardly seems to have limited its adoption. By 2009, it had become the world's most popular social network. Facebook's success is built upon finessing an existing concept, rather than being first to market with something new.

Time and again, you'll find examples in both the new economy and the old, where the finesser, who does it better, beats the first mover who has the right idea but fails on the execution. No one should be afraid of failure - after all, lessons of at least as much value are to be found in failure as in success. The trouble is, that when we fail in public, our competitors are at liberty to pick up on those lessons as well, and to learn from our misfortune.

THE DISADVANTAGES OF LEADERSHIP

Consider our jungle explorers again, and imagine they reach a river that they must cross. Luckily, there are a series of stepping stones. Our fearless leader crosses first, only to discover that one of the stones is wobbly, and he ends up getting washed away by the rapids. The others in the party know to watch out for that stone, and so they cross successfully. We might call this phenomenon "first mover disadvantage." It's really no different to our intrepid canary - the miners get "second mover advantage" by learning from the canary's misfortune.

A pecking order that we have all been a part of at one stage in our lives is that of sibling rivalry (unless, of course, you were an only child, in which case you were fortunately enough to occupy first, last and indeed every place in this particular ranking of your parent or guardian's affections). First born siblings often complain that they were treated more strictly than their younger brothers or sisters - my own older brother being a case in point. Recent research by a group of economists and sociologists at Duke University indicates that they may be right to suspect this.

The Duke University study posited that parents were strict with their offspring in order to discourage risk-taking behavior, and that parents would be strictest with their oldest children in order to set an example to those who followed. Since parents don't enjoy being strict with their children (the old "this is going to hurt me more than it hurts you" argument), their discipline will become more lax as most of their children have left home. Resulting in the archetypal "spoiled" youngest child, since there are no remaining children to whom an example must be set. To test their ideas, the researchers analyzed data from U.S. Bureau of Labor Statistics, focusing on two examples of risk-taking in teenagers (pregnancy and dropping out of high school) and two examples of disciplinary behavior in parents (not allowing children to live at home, and providing limited or no financial support). Perhaps unsurprisingly, the results did indeed support my older brother's gripe. The first born is indeed more likely to receive punishment for risk-taking behavior. Parental discipline falls neatly into our secondomics view of the disadvantages of second place - younger siblings can follow safely in the trail of their elders, much like our jungle explorers can follow the path beaten by their leaders. But in the case of siblings, the story is note quite so clear cut.

Evolution provides us another perspective on sibling rivalry, thanks to the work of evolutionary biologist W. D. Hamilton, who gave us *Hamilton's Rule* of kin selection. Siblings of any species tend to find themselves in contention for their parents' attention - whether this is their mother's milk, cuddles, protection from predators or any other attention that a parent may bestow upon its offspring. Hamilton's Rule tells us that individuals may behave altruistically towards their kin if the cost to the giver is outweighed by the benefit to the recipient, and only in proportion to their genetic relatedness. Since parents are equally related to each of their children, we might expect them to be even-handed in their treatment of their offspring. However, we should also consider the relative benefit to the recipients. Another study, conducted at Manchester University, indicates that parents may favor older children over younger children, since they have a better chance of survival, and will therefore receive greater benefit from acts of altruism. Although the Manchester study concerned dung beetles, we may expect humans to behave in a similar way. So whilst my brother was probably right that our parents were stricter with him, it's unlikely that he received less parental investment - indeed, it seems if anything we can expect leadership advantage, plain and simple. This is perfectly illustrated by the system of primogeniture, the tradition whereby the oldest child traditionally inherits more of their parents' estate than their younger siblings. So whilst we may find some trace of secondomics at work in parental disciplinary behavior, the overall picture of sibling rivalry is less clear cut. We must look elsewhere for the true disadvantages of leadership.

The Powell Principle

The story of almost any political leader perfectly illustrates the disadvantages of first place. Enoch Powell, a British politician whose career was damaged by his much-criticized "rivers of blood" speech on immigration, famously said:

> *"All political lives, unless they are cut off in midstream at a happy juncture, end in failure, because that is the nature of politics and of human affairs."*

Is it true that all political careers end in failure? Certainly, once you have won an election, all that's left to do at subsequent elections is to defend your position. Sooner or later, perhaps it is inevitable that a younger, hungrier politician will come along and knock you off the top spot. Defending an entrenched position can often be more difficult than fighting to gain ground. Put simply, when you've reached the top, there's no way to go but down. The media compound this phenomenon by following their instinct to "build 'em up and knock 'em down". This seemingly contradictory behavior is an inevitable function of the journalist's role of finding a story. For a story to be newsworthy, it

THE DISADVANTAGES OF LEADERSHIP

must tell the reader something that they didn't already know, and this means that journalists are on a perpetual hunt for change. Therefore, anyone in the media, through the lens of a journalist, must either be going up, or going down. Hence the classic stories of "working class boy made good" followed by "pride comes before a fall". From a journalists point of view, therefore, if someone is at the top and remaining at the top, there's no story there. Can you imagine a story like "popular prime minister continues to do well"? Of course not.

But in political careers, as in any career development, there's another principle at work which makes a position at the top particularly perilous. The Peter Principle. In 1968, Dr Laurence J. Peter & Raymond Hull published a hugely popular book on management. Despite the book's humorous style, it set out a valid and challenging (albeit rather cynical) argument. The Peter Principle states that everyone is promoted to their own unique level of incompetence. This happens because employers have a tendency to promote employees as a reward for doing their existing job well, rather than because they are necessarily suited to the next job up the line. This is a particularly perverse example of secondomics at work, since the Peter Principle indicates that you should expect the height of your career to be your second to last promotion - before you are ultimately promoted above your level of competence (or in Peter's terms, you've reached "Final Placement"). An even more cynical (if that were possible) extension of this argument is the Dilbert Principle, advanced by the eponymous cartoon office worker. The Dilbert Principle suggests that employers promote employees who are less qualified in order to stop them causing trouble. In other words, middle-management roles are ineffectual positions given to ineffectual employees in order to stop them from causing trouble. It's an amusing idea, but there's very little reason to suppose that it happens in practice. Whilst the Peter Principle is supported by the fact that promotions are indeed given on occasion to reward good performance, the premise at the heart of the Dilbert Principle, that middle managers can't do harm, seems far less certain! A particularly prominent example of both the Enoch Powell Principle and the Peter Principle currently in action in the UK, is the story of Gordon Brown and Tony Blair, and it serves as a salutary lesson on the disadvantages of leadership.

In 1997, Labour won a landslide victory in the British general election, and the party has been continuously in power ever since. Initially, the new government formed under Prime Minister Tony Blair was immensely popular. Much of the electorate was tired of more than a decade of Tory government, and as a result, there was immense good will for the fledgling administration. Flushed with their success, the new government seemed both strong and united. But beneath the surface, the party was not as united as it seemed, and at the heart of this disunity was a power struggle between Number 10 and Number 11 Downing Street, or in other words, a conflict between first and second.

Legend has it that before the 1997 general election, Tony Blair and Gordon Brown, whilst dining at Granita, an exclusive restaurant in fashionable Islington, struck a deal concerning the leadership of their party, and ultimately the leadership of their country. Both men were keen for the top job (this book had not yet been published, so sadly, they didn't know any better,) and they were prepared to use all of their political clout in order to get it. Gordon Brown had more experience, whilst Tony Blair had more charisma, and a flair for campaigning. Their solution was to take it in turns - Blair would go first, and Brown would go second, succeeding Blair at the end of the second term in government.

In retrospect, it seems pretty presumptuous for two men, dining alone, to be divvying up the fate of a nation between them. Their presumption did not go unpunished, however, as events conspired against these aspiring leaders' plans. Tony Blair's premiership was initially a happy one, and after his first four years in power, he was returned to office for a second term with a comfortable, albeit slightly smaller majority. But the attacks on New York and Washington DC on September 11, 2001 took Tony Blair's leadership in an entirely new direction. His unwavering support for the administration of George W Bush proved to be extremely unpopular with the British electorate, particularly as it took the country into wars with Afghanistan and subsequently, more controversially, Iraq. There's no evidence that Gordon Brown, had he have been in power at the time, would have handled the country's foreign affairs any differently, and indeed, as a part of the government, he had professed his support for Blair's foreign policy on more than one occasion. Nonetheless, Brown's political career benefitted enormously from Blair's new found unpopularity. Blair was blamed for taking the country into an unpopular war. Whilst Brown was the second most powerful person in the government that was responsible for this policy, somehow he was held less accountable.

Towards the end of Blair's second term in office, pressure from within the party for him to step aside in favor of Brown became hard for the prime minister to resist. At this point, in retrospect, Brown's political power was at its zenith. He commanded enormous goodwill from his party, who reasoned that a change in leadership would free them from the baggage associated with an unpopular war. He had perfected the art of superficially supporting the prime

THE DISADVANTAGES OF LEADERSHIP

minister, whilst allowing his supporters to tell the media a different story. It's a classic second place strategy that can be found throughout history. During George Washington's second term in office, Thomas Jefferson claimed to still support the celebrated general's administration. However, as Washington increasingly favored the federalists' cause in government, Jefferson encouraged his political allies to raise questions about the president's fitness for office. Jefferson could not afford to publicly fall out with the nation's greatest hero, but he could allow his lieutenants to do the dirty work for him. Sadly, however, I suspect that Gordon Brown is not a prolific letter writer in the same vein as Jefferson, so we may never know what involvement, if any, Brown played in Blair's downfall. But fall, he most certainly did.

Pressure from within Blair's own party forced him to set a timetable for his own departure from office. The prime minister announced that he would lead his party through a third election, and then at some point towards the end of his third term, he would step aside in favor of his successor, allowing sufficient time for his successor to prepare for the next election. Early into his third term in office, pressure from Brown's supporters increased substantially. The reasoning was that if Blair was going to leave, then the sooner the better, allowing Brown as much time as possible to get his government ready for the next election. Blair insisted that he would leave at a time of his own determination, rather than being forced from office. And whilst he can credibly claim that this is what ultimately happened, it was certainly a good deal earlier than his previous timetable had indicated.

In the same year that Gordon Brown took over from Tony Blair as prime minister, the country received two pieces of bad news. A global "credit crunch" resulted in the collapse of a major UK mortgage lender, Northern Rock, and the government inadvertently lost the personal data of over a million benefits claimants, raising serious questions about its competence. As the events in 2001 were not of Blair's making, so the events of 2007 were not the fault of Gordon Brown. But Brown was no longer in the comfortable position of number two, so whilst these events were not his fault, they were his responsibility. Both the media, and ultimately the electorate were prepared to hold him accountable. In the local elections of 2008, the Labour Party suffered its worst electoral defeat in forty years.

The sad tale of Blair and Brown perfectly illustrates some key themes of Secondomics. Consider how much more powerful Brown might have remained if he had stuck to his role as chancellor - Britain's number two in political power. In second place, Brown could have continued to exert enormous influence upon the direction of government, retained huge support from within his party, and not taken responsibility for any of the government's problems. But as the Peter Principle points out, people just can't resist the desire to ascend the hierarchy until they reach their final placement, and Brown was no exception. Political careers tend to end in failure because politicians rise to a point from where there is nowhere to go but down; they suffer perpetual underhand sniping from their ambitious subordinates; and they are held accountable for events which are often entirely outside of their control. We tend to be so critical of politicians that I can't help wondering sometimes why anyone would want to be one. But these principles extend far beyond politics. Similar events are playing out in workplaces, families, clubs or indeed any group of social animals, the world over. Rather than saying "who would want to be a politician," the more insightful question would be, "who would want to be a leader?"

The winner's curse

Leadership is not the only example where coming first can turn out to be a mistake. Let's now turn to the strange and contrary world of auctions. In a traditional marketplace, we find sellers competing for buyers, whereas in an auction we find the opposite - buyers are instead competing for a seller. The difference is that in a traditional market place, we assume relatively unconstrained supply, whereas in an auction, supply is very limited. So for example, if you're looking to buy a banana, they're in plentiful supply, and so you can choose the supermarket offering them at the lowest price. Whereas if you're looking to buy a Picasso, there's only a finite number of unique works available, and so prospective buyers must compete against each other, by offering progressively higher prices. If I'm a price sensitive banana shopper, I merely need to pick my store carefully in order to get a bargain, whereas if I'm a price sensitive Picasso shopper, I may have to make do with a poster. The winner in an auction is the one prepared to pay the most money, which means that all the bidders in an auction must judge how much the painting is worth to them, and to their competitors before making a bid.

Whilst great works of art, such as a Picasso painting, may be described as "priceless," because their value is purely a function of how much the bidders desire the item, not all items put up for auction are truly priceless. Some auction items have a value, but that value may be difficult to calculate, and it is down to the individual bidders to determine what it may be. In these circumstances, if the highest bidder wins, they have probably overestimated the value of the

THE DISADVANTAGES OF LEADERSHIP

item, since their valuation is so much higher than that of their competitors. This is called the "winner's curse". And a classic example of the winner's curse in action is the auctioning of licenses for wireless spectrum for 3G mobile phone services, which took place in many countries around the world at the turn of the millennium. Governments invited mobile phone operators to bid against each other for the mobile spectrum that they would require in order to operate the next generation of mobile phone services. There's no better motivator in life than survival itself, and for a mobile operator, the inability to offer these services would be the death-knell of their business. And at the time, it seemed as if this was precisely what was at stake. And so, mobile operators around the world hired the smartest minds available to calculate what the value of the mobile spectrum would be.

This calculation was extremely complex, since it must factor in an enormous range of variables. What would the demand for mobile services be? What impact would new 3G services have on demand? How much would customers be prepared to pay? What future trends in usage should be anticipated? How much would handsets cost in the future? And underlying all of these proximate considerations were more fundamental concerns, such as what would happen to the global economy during the term of the license? With so many complex factors at play, arriving at an accurate value was impossible. Whatever the real figure might have been, it's certain that the highest bidder was the one most likely to have overestimated the value of the license - and hence, overpayed as the winner. And there you have the winner's curse.

From the tax payer's perspective, you could argue that no harm has been done. The government has secured best value for the tax payer by selling to the highest bidder - indeed, the government has probably managed to sell the license for more than its real commercial value, although we can only be certain of this in the longer term. But as most economists will tell you, there's no such thing as a free lunch. The winning mobile operators will have to recover the cost of the license somehow, and of course, the inevitable way to recover this cost is by passing it on to the end user through higher mobile phone bills. Customers with phone bills are also tax payers, and ultimately voters. Governments have been known to be highly critical of mobile operators "excessive" charging, but in a sense, they are trying to both having their cake and eat it, on the one hand forcing mobile operators to pay over the odds by making them bid for their very survival, whilst simultaneously criticizing them for passing the cost on to their customers. A better way for governments to allocate their mobile spectrum could be to follow the rules of secondomics.

I would argue that when auctioning off mobile spectrum, the prize should go to the second highest bidder. This not only spares the highest bidder from their own error in overestimating the value, but it impacts upon the entire bidding process. In most mobile spectrum actions, the bidders are required to submit their bids in secret. There is not usually an option to respond to a competitor's bid. In these circumstances, if you're bidding for your survival, you'll not only be thinking about what you think the license is worth to you, but you'll also be considering how you think your competitor might calculate its value. If you believe that your competitor might value the prize more highly than you, you may decide to swallow hard and put in a bid that is higher than what you believe that your competitor will bid - even if this is considerably more than you believe that the license is worth. After all, your survival is at stake. However, if you know that the highest bid will be rejected, you'll take more care not to overestimate your bid. The secondomics bidding process should lead to a more realistic estimation of the license's true value.

A very different kind of auction where we may also find the principles of secondomics at play is taking place on the internet as you read this sentence. The advent of the internet as a mass medium has introduced an entirely new form of auction. One which was pioneered by a company called Goto.com, which was later renamed Overture, and ultimately acquired by Yahoo!. Goto.com invented the concept of auctioning "sponsored" results on search engines. Whilst Goto.com initially only achieved modest success with this invention, it was propelled into the mainstream with its subsequent adoption by a little-known search engine called Google. (Once again, so much for first mover advantage!)

Over the years, Google has evolved a unique and sophisticated method of auctioning their advertising space, called "AdWords". Participating in the AdWords scheme requires advertisers to bid against each other in order to achieve higher rankings in Google's search results. As in the previous example of mobile spectrum auctions, each advertiser must calculate the value of a particular keyword to their business. But there's a twist. Google charges on a per-click basis. So, for example, if you are an insurance broker selling insurance online, you may advertise on the keyword "insurance". Your ad may appear 10 times, but if only one person clicks on it out of those 10 times, you only pay once. And you don't pay the full value of your bid. The cost to you is calculated based upon the bid of your nearest competitor, and then adjusted for the "quality" of your ad, and that of your competitor. Google users a variety of metrics to calculate quality, but they're essentially all designed to determine the rele-

THE DISADVANTAGES OF LEADERSHIP

vance of your ad to the target keyword, and consequently, the click-through rate that it is likely to achieve. Poor quality ads will be penalized with higher charges, to compensate for their lower click-through rates. So, for example, if your bid is $10, and your closest competitor's bid is $5, then your cost will be around $5 per click, adjusted to allow for the relative quality of your ad. Google then uses a combination of your bid, your quality and your budget to determine the rank of your ad in their search results.

So how much should you bid? To answer this question, you should start by determining how high you can afford to go, and in order to do this, you must calculate the value of a click. This is a fairly straightforward calculation:

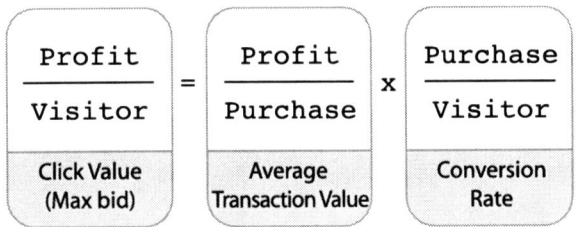

Or in other word, profit per visitor equals profit per purchase multiplied by purchase per visitor. So if you make an average $10 profit on every online sale (your *average transaction value*), and one in twenty visits to your site result in a sale (your *conversion rate*), that means that a click from Google to your site is worth 50c. This is the maximum value that you can afford to bid on Google for a keyword before you start making a loss.

Since Google allows you to set a "maximum bid" in its system, and in practice you will pay something closer to the bid immediately below yours, it may seem safe to put the full value of a click in as your maximum bid, and then leave Google to work its magic. After all, you'll never pay the full value of your maximum bid unless you competitor's bid is just below yours. The trouble is, that is precisely what your competitor's bid is likely to become, when they work out what level you've set your bid at. After all, your competitor wants you to burn through your marketing budget as quickly as possible, so that they can have all the prospective business for themselves. Whilst Google, at the time of writing, does not publicly publish individual advertisers' maximum bids, this can be determined through experimentation. By adjusting your own bid, and observing the impact that this has on your ranking, you can infer what the bids of your competitors might be. Once you have determined this, it is a simple matter to set you bid as high as it can possibly be whilst still ranking below your competitor's ad. That way, you know that your competitor is being forced to pay the full value of their maximum bid each time their ad is clicked on.

In my day job, I work at a web design agency. Frequently, our clients ask us what they need to do to be number one on Google. The reason that they ask this is more than sheer hubris. Clients who advertise on Google frequently discover that there is significant commercial value to being number one on Google. Click-throughs from a top-ranked listing are often of a higher quality in terms of conversion rates and average transaction values. This is often an area where leadership has its advantages. However, we advise our clients to avoid a strategy of pursuing the number one position at all costs. Such as strategy will inevitably result in an artificial inflation in the cost of advertising, that ultimately only benefits Google. Your competitors will soon get wise to your strategy, and exploit it for all it's worth, punishing you for your high maximum bid, by forcing you to pay its full value. In other words, in the Google system, the underdog gets to determine how much the leader must pay per click - putting those in second place in a particularly strong position.

What is the solution then? How do you get the benefit of the top spot, without paying over the odds for each click? Imagine a hypothetical scenario where three companies are all bidding against each other and their ads are of the same quality. Uno Inc is the first place advertiser, with a maximum bid of $10 per click, whilst Duo Inc is the second place advertiser, with a maximum bid of $9 per click. In practice, Duo's bid means that Uno pays $9 every time that they receive a click. Duo, however, are currently only paying $4 per click because that is what Tres Inc, (the third place advertiser,) has set their bid to. Duo are a crafty bunch. By setting their bid so close to Uno's, they force their competitor to burn through their marketing budget faster, whilst they pay substantially lower, and still get pretty close to the top spot. It's a quintessential secondomics strategy. However, of course two can play at that game. Uno are no fools either, and they want their share of the spoils of second place, so from time to time, they switch their strategy to targeting second place in order to punish Duo. They change their bid to $8.99. Suddenly, Duo's cost per click has risen from $4 to $8.99, and it doesn't take long for their ad to disappear altogether, and for Uno to regain the top spot. Why does Duo's ad disappear? This is due to another feature of Google - the ability to set a maximum daily limit, which enables advertisers to ensure that they don't inadvertently exceed their marketing budget if their ad is clicked on with greater frequency than normal. In any given day, if you begin to approach your maximum daily budget limit, Google will automatically stop serving your ad. Since Duo had become accus-

THE DISADVANTAGES OF LEADERSHIP

tomed to paying $4 per click, they set their maximum daily limit to reflect this. Now that their cost per click has suddenly doubled, they exhaust their budget in half the time, and so their ad has started disappearing by lunchtime, allowing Uno to enjoy the top spot at a cost of $4 per click for the rest of the day.

Uno are perusing a mixed strategy - alternating between first and second place. Like our example of jungle explorers earlier, changing ranks over time can have a big impact on the relative merits of first and second place - a theme we'll be returning to in chapter six. For now, let's just observe that advertising on Google provides another fine example of the disadvantages of first place.

Mating and dating

Finally, in this chapter, let's turn our attention to mating rituals - not the birds and the bees, but the toads and the monkeys. Mating is perhaps one of the most important naturally occurring ranking scenario, since it determines the genetic makeup of future generations. Sexually reproducing creatures of all kinds have a tendency to attempt to seek out their optimal mate. Optimal in the context of evolutionary biology means the mate who possesses genes that are best adapted to reproduction. Complex mating rituals have evolved to enable this process. These rituals can vary enormously from one species to another. In some cases, their significance is obvious - for example, females may be attracted by males with large muscles, because genes for strength will presumably increase their offspring's chances of survival. But the meaning of other rituals is less clear. Male peacocks, for example, have eye-catching displays of feathers, that attract females, but the only obvious advantage that a fancy plumage will have to their offspring is a greater chance of attracting a mate through similar displays. Reason enough, certainly, but seemingly of no intrinsic value beyond the sexual display itself - how these fancy feathers evolved in the first place is therefore more difficult to explain.

Mating rituals are not limited to visuals displays. Mating calls, for example, may also be involved. Male Great Plains Toads make a loud mating call to attract females, and there's a real art to in. Female toads are connoisseurs of mating calls - perhaps in the same way that some humans can distinguish between a good singer and a true virtuoso. Female toads are literally drawn to the best croaking that they can hear, giving the best toad-singer an advantage, you may think. But in practice, it turns out that this is not always the case. Imagine that you're the second best croaker, and your buddy is the number one crooner in town. What do you do? Well the answer, it seems, is you stick as close to your buddy as you can. Non chart-topping toads, crowd around the best croaker, establishing a perimeter - far enough away not to put their buddy off his warbling, but close enough so that they can intercept any females flocking his way. Like being a roady on a boy band tour, these clever toads get their mates by sticking close to the talent. They're called "satellite toads" because they gather around the best croaker in a satellite formation.

A similar phenomenon is found amongst male Rhesus Macaques. The strongest, smartest macaque in a given group (the "alpha male") will typically take the fittest female as his mate and guard her. The other males ("beta males") must make do with the remaining lesser females, or no female at all. In order to increase the chances of their genes, beta males have evolved the behavior of furtively mating with the alpha male's mate when he's inadvertently off guard. In doing so, they not only increase their chances of having offspring with the fittest female, but they also trick the alpha male into helping to raise their offspring. Just as a political leader must be constantly on guard for back-stabbing politicians on their way up the ladder, so an alpha male baboon who has taken the best female must be constantly on the lookout for those who covert his mate.

But it's not just politicians and other animals who play these games. Humans exhibit a wide variety of complex mating rituals. We are attracted to others by their looks, and in some way we have presumably evolved to use good looks as an indicator of fitness for procreation (our genes being quite single-minded in this respect). We might therefore imagine that those who are blessed with better looks will, in turn, have a better chance of attracting a good looking mate. And of course, this is true, to a point. It's commonly observed that most people have a tendency to date those with a similar level of attractiveness. Supermodels date supermodels, whilst the less attractive amongst us must sadly make do with each other. It's easy to understand why this might happen. If you date someone whom you consider to be substantially better looking than yourself, it's natural that you may become insecure in your relationship, and increasingly paranoid that your partner may be tempted to leave you for someone more attractive instead.

THE DISADVANTAGES OF LEADERSHIP

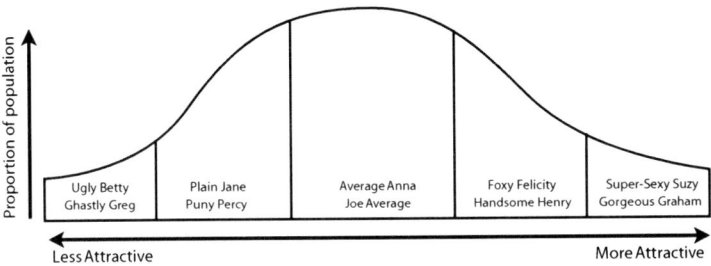

So dating must be a breeze for good looking people, right? Wrong. The sad truth is that good looks are not distributed in equal measure. As any statistician knows, we should expect good looks to be distributed in a bell curve (see diagram) where a lucky few Sexy Suzies and Gorgeous Grahams, and an unfortunate handful of Ugly Betties and Ghastly Gregs are massively outnumbered by all the regular looking people in between. When you consider that people have a tendency to date those of a similar level of attractiveness to themselves, you realize why it can be a tough life being good looking - there are less potential mates about. Whilst average looking people in the middle of the bell curve have many possible mates to choose from, our good looking types will normally need to look much further to find a suitable partner. So the best looking guy or gal suffers from the same disadvantages as our crooning toad and our alpha male rhesus monkey. Their leadership in their respective mating fields can actually disadvantage them in the mating game.

So what have we learned? A gentleman may allow a lady to go first in order to ensure that the room that they are entering is safe. A politician's career comes to an end when he reaches the top. The winner in an auction often pays too much for his prize. The top advertiser on Google is often forced to pay over the odds by his competitors. All of these examples serve to illustrate the simple point that leadership is not always as great as it is cracked up to be, and they essentially breakdown into eight characteristics of the disadvantages of leadership:

- **The winner doesn't always take it all** - Abba was wrong - sometimes the winner is forced to share the prize
- **Breaking new ground is harder work** - when trekking through the jungle, the guy at the front carries the machete
- **No cover from threats ahead** - whether you're a canary in a mine shaft, Prime Minister Blair, or the first penguin into the sea, whatever danger lurks ahead, it is coming you're way first

- **Back-stabbing from behind** - a leader's success will inspire strategies in those behind to seize the spoils - keep an eye out for those beta-male rhesus monkeys
- **Setting an example** - your competitors may benefit by learning from your mistakes
- **Nowhere to go but down** - the generalized Peter Principle tells us that resources will be increasingly exploited until they ultimately fail
- **Over investing in winning** - by out-bidding your competitors, you have probably over-valued the spoils of leadership - the "winner's curse."
- **Punishing the winner** - when perceived as proud or arrogant, leaders may well become the targets for punishment

But why does this matter? A common objection that I frequently encounter to Secondomics is that coming second can never offer as many benefits as coming first. The collection of examples in this chapter is by no means exhaustive, but it does serve to illustrate the principle that it is not always best to be in first place, and that in fact, first place brings with it quite specific disadvantages. A common theme to all of the examples in this chapter is that first place is uniquely different to every other place in a ranking. Since only one within a group can be first, that leader comes in for undue, and often unwanted attention, and they may suffer all kinds of disadvantages as a result. I've hopefully demonstrated that first place is not always all that's it's cracked up to be. Now that we've got that out of the way, we can turn to the main focus of this book: second place. What make's it such a great place to be? That's what we'll be exploring in the next section.

Part 3 - The advantages of second

The disadvantages of first place, and the advantages of second are intrinsically linked. After all, payoffs are distributed by rank: the higher your ranking, the greater your share. So all we need in order to establish second place as special is to demonstrate that, in some cases, the disadvantages of leadership outweigh the difference in payoff between first and second place. In other words, since second place gets a greater payoff than all other ranks except first, if the disadvantages of first places are greater than the advantage of first over second, then second place has the greatest benefits of all. But determining situations where this is the case is tricky, since it often involves mixing apples and pears.

To illustrate this point, let's consider the newsstand owner's curse. Naturally, if you're a newsstand owner, you want to sell newspapers and magazines. You're prepared to tolerate a little browsing, because you anticipate that this will eventually lead to sales - effectively, you're allowing your customers to try before they buy. By allowing your customers to browse, you hope they'll find an article in a publication that interests them and choose to buy the magazine, (in order to read the entire article in the comfort of their own homes). A browser, however, may have a different strategy in mind - hoping to read the entire article at the newsstand without paying. The challenge is to finish the article before the guy at the newsstand tells you to get lost, perhaps remarking that "this ain't no library." But for those who *do* intend to buy a magazine if they find one that interests them, a different, arguably more modest "cheat" strategy emerges. Like all browsers, our serious browser will tend to browse the magazine on the top of the stack, since this is closest to hand, and therefore easiest to pick up. Of course you're not going to dig down to pull out a copy from the back of the shelf. Why bother? However, once you'd made the decision to purchase, the game changes. If you're going to pay good money for a magazine, you don't want a copy that's been thumbed by all and sundry. It may have creases, thumb prints, smudges, missing pages, or even germs. Who knows who has had their dirty paws all over it. Suddenly, it's become worth your while to start mining: going deeper into the stack in order to find a virgin copy that has been un-thumbed by the great unwashed masses. But where do you find such a copy? How far down the stack must you mine? I suspect that you already know the answer to this. Not only because it's implied by the title of this book, but also, as a patron of your local newsstand, you've probably done it on numerous occasions. You take the second copy - the one that sits beneath the top copy. Since everyone tends to follows this unspoken strategy, the top copy effectively becomes the trial copy. Thumbed by all browsers, it quickly becomes tatty, and unwanted. Whereas the second copy, below the top "trial" copy is usually still pristine.

In fact, the picture is a little more nuanced than that. Whilst the biggest cheaters at the newsstand are the ones that attempt to read an entire article without paying, and the small cheaters are the ones that choose not to buy the copy that they themselves have soiled, there's another breed of cheaters that fall somewhere in-between the two. These despicable fellows might forsake the pre-thumbed trial copy and decide that they wish to browse a virgin, pristine copy from further down the stake. It's essentially another secondomics strategy - the only difference is that one selects the second copy to browse, rather than to buy. One might reasonably presume that such a slippery customer will then do the noble thing and buy the formerly virgin copy that only they have soiled, and of course, some may do just that. But the even sneakier ones may decide that they don't wish to purchase the one that they themselves have browsed, choosing instead to mine yet further down the stack, in order to find a fresh virgin copy to sully again when they get home. The kind of newsstand patron that thinks this way tends to be pretty self conscious about the strategy that they are employing, and as such, they may well anticipate that other newsstand patrons are doing exactly the same thing. As such, they may choose to delve even deeper down the stack of magazines in order to be confident that they've found a genuinely untouched copy. I call this kind of process "recursive secondomics" - working your way recursively down the rankings by continually selecting the second candidate.

When we factor recursive secondomics into the picture, we may expect the top copy to be the most thumbed, but the second copy will also be lightly thumbed, and even the ones beneath may have known a browser's touch. So your odds of finding a virgin copy progressively increase as your work your way down the stack.

In deciding which copy you wish to purchase, you must weigh up two disparate variables - the "apples and pears" scenario that I mentioned earlier. The first variable is your desire for an unsullied copy of the magazine, and the second is the convenience of taking a copy that is close to hand. How do we reconcile the two? This is where the economist's concept of utility comes to the

THE ADVANTAGES OF SECOND

rescue again. Whilst pristineness, and convenience are two entirely different sorts of things, and they therefore can't be counted together, we can attempt to count how highly you prize their relative merits. How much utility do you derive from having a pristine magazine, and how much utility do you derive from not having to dig too deeply down the stack in order to find your copy? Your answers to these questions may be very different to mine, or to somebody else's. After all, we're all unique in some respects. Nonetheless, we should be able to express the relative utility that you derive from each of these things numerically - in terms of "utils" - or units of utility. If you assign more utils to having a pristine copy than you do to the convenience of taking the closest copy to hand, then taking the second copy will offer you greater overall utility than taking the first.

Other people will assign different utils, and as a consequence they will arrive at different conclusions. So we should not expect everyone to choose the second copy - and indeed they don't. This does not undermine the secondomics argument - it would be nonsense to say that everyone in all circumstances will always buy the second from top magazine. But in practice, I believe that the second from top magazine is a disproportionately popular choice for purchase. Whilst I don't have a scientific study to cite in support of this assertion, I have spent (a little too much) time at newsstands observing browsing behavior, and I've witnessed this behavioral pattern emerging time and time again. And even in situations where the second copy is not selected, it's more likely to be one lower down in the stack, rather than the top copy - and this is probably indicative of recursive secondomics at work.

The newsstand owner's curse gives us a simple model that illustrates our core principle, which we may now express in terms of utility:

> *The negative utility associated with first place may be greater than the difference in utility between the advantages of first and second place, and under these conditions, second place may afford a greater net payoff than first.*

By negative utility, I mean the disadvantages of leadership that we explored in the previous chapter, that **ultimately** boiled down to our eight disadvantages of leadership. For each of these eight disadvantages, there is, perhaps unsurprisingly, a corollary - eight advantages of second place. We will explore each in turn, in this chapter:

- **Disproportionate share of payoff** - the first and second slice of the cake are often substantially larger than all of the other slices, allowing you to

feast like a king
- **Coasting in the slipstream** - when you follow a leader, you can sometimes literally get dragged along in their wake... or even hitch a ride
- **Cover from threats ahead** - by sticking behind the leader, you remain safely out of the line of fire
- **Enemy in your sights** - in an arial dog-fight, the last thing you want is a bogie on your six - get behind the guy in order to shoot him
- **Learning from the leader** - if there's a concealed banana skin on the road ahead, the guy in front of you is sure to show you where it is - and give you a cheap laugh in the process
- Room for growth - **having ambitions for the top spot gives you** something to focus on - it's more fun to be a challenger, rather than an incumbent
- **Lower total cost of ownership** - coming first can involve investing substantially more than your opponents, whereas setting out to come second can cost a lot less
- **Everyone loves an underdog** - we seem to have an innate desire for balance, which sometimes makes it irresistible to give a helping hand to the runner up

Chapter 3: Disproportionate share of payoff

How much is first prize worth? How much is second prize worth? Maybe they are similar, but there's a big drop in value when you get to third prize. Maybe first prize is substantially bigger than all the other prizes put together, or perhaps the runners up get no prize at all.

As we saw in section one, a wide variety of factors influence payoff distribution - for our thirsty wildebeest, the size of the watering hole was a major determining factor. There was an effective cutoff point, which determined how many wildebeest would get to drink, and how many would not. Lucky wildebeest whose position within the herd enabled them to drink were on one side of the cutoff, whereas those whose position was on the other side did not drink at all. This kind of cutoff is a naturally occurring feature of payoff distributions, and there may be enormous variety in how they occur. Sometimes a cutoff may be entirely polarizing - with the payoff being all or nothing, depending upon which side of the cutoff you fall. For example, if you're standing in line for theater tickets - since there's a finite number of seats in the auditorium, there's a cutoff point in the line - a lucky number at the front of the line will get tickets, whilst the remainder after the cutoff will not. In other situations, we may find multiple cutoffs of varying degrees.

In every circumstance, we may expect second place to afford the greatest payoff available after first place. Depending on the position of the cutoff, however, second place may afford an identical payoff to first. For example, the second wildebeest probably gets space to drink alongside the first wildebeest, and the payoff in this instance is therefore identical. In other situations, such as a presidential elections, there's only space for one man (or woman) at the top, and there's no prize for second place (although in presidential primaries, or course, there may well be a prize for second place as running mate for vice president).

Whilst we may expect to find an endless variety of different payoff distributions, as we explore the variety of ways in which rankings emerge, patterns do start to appear. One such pattern is that second place is often a disproportionately privileged position. Whilst presidential elections may only have one winner, more generally, "first past the post" electoral systems employed in democracies such as the United States and the United Kingdom, give a specific disproportionate advantage to second place. The nature of first past the post voting creates an inevitable and substantial cutoff between second and third place.

In first past the post systems, there is only one winner in each constituency. Therefore from an individual candidate's perspective, the cutoff represents an all or nothing split between first and second place. However, from a political party's perspective, the cutoff tends to rest between second and third place. The explanation for this is twofold - firstly, votes for losing candidates are discarded. If a party fields many losing candidates, these may still have received a lot of votes in combination, but simply not enough to win in any given constituency - as a consequence, that party may have no representation in an elected assembly even though they have received a lot of votes. Secondly, politics tends to be a polarized debate between left-wing and right-wing candidates, broadly speaking, representing the interests of the poor and rich in turn. Since populations have a tendency to group into wealthy areas and poor areas, the two parties to the left and right of the political spectrum will benefit from "heartland" voters. For example, urban voters have a tendency to vote for left wing parties such as the Democrats or Labour, whilst rural voters have a tendency to vote for right wing parties such as the Republican's or the Conservatives. A center party, such as the Liberal Democrats in the UK has no heartland, and as a result, their vote is spread fairly evenly across the entire country. Even though they tend to get a substantial share of the vote, the party gets a disproportionately small share of seats in the UK parliament. In America, the effect is even more pronounced, with political debate entirely dominated by the two main parties.

Interestingly, both two-party systems have their roots in the British Whig and Tory traditions that emerged in the late 17th century. Whilst the Tories tended to be strong supporters of the crown, and vociferous defenders of the elite rights of the rural landed gentry, the Whigs were progressive intellectuals, advocating the rights of parliament and the merits of financing and ultimately industrialization. Over the centuries, the Tories evolved into the modern Conservative party, whilst the Whigs evolved into today's Liberal Democrats - although the Labour party are arguably the true inheritors of the Whig tradition. In America, two party politics swiftly began to emerge after the revolution - much to President Washington's dismay. Initially, the Democratic-Republicans (precursors to today's Democratic Party) and the Federalists (who later disbanded) bore little resemblance to the Whig and Tory parties. Whilst the Democratic-Republican party shared common cause with the Whigs over supporting the rights of individual citizens over those of nobles and monarchs, they were deeply mistrustful of urban life, industrialization and the emergence of finance and banking. Equally, the Federalists, whilst leaning towards the privileges of nobility, and even striking an alliance with their formal colonial oppressors, were unlike the Tories in their appetite for cities, industry and finance. As American politics matured, however, the parties increasingly settled into the familiar Whig and Tory mould. A third party in American politics never got a look in.

It seems that the domination of American and British politics by two parties is entirely due to their first past the post electoral systems, since there is no intrinsic reason for political debate to be polarized in this way. The concept of politics as a polarization between left and right wing views is both arbitrary and limited. On any given political issue, there may be any number of legitimate views that one may adopt - a far more nuanced and sophisticated perspective than could possibly be represented by a polarized two-party system. Nonetheless, two party politics continues to thrive wherever first past the post systems give it the opportunity to do so, giving a disproportionately high payoff to the second party.

First past the post electoral systems are just one example of a mechanism for allocating payoffs that creates a polarizing cutoff after second place - there are plenty more. But equally, cutoffs could occur further down the rankings - one specific example of this is the balance of power in a hung parliament, where no single party has a majority of seats. In this situation, one of the two largest parties will seek to make a deal with the third party in order to form a coalition with a working majority. This gives the third-ranking party a disproportionate payoff relative to their share of seats. However, interestingly, this is yet another example of secondomics at work, since in this instance, it's quite possible for the second largest party to form a coalition with the third, leaving the winning party out in the cold. In this circumstance, the second-ranking party is also benefiting from a disproportionately high payoff.

Tipping points, long tails and black swans

Traditionally, statisticians have not enjoyed a glamorous life. Scorned as purveyors of lies and damn lies, the problem has been that statistics are hard work to understand correctly, and can so easily be misconstrued. They also have a frustrating tendency to undermine our comfortable assumptions and make us think. It's all to easy to dismiss something that one struggles to understand, opting instead to leap to self-serving, but unreliable, conclusions. In recent years, however, statistics have enjoyed something of a renaissance, with books such as Malcolm Gladwell's *The Tipping Point*, Chris Andersen's *The Long Tail* and Nassim Nicholas Taleb's *The Black Swan* successfully making statistics sexy. And it is to these statistical sages that we now turn, as we explore what patterns of payoff distribution we may expect to find, and where this might favor those in second place.

Broadly speaking, payoff distributions may be characterised as belonging to one of two types - constrained by physical limitation, and unconstrained. Taleb's book, "The Black Swan," describes the characteristics of two types of data as "Mediocrstan" and "Extremistan." These two fictitious counties operate in contrasting ways. In Mediocrstan, all data tend to be similar in value, and tend to follow observable trends. By looking at historic data, you can reliably forecast will will happen next in Mediocrstan. In Extremistan, by contrast, data tend to be more random, and less predictable. The terrain of Mediocrstan is filled with gently rolling hills and valleys, whilst Extremistan is contains treacherous mountains, unexpected peaks and sheer cliff faces. The beguiling thing about Extremistan, however, is that it also contains gently rolling countryside that could fool you into believing that you're actually in Mediocrstan... until, that is, you take one step too far, and fall off a cliff. Taleb explains that data types following the Mediocrstan pattern tend to be constrained by some physical limitation - for example, people's weight, the height of trees or 100 meter sprint records - whereas Extremistan-style data concerns things that are scalable and not constrained by the physical, such as money in a bank, or hits on a web site.

So Extremistan-style payoff distributions, unconstrained as they are by the laws of physics, can provide enormous cutoffs, and these can, in turn, disproportionately favor second place when it finds itself on the same plateau as first. But even when we're more constrained by the physical world, we may also find that second place gets an unfair advantage over those beneath. One such naturally occurring payoff distribution is the power curve. Cleverly explored by Chris Andersen in his book "The Long Tail," power curves are the result of multiplying a number by itself, so for example, 2 to the power of 4 equals 16. In the case of payoff distribution, imagine that each rank gets a prize that is half the value of the rank above. So if first place gets 1,000 points, second place gets 500, third gets 250 and so on. The chart below illustrates what such as payoff distribution looks like. You can see the characteristic "long tail" described by Andersen, as the payoffs taper off into very low numbers to the right, whilst to the left, you can see the disproportionately high payoffs allocated to those with the highest rank. We find many examples of this type of payoff structure. For example, income distribution. It's a widely held belief that "the rich keep getting richer, and the poor keep getting poorer." Whilst the former statement is undoubtedly true, it's certainly not true to say that in most western countries, the poor are getting poorer - standards of living continue to rise. It is true, however, to say that the difference in income between the richest and poorest is increasing. Economists measure the distribution of income using the Gini Coefficient - a rise in this measure indicates an increase in income differential. And it seems to be relentlessly rising.

It's natural for this differential to emerge, since skilled workers at the top of the earnings ladder are in increasingly high demand, whilst technological advancement combined with globalization are resulting in a surplus of unskilled labor. If these trends continue, we can expect income distribution to follow an increasingly exaggerated power curve. So top footballers will earn ever more stratospheric salaries, shareholders and rank and file employees will continue to bemoan the fat cats creaming off the profits, whilst the bottom of the earnings scale will increasingly be filled with low-paying McJobs.

THE ADVANTAGES OF SECOND

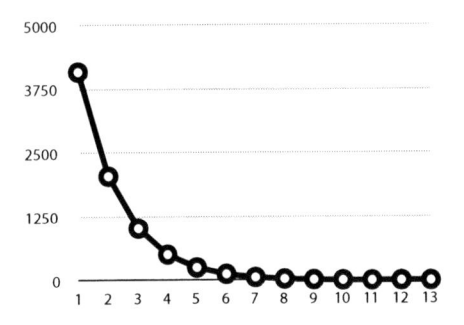

[Chart showing a power curve distribution with y-axis values 0, 1250, 2500, 3750, 5000 and x-axis values 1 through 13, with values decreasing sharply from ~4000 at x=1 to near 0 by x=5]

Another type of data that follows this power curve distribution is book sales, with a few best sellers at the top disproportionately dominating the rest. This kind of distribution is largely a function of how readers choose which books to buy, and how the books themselves are marketed. Readers are enormously influenced by word of mouth, which means that they buy books because other people recommend them. The fact that readers influence each other's purchasing means that book recommendations spread like an epidemic within a community of readers. And in the case of some particularly virulent book recommendations, they spread until everyone has been infected. Think Harry Potter or The Da Vinci Code. Other books, which may be excellent works but never managed to get picked up in one of these recommendation epidemics, will continue to languish somewhere down in the long tail. This is the type of epidemic that Malcolm Gladwell describes in his book "The Tipping Point," in which he explores the point at which something moves sufficiently up the ranks to escape the long tail and enter into the best sellers spike.

The marketing of books introduces another important component to the distribution of book sales - one which may appear more like a cutoff than a power curve. A retailer has a finite amount of space within which to sell books. That means that they can only stock a finite number of titles at any given time. In some situations, the number of titles may be very limited - such as in a supermarket, where there is only shelf space enough for best sellers. Other constraints also introduce arbitrary cutoffs, such as The New York Times Top 10 Best Sellers. We may expect a book placing just below the top ten to experience disproportionately lower sales as a consequence of the lower level of media attention that it receives. In this situation, the distribution will reflect a combination of power curve distribution and arbitrary cutoffs. These various cutoffs will introduce a certain lumpiness to our otherwise smooth power curve.

Second place will always sit comfortably high up the slope of Best Seller's Peak. Certainly, first place will earn a substantially higher payoff, but second place will in turn receive a disproportionately greater payoff than any other rank. Where power curves and cutoffs are combined, best sellers will get an even more disproportionate advantage.

Chapter 4: Coasting in the slipstream

What do Doctor Watson, Sancho Panza, Mr Spock, Cyrano De Bergerac, Abigail Adams and Hilary Clinton have in common? The answer is, of course, obvious. They're all sidekicks. That's a term that we may comfortably apply to the first four individuals, since they are all fictitious and male. Applying this soubriquet to the latter two, however, may give cause to wince. After all, both Abigail Adams and Hilary Clinton were surely more than mere sidekicks. But that is precisely my point. Hilary Clinton went from being First Lady to mounting a convincing campaign to be the Democratic nominee for the presidency in her own right. Whilst her campaign did not ultimately succeed, it came very close indeed. This achievement was doubtless in no small part due to her many notable talents, but her previous tenure in the White House, and her association with her immensely popular husband certainly benefited her campaign's chances.

In the sidekick role, someone in second place actively collaborates with the leader in order to achieve a common goal. In literary fiction, the secondary nature of the role may be emphasized through an exaggerated portrayal of lesser ability. For example, Doctor Watson was consistently one step behind his brilliant mentor, Sherlock Holmes. In this context, the sidekick is used as a foil - simultaneously contrasting and in so doing highlighting the merits of the hero, whilst providing a perfect narrative contrivance for explanatory dialogue. How would we know what Holmes was planning next, if he didn't have Watson by his side, in order to ask the obvious questions. Indeed, Watson may even serve as some comfort to the reader who is dazzled by Holme's tiresome brilliance. The humble reader may not share Holme's genius, but at least he can take some solace in the fact that he's smarter than Watson.

But the secondary status of the sidekick need not be indicative of a lesser ability. It may simply illustrate that age old truism "life isn't fair." After all, who didn't feel for Mr Spock - a man with remarkable intellect and enviable self control (apart from the odd indiscretion during pon farr,) who is nonetheless expected to play second fiddle to that posturing overweight womanizer, Captain

THE ADVANTAGES OF SECOND

Kirk. A predicament that Hilary Clinton herself may well empathize with.

So whilst Hilary Clinton's ability may not be any less than that of her husband, we may still allow that her career probably benefited from her time at the White House, standing by her man (albeit once, in an ungenerous slur on Tammy Wynette, she claimed this this is precisely what she would not do). Another highly regarded First Lady, who certainly did stand by her man was Abigail Adams. Born in an age where women were not even allowed to vote, she nonetheless exerted considerable influence upon the politics of her country during its formative years. Highly regarded for her intellect and insight, she was the trusted advisor and confident to her husband, America's second president, John Adams. The president depended on the trusted counsel of his wife to such an extent that some even came to refer to her as Mrs. President. Despite Abigail Adam's many obvious talents, in those days there was no chance for her to take the number one post herself - and indeed, at the time of writing, no woman has ever served as president of the United States. Nonetheless, in her secondary role of sidekick, she was able to bring her talent to bear in guiding that nation's successful formation.

So the sidekick role may at times be a secondomics strategy of standing close to power in order to exert disproportionate influence upon events. Someone whose evident ability may go unnoticed due to the whimsical prejudices of society, may still get an opportunity to exercise their talents by positioning themselves in second place, and channeling their abilities vicariously through the leader. The example of Cyrano de Bergerac springs to mind. Cyrano, a sensitive and sophisticated, yet nasally challenged man, in an era before today's sophisticated cosmetic surgery techniques, falls in love with the beautiful Roxanne. Although Cyrano never had the chance to read chapter two of Secondomics, where we explore the bell curve of attractiveness (or belle curve, as Cyrano may have referred to it), he was nonetheless aware of the negative utility associated with dating a man with a large nose. However, he failed to accurately account for the utility that Roxanne may have ascribed to dating a man with his many other talents (dueling, poetry, brooding, etc) and as a result, he concluded that Roxanne may prefer to date a guy (Christian) that perpetually lies to her, by drawing upon his friend Cyrano's poetic skills in order to express his amorous intent.

Roxanne explains how her feelings for Christian have developed, in Act IV, Scene V of Edmond Rostand's play:

At first I loved you only for your face!...

> *And later, love—less frivolous...*
> *Arrested by your beauty, by your soul*
> *Drawn close—I loved for both at once!...*
> *And now, I love you only for your soul!*

So, the story of Cyrano and Roxanne is a strange twist on the tale of our satellite toads in Chapter 2. There, the satellite toads who were bad at croaking would gather around the talented croaker, and intercept the females that approached him in the process. Here, Cyrano is clearly the skilled croaker, whilst Christian intercepts the female. The difference, however, concerns who is doing the exploiting. The satellite toads are clearly the exploiters - stealing potential mates from the top croaker. But in the tale of Cyrano De Bergerac, I can't help feeling that Christian is ultimately the one being exploited. Cyrano is (perhaps unconsciously) borrowing his good looks in order to get an opportunity to woo the lovely Roxanne. As Roxanne, herself explains, she is initially drawn to Christian's good looks. If Cyrano had approached her directly, would she have seen past his enormous nose, to discover his "beautiful soul"? Perhaps not. By piggybacking on his friend's good looks, Cyrano consigns Christian to a soulless existence in a meaningless relationship, and ultimately dying in the knowledge that his partner does not truly love him. So Cyrano is more like Hilary Clinton and Mr Spock than he is like a toad. By playing sidekick, he is able to exert greater influence. Indeed, Cyrano so successfully exploits his sidekick position that he ultimately succeeds in usurping Christian in Roxanne's affections. In this sense, the sidekick role may instead be a staging post in a covert campaign for the top spot. In this sense, perhaps Cyrano is more like Gordon Brown. As Sun Tzu wrote way back in 500BC, in his influential text The Art of War, "Keep your friends close, and your enemies closer."

Adopting the role of sidekick is one method of coasting in the slipstream. Migratory birds have discovered another. Flocking birds have a tendency to assume V-formations, with a leader at the front, following by two lines (or "skeins") of birds, trailing out behind, on either side. Since this kind of flocking formation is consistently observed across a variety of avifauna, we can reasonably assume that the birds derive some utility from it, which has resulted in this behavior evolving through natural selection. But what utility are the birds deriving from it, and which birds are receiving the greatest utility? No surprise, perhaps that the second bird appears to get the greatest benefit.

Evidence indicates that energy saving is an important advantage of the v-formation. This energy saving is achieved by each bird flying in the vortex

THE ADVANTAGES OF SECOND

wake of the bird in front. When the bird in front forces its wings down, this pushes the air beneath the wing downwards, and creates a brief pocket of thinner air above the wing. As a consequence, an uplift of air occurs behind and away from the wing, as air rushes to balance this displacement. And it's this uplift that makes the task of flying just that bit easier. It doesn't make a huge difference - the bird could certainly manage to fly without it. Just a very small difference. In a single bird's lifetime, this kind of advantage may not have much impact. But if you look at a large enough sample of birds - the quantity of birds that might have existed over millions of generations, then sufficiently more birds that adopted this v-formation must have successfully reproduced versus those that did not for the behavior to ultimate come to dominate the population.

It must be a lonely job at the front - you can't see any of your bird-buddies, and it's slightly harder work to fly. Why would any sane bird volunteer for such a task? One common example is parents - who may be willing to take on this burden in order to improve their offsprings' chances of future reproduction. This kind of parental generosity is referred to as kin selection. Another solution is that the bird might take it in turns to share the burden of leadership - a topic we'll return to in Part Five.

So the bird at the front is clearly at a disadvantage, but what of the bird in second place? Since birds are flying in formation for a reason (migration) there is some purpose to their destination. This might be finding the optimal nesting spot, catching the best bite to eat, or whatever. Clearly, the closer you are to the front of the flock, the sooner you'll get to wherever your going, and this may in turn give you a better chance of exploiting whatever resources you find there, at the expense of the birds behind. The leader bird then has the best opportunity to exploit the resources at their destination, but he has the disadvantage of having no vortex wake to fly in. Once again, it comes down to the utils that we might assign to first pickings at the destination, versus the benefit of some free uplift. That may be a calculation that only a bird can make (or millions of birds over thousands of years of evolution), but I suspect that the second bird on the skein knows exactly what he's doing (or at least his genes do).

Before I let the birds fly away (for now at least), it's worth noting that the shape of the V is of some significance. The advantage of flying in the wake of the bird in front is most pronounced when a flock flies in a very acute formation (a very pointed, narrow V shape). The shape of the V varies somewhat from one flock to another, and from one species to another. Some formations may have a more obtuse shape (less pointed). In these cases, the advantages a less pronounced. Some V formations become so obtuse that the point becomes almost rounded, so that the lead bird is not much in front of the birds that flank him on either side. In this instance, the bird at the front might even get a slight advantage from his neighbors' vortex wake. In these special circumstances, clearly the second bird in the skein is unlikely to gain the maximum utility. We should instead look for the bird at the back. However, where animals at the periphery of a pack are more likely to be attacked by predators, the second from last bird on the skein may be getting the maximum advantage in this type of formation.

Birds are, of course, not the only species to engage in this kind of freeloading. Humans have a name for it too - drafting, or slipstreaming. The faster we travel, the more benefit there is to gain from drafting - and we humans have a penchant for traveling fast. This addiction to speed is perhaps something to do with our competitive natures. All animals compete in the evolutionary sense - they're competing to be most adapted to their environment, and to monopolize the resources that they find around them. As we explored in Chapter 1, this competitive behavior has its origins way back in the primordial goo, where self-replicating chemicals found themselves in contention to utilize the raw materials within the goo to reproduce. Many animals exhibit playful competitive behavior. Packs of dogs, for example, will chase each other, seemingly just for the fun of it. But the difference between us humans and all the other organisms that evolved from the goo is that we have the capacity to compete self consciously. When dogs in a pack compete for fun, they don't appreciate that they're doing so in order to exercise themselves, establish a pack hierarchy and prepare to defend against an attack from an external aggressor. This playful behavior is just instinctive to them, and that instinct has probably evolved over many generations because dogs that exhibit it have a better chance of survival over those who don't. In just the same respect, birds do not consciously decide to fly in a v-formation. They're merely following instincts that have evolved over many years.

Human competition is doubtless fulfilling some instinctual need for us too, but the difference is that we have the capacity to consciously enter into it - and we describe this kind of behavior as games or sport. It seems reasonable to speculate that running races would be one of the earliest forms of sport - perhaps together with wrestling, since these activities require no special equipment, and no complex linguist communication to arrange. At running speed, the benefits of drafting are limited, but when you start to move faster it becomes more significant. As human society has developed, our methods of transportation have become more sophisticated. At cycling speed, there is a noticeable advantage to drafting, which is why in cycling races, we so often see cyclists grouped together in tight packs referred to as pelotons (a French word for a scrum). The formation of pelotons is noticeably different from the v-shaped formations observed in birds. The reason for this is not simply that the v-shape would not be very practical on the road. Whilst birds in v-formation are exploiting the vortex wakes that occur behind the wings of the bird in front (which are in their nature to the side), cyclists are riding in the lower air pressure directly behind the cyclist in front. So instead of the dual skeins with birds, we observe a single line or cluster.

Pelotons provide a perfect model of secondomics at work. The cyclist at the front of the group expends the most energy, since he must contend with the wind ahead. However, providing you're not at the front, being towards the front is the optimal place to be - it's referred to as the tête (meaning "head" in French). Being towards the front, it is easy to adjust to the leader's speed changes, and there is less risk of being involved in a crash, since there are less cyclists in front of you to fall over. Conversely, towards the back, in the "tail," the cyclists tend to be more tired and less skilled, making accidents more likely. Also a phenomenon called the elastic band effect, where compounded reaction time results in the back responding sluggishly to changes in speed at the front, can result in the tail breaking off from a peloton altogether.

Cyclists may also form extended single-file formations (rather than the bunched-up peloton) - these are known as pacelines. And in order to compensate for crosswinds, diagonal pacelines may also emerge, which are known as echelons. And indeed, the phenomenon of drafting is not unique to cycling - it also emerges in other high-speed racing activities, including motor racing swimming and speed skating. In all these cases, secondomics applies - being in the tête, right behind the leader affords the greatest payoff.

A cyclist who routinely follows the leader without doing his fair share at the front is sometimes referred to as a "wheel sucker". Interestingly however, in cycling as in all the examples of drafting that we have explored, wheel sucking is a victimless crime. By following in the wake of the leader, you do not apply any drag to the leader. In effect, you are taking advantage of a by-product of his activity that is of no value to him. In game theory terms, this is a non-zero sum game. Whilst, in a competitive racing scenario, an advantage to your competitor is by definition a disadvantage to yourself, cyclists may also race in teams or for fun, and so once again, cooperative mixed strategies may emerge, where the participants take it in turns to share second place.

Whilst a wheel sucker may not actually be stealing anything from the guy in front, there is of course a variant of this strategy, made famous by Marty McFly in the movie "Back to the Future" in which he introduces skateboarding to 1950's America. In the film, Marty masters the dangerous art of hitching a ride by grabbing hold of the rear fender of a car, and allowing it to pull you along on your skateboard. Rather than following in the wake of the guy in front, in this context, Marty is freeloading on a little of the car's energy. However, so little additional energy is expended by the car in pulling Marty, relative to the overall energy required to move the car, that the duped motorist doesn't notice. Whilst he has to put his foot down ever so slightly more on the gas in order to maintain the same speed, the difference is so tiny that he's presumably entirely unaware of it. This is a variant of our slipstream situation, therefore - whilst it is essentially freeloading at the leaders expense, the marginal cost to the leader is so tiny as to go unnoticed.

In all manner of situations, there are advantages to be gained by positioning oneself in close proximity to the leader. We may benefit from their hardwork, like birds and bicycles, we may influence their behavior, like Abigail Adams. But in all cases, we may avoid the disadvantages of leadership, even as we vicariously benefit from the advantages.

Chapter 5: Cover from threats ahead

Cover from threats ahead is related to our peloton example, if we think of wind resistance as a threat. However, whilst the wheel sucker's good fortune does not come at the expense of the leader, if the threat ahead is a soldier with a gun, and you're emerging from the trenches, your fellow soldier in front of you may well end up taking a bullet on your behalf. In these circumstances, your gain is very much your leader's sacrifice. We might also think of the captain who is expected to go down with his ship, whilst the second in command gets to flee with the other passengers. But under what circumstances will this kind of situation emerge? Are these genuine acts of altruism on the part of those providing cover, or is something else going on?

Imagine that you are a protein molecule, floating in a pan of warm milk. You're probably a casein molecule, since this accounts for about 80% of all the protein in milk. Most of your molecular buddies are also casein, apart from the smaller awkward-squad of lactalbumin oddballs. As the temperature slowly rises in the pan, past 40°c, something interesting starts to happen. Some of your buddies start to become "denatured". Protein molecules are like bundles of string - when they are denatured, they unravel, and then form a new shape instead. A combination of the rising heat, and the evaporation of moisture from the top of the pan is causing your buddies at the top to literally change shape, and as their shape alters, they join together to form a solid membrane. It's pretty decent of them to do this for you, as it turns out, because this membrane is now protecting you from further evaporation, so that you are less likely to become denatured yourself (you like your nature just the way it is). Not only that, but the "skin" on the surface of the pan allows you to enjoy a little more warmth and pressure - a nice, relaxing protein sauna.

Like every milk molecule, your purpose in life is ultimately to be drunk by some thirsty youngster. Since you're a bovine milk molecule, you're expecting to serve as the nourishment for a lucky calf. Little do you know, that you're being heated up in order to be served to a greedy ape-infant, alongside a plate of cookies. Whilst this may be the great tragedy of your milky existence, at least you'll get to provide some nourishment to someone. Your selfless pals up above are afforded no such respect for their efforts. With the brief words "Yuck! I hate skin on my milk," they are scooped off the surface and discarded. "Why did they perform such as selfless act?" you muse, as you are transferred from the pan's embrace to the more confined enclosure of a glass. You were so close to the surface, that you very nearly became denatured yourself, and you certainly would had done, had it not been for the swift and decisive action of the molecules above.

As hard as it may be for your non-existent molecule-brain to accept, the skin-forming antics of your brethren was not selflessness on their part. Like you, they have no sense of self - they cannot act of their own volition - they're just molecules. They formed a skin because of their context within the pan - they were on the surface - at the top - first amongst many. If you were in their position, you would have done exactly the same thing.

In fact, you're not a milk molecule - if you were, you would not be reading this. I'm going to guess that you're actually a person - comprised of many billions of protein molecules, and more besides. Nonetheless, like our molecule, you may also at times be vulnerable to fundamental attribution error. We have a tendency to identify specific behavior we observe in others as indicative of more general personality attributes. In other words, if we observe someone to be exhibiting heroic behavior, we are likely to conclude that they are a hero, when in fact, their behavior is merely a matter of context. We would probably have done the same thing in the their situation.

When we observe a captain who refuses to desert his sinking ship, we may assume that he is a hero. In fact, there are many reasons why a captain may prefer to go down with his ship - some more heroic than others. He may simply be electing to commit suicide rather than face the consequences of his failure to save his floundering ship. Or perhaps he is a hero after all - electing to be last to disembark, to maximize the survival chances for his passengers and crew.

As we saw in Chapter Two, Prime Minister Gordon Brown may not have been responsible for the collapse of British mortgage lender Northern Rock, but as the leader of the government, he was held responsible. There was nowhere for him to hide. He was in the front line. In this instance, the problem was not really of the UK government's making - it was the result of the credit crunch that was occurring globally, and would probably have happened regardless of UK government policy. Nonetheless, journalists and voters are never satisfied with the explanation that some bad things just happen, and it isn't necessarily someone's fault. No, someone must take the blame. Someone must be held to account. Someone must be punished. It had been plain sailing for Gordon Brown in his number-two role as Chancellor of the Exchequer, but as prime minister, he is held to account for events that are not necessarily anyone's fault.

In other circumstances, Gordon Brown found himself held responsible for a problem that was indeed someone's fault - but not his. In November 2007, in the British parliament, members gasped when Chancellor Alistair Darling announced that there had been an "extremely serious failure on the part of [the Inland Revenue] to protect sensitive personal data entrusted to it in breach of its own guidelines." What this meant in practice was that some office junior had decided to slip two CDs containing the banking details of 25 million people into a jiffy bag, and mail it to another government department. The British mail service is notoriously bad, and so it comes as no surprise to discover that the discs in question never turned up. It's a classic example of a small mistake having very large consequences. And our brains seem hard-wired to struggle with the concept of a small mistake precipitating a much larger consequence. In this instance, millions of people had to be extra vigilant for possible fraud. How could one humble clerk possibly be to blame for such a big mistake? A big head must surely roll for a big mistake. And in British politics, there is no head bigger than that of the Prime Minister, Gordon Brown.

Like the protein molecules at the top of a pan of warm milk, Gordon Brown was effectively forming a protective film around his government. The press and the public questioned his competence, despite the fact that this error was not his fault, and was only marginally his responsibility. Gordon Brown was not heroically defending his government. He did not volunteer to take the blame. It was thrust upon him, and in the process, he deflected the heat from those people within his administration who were really responsible. But the politicians below the surface, benefiting from this kind of protective skin should beware. The molecules in a pan of warm milk are excited by the heat, which causes them to jiggle around - an effect (ironically) known as brownian motion. This jiggling causes the molecules to move around within the milk - so a protein that is safely away from the surface at one moment, could randomly find its way to the surface the very next moment, and as a consequence, find itself at risk of being denatured. Just like Gordon Brown's political career, it doesn't take much for a protein molecule to become unravelled.

As we discussed in chapter one - classical economists tend to agree that individuals act in their own best interest. In practice, they act in what they *perceive to be* their own best interests, which means that they may be wrong. The decision of a captain who decides to go down with his ship may at first glance appear to be just such a situation where self interest is not served. However, when we factor in the utility that my be afforded to the captain by the posthumous preservation of his reputation, or the avoidance of a subsequent uncomfortable legal wrangling, we may suppose that the captain is indeed acting in the furtherance of what he perceives to be his own self interest. And as discussed, a leader who gets flack from the front, like Gordon Brown, may better be compared to a molecule, that has not chosen to nobly protect his brethren, but simply cannot get escape the denaturing effects of moisture evaporation and heat. In most cases, however, we might reasonable expect those in power to avoid the frontline altogether.

In most of our examples so far, we have focused on first place as a leadership position, and as such, we have assumed that the leader is the most powerful individual within the group. Of course, in practice this is not always the case. George Bush was certainly not in the front line when he ordered the invasion of Iraq in 2003. He was safely ensconced in a maximum-security military facility in Washington DC, several thousand miles from the front line or FLOT (US military parlance for Forward Line of Own Troops). Whilst history tells many illustrious tales of great rulers who lead their troops into battle, I doubt many of these would bare up to any degree of scrutiny. The truth is that those on the front line are most likely to die in battle, and as such, any general who routinely places himself on the front line is unlikely to participate in many battles. In fact, it's arguable that, the more experience a leader has of battle, the less likely he is to have positioned himself in the front line.

The chess board provides us with a perfect illustration of this. The most powerful pieces on the board are positioned in the second row - safely behind a first row of more expendable "pawns". Any soldier in battle who finds himself on the front line may reasonably surmise from this that he too is a pawn. He is expendable, and therefore does not earn the luxury of second place. In the case of a chess board, the pieces are not powerful in themselves - their power is measured by the utility that they afford to the players who play with them. And it serves the players best interests to protect his most valuable assets with his more expendable pawns.

Once again, those at the front - the pawns - are not brave, they are simply forced to face death as a consequence of their context, which is outside of their own control. Like Gordon Brown, a pawn on a chess board does not seek out the threats ahead, he merely cannot avoid them, because of his context. The difference is, however, that one is supposed to be the most valuable piece on the board - the Prime Minister - whilst the other is the least valuable - a mere pawn. This serves to illustrates that it matters not how you arrive on the frontline. It is merely the fact that you are there that counts. Whether through an act of your own volition, the concerted act of your leader, or just a quirk of fate, if you're at the front, you'll be providing a protective a shield from the threat ahead for those behind.

In some situations, this becomes so exaggerated, that the extent of the battle for second place becomes readily apparent. I was recently riding a subway train on London's Underground system. I was on the Piccadilly Line, which has cramped, claustrophobic carriages, and is typically overcrowded. On this occasion, the carriage was only half full, so I and all the other passengers, were taking advantage of the extra space. Most of us had bags, coats, umbrellas or whatever, on the seats next to us. Some of us were taking advantage of the extra elbow room, our arms slumping over the armrest and into the space of the adjacent seat. Londoners are rarely afforded the luxury of extra space on the Underground, but on the rare occasions when they have it, they don't waste any time in taking advantage of it. It gets interesting, however, when the train starts to get more crowded.

We stop at a particularly busy station - Knightsbridge - a honeypot for tourists, drawn to the excesses of Harrods, where they can buy branded teddy bears, and weak English-style teas. A throng of these tourists pile onto our train. Most of them are able to find seats, but there is still one who is left standing. An uncomfortable moment ensues for the rest of us, seated passengers, who

THE ADVANTAGES OF SECOND

have sprawled ourselves and our luggage onto multiple seats. Basic human decency requires that we make room for the remaining passenger - that we remove our luggage from the seats, and bring in our elbows so that we're not using more than our fair share of space.

But the truth is that ultimately only one of us needs to surrender some space, since there's only one passenger standing. How do we resolve who this will be? To find the answer, let's look at the various motivating factors. There are two opposing incentives in this scenario - on the one hand, the seated passengers wish to retain their extra space, whilst on the other hand, they do not want to appear impolite. The solution to this dichotomy is obvious - make an exaggerated display of making room, whilst ensuring that the space that you've ceded does not look as attractive as that of other seats on the carriage. As a result, you'll hopefully appear to be willing to make room, whilst ultimately not being required to do so.

We can consider this situation as a kind of game, where on one level, all seated passengers are competing to make the space adjacent to them as attractive as possible to the standing passenger. The more ostentatious your display of making room, the more generous and polite you appear to be. But there's a sting. In this kind game, the winner is punished, since the seated passenger making the best display of making space will lose some space. The seated passenger who comes second - gets a much better payoff, since he appears to be very generous, without having to give up anything. The aim of the game, then, is to receive a "that's a generous offer, but..." response.

This is a special case of the *cover from threats ahead* scenario. In this case, all the participants are acting as if they want a prize that they actually do not wish to receive. They just wish to *appear as* if they want to win it. The *threat* is ceding space, whilst the *cover* is the illusion that you were willing to cede space without actually having to do so. If you simply wanted to retain your extra space, you would sprawl out even more - depositing arms, bags and even feet in the way of a passenger who may try to sit next to you. This strategy will almost certainly ensure that you get to sit by yourself, but at the expense of your cover - and as a result, your esteem amongst your fellow passengers, who will think that you are rude, inconsiderate and offensive.

I call this secondomic generosity, were the aim is to make an offer that sounds as generous as possible, in order to maximize the esteem that one receives from one's peers, whilst ensuring that your offer will ultimately be rejected by an even more generous offer. This may seem like an excessively cynical view of human behavior, but I'm not necessarily arguing that this is conscious behavior. When I'm sitting on the train, making space for someone to sit next to me, I'm not consciously reasoning before acting. This is about manners, and it's almost an automatic response - I'm making room "without thinking," as if it's instinctive behavior. I don't know that it's truly instinctive, rather than learned behavior, but if it's the latter, then it's been learned by rote, to such an extent that I no longer have to think about it. It's clear that however much effort I undertake in making space, there's always more that I could do. I could move my elbow entirely off the arm rest, or I could even dust-down the adjacent seat, for example. But I don't do those things. I only do as much as is necessary in order to been seen to have done the right thing by my peers. But I haven't made a conscious decision to do this - it just happened. This unconscious proportionality of my response may well be some instinctive ability to weigh up the conflict between group esteem and sacrifice, that has evolved over time.

So in some situations, it may be to our advantage to act as if we want to win, without actually winning. We benefit from appearing to compete, whilst being protected from the disadvantages of success by the winner. And in order to achieve this, we must finely judge our proportionate response - making as elaborate a display as possible of participation, without going so far as to risk achieving victory. Thus, we maximize the prestige we may gain from within our group, whilst minimizing the associated costs. Interestingly, however, in many situations, we not only make elaborate displays of participating, we also make similar displays of victory or defeat.

Recent research by Jessica Tracy of the University of British Columbia and David Matsumoto of San Francisco State University, provides evidence that these displays of pride or shame may be innate behavioral responses. The research looks at at Judo competitors in the 2004 Olympic and Paralympic Games. Winners tend to make the same behavioral displays - tilting back their heads, expanding their chests and raising their arms. The research found that blind judo competitors in the Paralympics make much the same displays. Whilst some aspects of these displays may be learned (sighted friends may have told blind athletes that it is customary to raise one's arms in a victory salute), other more subtle aspects of these displays are unlikely to be learned through verbal accounts, and could not have been observed visually. The researchers conclude that this provides evidence to support the premise that these displays are biologically innate responses, which would indicate that they have or had some evolutionary benefit. Presumably they served as a method to claim prestige and therefore status within the hierarchy of the group. The clear and early confirmation of a consensus between victor and vanquished in a conflict situation may also serve to reduce damage inflicted to both parties by shortening the duration of the conflict.

But, whilst there are advantages to victory displays, their are clearly also disadvantages. A motorist making an ostentatious show of wealth, by displaying a valuable gadget on the dashboard of his unattended car, will make him all the more likely to be singled out as the victim of crime. A home owner that allows his valuables to be seen through a window from the street is more likely to be the victim of burglary. And by making such displays, the victor draws this unwanted attention away from the other competitors.

In other words, those coming second may benefit by not making victory displays - allowing those who seek to take (or steal) the spoils of success to be drawn to those who did slightly better, and are ill-advisedly making a song and dance about it. Quietly coming second allows one to take as big a share of the payoff as possible, whilst minimizing the risks associated with unwanted attention.

Chapter 6: Enemy in your sights

Our next advantage of second place is the opportunity to have your enemy in your sights. Here, I'm using the term second to refer to spacial context within a group, rather than competitive ranking - so, taking someone at the front to be first, and someone behind first to be second. At this point, you may protest and say that this is stretching the definition of second. You'd be right, of course, but what is important here is that competitive rankings often result in spatial context. For example, if you're in a race, first will physically be in front of second, whilst second will be physically in front of third. In this sense, spatial context is very relevant to competition.

Attacking a guy from behind is normally frowned upon. After all, it's hardly heroic behavior. We might make an exception, however, when it comes to air combat maneuvering, where it's quite the done thing to attack from behind. Air-to-air combat has had a colorful past. In the first world war, aircraft were first used as war machines. The Germans excelled at this, with their invention of the synchronization gear, enabling machine guns to be mounted onto planes, with the ability to fire in-between the spinning blades of a propeller, without damaging them. Of all the great dog-fighting German pilots, perhaps the most famous was the "Red Baron", Manfred Albrecht Freiherr von Richthofen, the most celebrated fighter pilot of the Great War. As you might expect in a book on secondomics, however, behind every great man, there is another great man. In this case, that man is flying ace Oswald Boelcke.

Oswald Boelcke was the first to attempt to formalize the tactics of air-to-air fighting with his "Dicta Boelcke." These eight rules defined the early principles of dog fighting - and the Red Baron followed his teacher's rules religiously. Oddly, nowhere in these rules did it say that posh Germans should not paint their planes bright red, turning them into rather obvious targets. What it did say, however was that:

"In any type of attack, it is essential to assail your opponent from behind"

At first glance, it seems as if Oswald Boelcke is stating the obvious here, since fighter planes in the First World War had forward-mounted weapons, but not aft-mounted. But there's more to the advice than that. Attacking the enemy from the side requires an adjustment to be made for speed - you must fire at where the enemy is going to be when your bullets reach their target, rather than where he is when you squeeze the trigger. Whilst it's clearly possible to for a skilled pilot to make this calculation, it's a lot easier if you can just fire at the guy in front of you. No adjustment is necessary for speed, so you have a better chance of hitting your target. In addition, when attacking from the side, a lucky enemy may manage to cross your line of fire by slipping between the bullets. From behind, however, there's no chance of such a lucky escape. Whilst a head-on attack shares these advantages, there is of course the disadvantage that the bad guy will be able to fire right back at you. Second place is undoubtedly preferable then, when you're dog fighting with the Red Baron.

A final, sobering note of caution from Boelcke, before we come in for a landing. In his Dicta, Boelcke also cautions:

"Always continue with an attack you have begun"

The thinking behind this advice is clear. If you turn tail and run, you allow your opponent to get behind you, surrendering any advantage that you may have had. Suddenly you're out in front and you gotta a bogey on your six (as Tom Cruise might have said in Top Gun). In a dog fight, you want to get into second place, and stay there until you've shot the other guy down.

But let's turn out attention now from fluffy white clouds, to fluffy white sheep. We've already explored how leadership is not always synonymous with being in first place - ask a soldier serving on the frontline whether he's a leader or a minion. Military leaders position themselves well away from the frontline as a matter of self preservation. Just as, in a game of chess, you preserve your most valuable pieces at all cost, so a military leader will avoid direct engagement at all costs. But there is another, less cynical reason why a military leader may choose to take a step back from the heat of the action. In order to supervise and coordinate his forces, a general must oversee them - he will need to find a vantage point from which to oversee the battleground. Far from being the first, at the front, in this context, the leader is the last - at the back. His messengers must run to and fro, passing his order on to the frontline. But this is all about soldiers, when I promised fluffy sheep!

Much like a general, you won't find a shepherd leading his sheep from the front. He'll follow the herd from behind, using his sheepdog to steer the sheep, just as a general users his messengers to communicate with the frontline. The reason for this is, of course, because the shepherd wants to keep an eye on his flock, and in just the same way that the Red Baron did not have guns mounted on the rear of his little red biplane, so the shepherd does not have eyes in the back of his head. Whilst the Red Baron is keeping an eye on his adversary, the general and shepherd are keeping an eye on their assets.

In Chapter Two, I questioned the true origins of the phrase "ladies first," suggesting that perhaps the gentleman might like to expose the lady to the unknown risks of whatever may lie ahead, rather like a canary in a mine. But this particular advantage of second place provides an alternative explanation. In patriarchal societies, married women become assets belonging to their male mate - effectively as sheep are to their shepherd. So the chivalrous gesture "ladies first" is perhaps an indication on the part of the male of their perception of a female as an asset to be monitored and protected by the male. Small wonder then, that these chivalrous gestures as so unequivocally rejected by many women's rights campaigners.

Chapter 7: Learning from the leader

Why is the leading edge of technology sometimes referred to as the bleeding edge? Why do some people insist on waiting for the "point one" release of a software package before upgrading? And what's all this business about "service packs" with Windows?

Trouble is, when it comes to gadgets and technology - especially anything with an Apple logo on it, I'm a sucker for the first release. I always want to have the latest shiny toy. But as is so often the case (and at the risk of repeating myself ad nauseam), there's a price to pay in being first. Of course, there's much pleasure to be had from the admiring glances that my super-thin Macbook attracts at the local Starbucks. But the downside of being an early adopter is that you end up being an unpaid guinea pig for the electronics or software company that probably brought their product to market a little earlier than it was ready. So whilst your shiny new toy looks great, and is really cool in theory, in practice, it doesn't quite... work. A minor detail, perhaps.

So the mainstream technology buyer tends to prefer to wait for the second release - or the "point one" revision, where all the initial teething problems are worked out. They get the benefit of all the feedback that the early adopters gave to the manufacturer, with none of the drawback. They also get an idea of what they do and do not want to purchase, based upon the word on the street. So whilst the early adopters buy based upon the claims of the manufacturers, the late adopters buy on the word of the early adopters. This is a classic example of our next advantage of second place - learning from the leader.

Another example might be when you find yourself in a curry house, and you try to persuade your partner to order a Goan Vindaloo that you think you might like, but you suspect it might be a little too spicy for your tastes. Rather than risk ordering it yourself, and sweating the whole way through your main course (not the best way to impress a date), you see what your date thinks instead, and maybe even try a bit, before you risk ordering it yourself on a subsequent visit to the restaurant.

So in this context, the early adopter, who is going first is not doing so for your benefit - they're presumably finding their own utility in being the first to experience the new, new thing. But their experiences have the result of indirectly benefiting you. Either by demonstrating to you that something is safe (if the guy in front got across the gorge on that dodgy rope bridge, then presumably you can too), or the opposite (since the bridge is now collapsed under the weight of the guy in front, you won't be crossing the gorge that way). And the feedback that the guy in front gives may even make the experience better by the time you get to it ("I suggest you tighten that rope, the bridge almost gave way when I was half way across!")

The technology industry has many such sob-stories. Consider the fate of thoe unlucky music fans who chose to purchase music from Microsoft's short-lived MSN Music download store. Launched in 2004, as a direct challenger to their arch-rival Apple's iTunes Store, the MSN store would provide digital music downloads, available on a per-track basis. Microsoft had big plans for the store. Apple was rapidly making inroads into territory that the software behemoth had coveted for some time: consumer electronics and online services. It was time to strike back.

THE ADVANTAGES OF SECOND

Microsoft believed that they had a winning formula with a new strategy ironically dubbed "Plays for Sure." Whilst Apple's success with the iTunes Store was predicated on the immense popularity of their iPod MP3 player, Microsoft believed that this tight integration would ultimately be Apple's downfall. The Plays for Sure strategy was intended to create a community of different vendors, all producing players and stores that interoperated, thanks to a common technology platform provided by Microsoft. At the time, both the company and most analysts felt sure that this strategy would ultimately unseat the iPod and iTunes store from the top spot. Surely consumers would favor the flexibility and choice afforded by Plays for Sure over the single-vendor lock-in of Apple's offering. There was a sense that history was repeating itself. Back in the late eighties, Apple's famous refusal to license the Mac OS to 3rd party computer manufacturers gave Microsoft an opportunity to dominate the market with Windows. (A theme we'll be returning to in greater depth in Chapter 23.)

But history was not repeating itself. The market for MP3 players turned out to be very different from that of PCs. Apple continued to dominate the growing MP3 player market, and the MSN Music store - the flagship of the Plays for Sure fleet, went down unceremoniously, like the Titanic, taking all it's customers music purchases with it, to the bottom of the deep sea, where so many early adopters have perished. Microsoft announced that tracks purchased from the store would no longer be supported. This meant that owners would no longer be able to transfer them from one device to another, if they ever decide to upgrade their music player or computer. Instead they had to back up their purchased by burning them onto CD, and if they subsequently ripped them back onto their a new PC, they would lose some audio quality as a consequence. Customers of the MSN Music store might have imagined that they would be relatively safe, since they were purchasing from the world's largest and wealthiest IT company, and the product was even labelled "Plays for Sure". But even they were not immune from the risks of being on the bleeding edge. Which just goes to show that there's no safe bet when it comes to early adoption. In technology, it's always safer to wait for the second release - learning from the example of the early adopters.

As it turns out, the second generation of music download stores has proved to be, surprise, surprise, far better than the first - dispensing with the cumbersome restrictions of digital rights management and often increasing the sound quality. So what happened? How could Microsoft have made such as huge blunder, and let down their faithful early-adopting customers in this way? The truth is that it's not just consumers who learn from the example of early adopters, software vendors do too - even the very big ones like Microsoft. Each time Microsoft releases a new version of Windows, it's plagued with bugs and problems. IT pundits the world over throw up their hands in horror, and everyone claims that they won't be upgrading. A few years later, of course, everyone has upgraded, and then the whole farce starts again. What's going on here? Is this part of some twisted marketing strategy on the part of Microsoft? Are they just having fun at their customers' expense, since they know that most of them will have no option but to upgrade in the end?

Of course not. Microsoft does not set out to produced flawed software. The trouble is, that with a product as complex and a user-base as vast as Windows, it's impossible to catch all the bugs before it is released. Imagine a bug that may only affect one in a million users. With Window's users, that bug will effect hundreds of users. It is simply not possible for Microsoft to test the product in sufficient numbers before it is released. There's really no alternative but for the vendor to release their product and learn from the feedback of the early adopters.

So both vendors and customers learn from earlier adopters, who find bugs on the vendor's behalf. But there's a second way in which customers may also learn from early adopters, which concerns consumer behavior, rather than the intrinsic properties of the product itself. In the IT sector, consumer behavior belongs to Nassim Nicholas Taleb's crazy world of "Extremistan" that we explored earlier. The seeming extreme randomness of consumer purchasing in IT is what tripped up Microsoft with their Plays for Sure program, and it relates to Metcalfe's law, named after Robert Metcalfe - one of the inventors of ethernet. It's also referred to as "The Fax Effect" by Kevin Kelly in New Rules for the New Economy. In mathematical terms, Metcalfe's law states that the utility of a telecommunication network is equal to the square of the number of users of the system. So, taking Metcalfe's (rather outdated) fax machine example. If there was only one fax machine in the world, it would be worthless, because there would be no one to send a fax to. If there were two fax machines, they both become useful. If there are ten fax machines in the world, they're 25 times more useful than if there are two (two machines are worth 4 utils, 10 machines are worth 100 utils, 4/100=25). The reason for this giant leap in value is to do with the number of potential unique connections within a network, which increases exponentially as a network grows.

Since all IT products tend to be networked these days, they all follow Metcalfe's law to some extent. As a result, IT products have a tendency to extreme success, or massive failure. If sufficient early adopters purchase a product, it will gain a critical mass, and everyone will be wanting one. If not enough early adopters purchase, it will never be adopted at all. Whatever the relative utility afforded to early adopters of the MSN Music store versus the iTunes Store, this difference would be magnified by Metcalfe's law, and consequently the second wave adopters would likely follow the behavior of the first wave.

No wonder then, that Microsoft struggles to coax their customers onto the latest version of Windows. These days everyone knows about services packs, and they'll wait for the first, or even second service pack before upgrading. Perhaps Microsoft would be better off incorporating the term "Service Pack 2" into their product branding, in order to encourage earlier adoption - if there's anyone from Microsoft reading this book, may I humbly suggest "Windows 7 Service Pack 2" as the name for their next release. It'll fly off the shelves.

Obviously, it's not ethical to call a first release "Service Pack 2" in order to trick customers into buying it. But stranger things have happened. The idea of a 2.0 release has captured the imagination of the entire IT industry over recent years. Suddenly everything looks better with "2.0" tagged onto the end of the name. "Web 2.0," "Business 2.0," "Culture 2.0," "Entertainment 2.0" and so on. The IT industry, more than any other, has fetishized the idea of coming second. Few phenomena in recent years better illustrates the power of secondomics, and the extent to which it exerts influence on our subconscious minds than the enormous buzz in the internet industry surrounding the cult of Web 2.0.

The idea of Web 2.0 achieved mainstream recognition and popularity in 2004, with the launch of O'Reilly Media's first Web 2.0 conference. Whilst it doesn't have a precise definition, the term Web 2.0 is typically used to evoke the idea that new technologies are facilitating a re-envisioning of the Web. Moving away from the notion of static pages linking together (like an electronic, cross-referenced collection of books), and moving towards a system that facilitates communication by connecting users in a rich variety of ways. Whilst the Web itself is not a single product with uniform release cycles, the notion of a 2.0 release is used as a metaphor to invoke this idea of re-invention: learning from release 1.0, in order to realize the full potential of the platform in the second release.

But there's more to the advantage of learning from the leader than the example of the IT industry, and it's 2.0 obsession. Let's turn now to the world of games, where the idea of who goes first and who goes second, and which is best, has captured players' imaginations for generations.

Game theorists will tell you that chess is a simple game, as opposed to the games that they prefer to play, such as Prisoner's Dilemma, Mutual Hostage and Ultimatum. The odd thing is that if you like actually playing games, as opposed to being clever with mathematics about games, then you may well find a game theorist's preferred games pretty tedious, whereas chess can be more of a challenge. The difference, from a game theorist's perspective, lies in the number of possible outcomes, and the extent to which you know what your opponent knows. In a game of chess, you can always see your opponent's latest move and there's a theoretically finite number of outcomes - literally, there are only so many game combinations that may be played. In this sense, chess is similar to Tic-Tac-Toe (also known as naughts and crosses). Children tire of Tic-Tac-Toe pretty quickly, and we frown upon adults with a taste for it. There are a maximum of 26,830 different possible games of Tic-Tac-Toe - in game theory terms, this is known as the game tree complexity. Tic-Tac-Toe is so simple, that a competent player should always be able to force a draw. On this basis, it's actually quite surprising that the supercomputer in the 1983 movie War Games took so longer to figure this out. Those numbers are hardly very big for a supercomputer to crunch.

Of course, chess is a good deal more complicated than Tic-Tac-Toe. In 1950, American Electrical Engineer and Information Theorist Claude Shannon took a stab at calculating the game tree complexity of chess, (that is, the number of possible unique chess games that exist). It is, after all, finite, just like Tic-Tac-Toe. He estimated that there were a possible 10^{120} games - that's a mind-boggling number. If we stacked chess boards on top of each other - one for every possible game, our chess tower wouldn't just reach the sun - it would stretch there and back a few million times.

So the number of possible sequences that a game of chess may take is finite, but vast. However, as the term "game tree complexity" suggests - it doesn't start out vast. All the possibilities branch from a single trunk. After all, in chess, the first move is rather constrained - there are only twenty legal moves. Eight pawns each have two possible moves, plus the two knights each have two possible moves. So one of twenty outcomes must take place in the first go. There are then a further twenty possible responses, which means that after both players have taken their first turn, there are 400 possible paths that the game may have taken (20x20). With each subsequent turn, further possibilities branch out from the trunk of the tree, and the number of possible outcomes grows exponentially. Nonetheless, it is theoretically finite.

But what does this tell us about the advantages of second place? In finite games such as Chess and Tic-Tac-Toe, we should be able to calculate whether

THE ADVANTAGES OF SECOND

there is an advantage in going first or second. It's easier, or course, with Tic-Tac-Toe, since there are so few possible outcomes. As it turns out, Tic-Tac-Toes is not an example of secondomics at work. Since there are 9 squares on the board, the player going first has the chance to fill up to five squares, whereas the second play may only fill up to four. So there is a slight advantage for the first player. We should, of course, temper this perceived advantage with the fact that a skilled opponent should at least be able to force a draw anyway. Most people, however, don't know what they're doing most of the time, a fact well known by casino owners the world over. The Tropicana in Atlantic City, and the Trump 29 Casino in Palm Springs, offered cash prizes to patrons who could beat a trained chicken, called Ginger (that's right - a chicken!) The lucky bird always got to go first (a casino must make it's money somehow), and since she was a well-trained fowl, she could always force a draw. What made money for the casino, however, was that by going first, she had a better chance of catching out a punter who made a single ill-judged move. So there's no doubt that Tic-Tac-Toe favors the first player over the second.

This advantage is intrinsic to the game of Tic-Tac-Toe, however. And whilst other games (such as Russian Roulette) follow a similar pattern, not all games favor the player who goes first. Reversi (also known as Othello) seems to favor second place. But what of chess, where black always goes second? Much has been written on this topic, and there seems to be little consensus. Theoretically, one day a computer may be able to "solve" chess - calculating with precision which color has the advantage assuming that both sides play a perfect game. But such a calculation could take hundreds or thousands of years to arrive at, and the advantage of one side might turn out to be extremely slight.

So if this kind of finite game does not shed much light on the advantages and disadvantages of second place, what of the other type of games - the games favored by game theorists? Typically, this type of game can have an unlimited number of turns, and both players tend to take their turns simultaneously, so neither player knows everything about what the other player is doing. This means that as you take your turn, you can only guess what your opponent's simultaneous turn may be.

Perhaps the most famous of these games is Prisoner's Dilemma. This is a two player game. In each round, both players are presented with a choice between two simple options: to cooperate or to defect. If both players cooperate in any given round, they will receive a small reward. If one cooperates, whilst the other defects, the defector will receive a large reward at the other player's expense. If both players defect, they win nothing.

Prisoner's Dilemma gets its name from a hypothetical scenario where two suspected accomplices are arrested for the same crime, and interrogated separately. Each prisoner is presented with the option of cooperating (keeping silent, in the hope that your accomplice with do the same), or defecting (testifying against your accomplice, so that you'll get off without charge, whilst your accomplice will service the maximum sentence). If both prisoners cooperate, they'll both receive a small sentence. The trouble is, since the two prisoners are held in separate cells, they cannot communicate with each other in order to agree a cooperative strategy. This game is similar to one played by Heath Legdger's character, The Joker, in the recent Batman movie, The Dark Knight, where two boats are rigged with explosives, and the passengers on each boat have the detonator to trigger the explosives on the other boat. The Joker explains that if one boat blows up the other - he'll allow the people on that boat to live.

What's interesting about this game, is that in each round, your opponent's decision is going to have a big impact on the payoff from your decision, and yet you don't know what your opponent's decision will be. You have to take a guess. If you trust your opponent, you might choose to cooperate - but if that trust is misplaced, you stand to lose a lot. But if you and your opponent both play nasty and defect, you win nothing.

This is clearly a very different kind of game to chess. The difference that is most significant for our purposes, is that there is no first or second player - and as a result, both sides are left guessing as to what the other side may do. In chess, of course, you have your opponent's previous move to scrutinize. You can also evaluate the game from your opponent's perspective, and anticipate what move they're likely to make next. In Prisoner's Dilemma, however, the players are very likely to consider their opponent's move in the previous round. If your opponent defected last time, maybe he will again this time. Perhaps you should defect this time, in order to punish him. So although there is no first or second player, the nature of the game is very much reactive - responding to your opponent's previous action.

In fact, the most effective strategies in Prisoner's Dilemma tend to reflect this second guessing based on your opponents previous move. Described as "friendly, provokable, forgiving," they tend to play cooperative in the first round, since there is no track record of opponent behavior to evaluate, it makes sense to start on a positive note, in the hope that your opponent will comply. In subsequent rounds, an effective strategy will involve punishing defections (by responding in kind), until your opponent begins to cooperate again, at which point you forgive them and switch back to cooperating again.

So it's not until the second round of Prisoner's Dilemma that you can start to interact with your opponent, giving the second round particular importance. Let's turn now to a different kind of game, where, like Prisoner's Dilemma, we don't have perfect information (neither side has complete knowledge of the other side's actions), but like chess, play alternates between players, rather than happening simultaneously. I'm referring to the fascinating world of negotiation.

Imagine a typical negotiating scenario, where two parties - a customer and a supplier - are trying to agree on a price for a service. At the start of the negotiation, neither side knows how much the service should cost. So the customer wants to pay as little as possible, and the supplier wants to charge as much as possible. Of course, it's a little more complicated than that, since both sides need to consider their longer term relationship a well. Good suppliers and customers are hard to come by, so neither side wishes to over charge/under pay the other side to such an extent that it does damage to the relationship. Nonetheless, we can safely say that the payer would prefer to pay less, and the payee would prefer to receive more.

People are buying and selling things all the time, of course. In Chapter Two, we explored auctions, where the price is set by bidding, and the winner may get stung by the Winner's Curse. But buying a Picasso painting or 3G mobile spectrum at an auction is very different to buying a service. It's also very different to buying sugar. If you're at your local grocery store, and you want to buy a pound of sugar, you have a pretty good idea of how much it should cost - and so does the guy who owns the store. Sugar is a commodity, after all. It's traded in huge quantities on commodities exchanges, by supposedly brilliant minds, who know a thing or two about how much sugar should cost. In fact, these commodities traders obsess about the price of sugar, (and other commodities like it,) to such an extent, that they invented futures trading, so that they could start speculating about the future prices for sugar as well, in futures markets, where you can buy and sell a commitment to supply or acquire sugar at some arbitrary point in the future.

Indeed, the price of sugar is much easier to determine than the price of performing a service, such a designing a website, building a football stadium or raising the Titanic. The price of sugar is one of the few things in life that economists are actually good at calculating. It complies with the classical economics principle of supply and demand. When demand for sugar rises, its price rises. When supply of sugar rises, its price drops. Few things in life are that simple, however. For example, supply and demand is not a particularly important consideration when determining a price for raising the Titanic. There's only one ship to raise, there are very few contractors in the world who could conceivably do it, (OK, perhaps there are none, in which case the service is priceless, but for the purposes of the example, lets suppose that there is at least one). The trouble is, that there is a shortage of information. Neither the customer or supplier knows exactly what's going to be involved in raising the Titanic. The contractor will presumably have some idea of how they're going to go about it. But they need to allow for the unexpected - their first plan may fail, in which case they'll need to try something else. The cost of the project will continue to rise, even as the ship remains at the bottom.

Of course, if someone ever did attempt to raise the Titanic, it is very unlikely that they would agree to do so under a fixed price contract. They would instead propose to charge for it on a time and materials basis - that is, they would want to charge as much as it costs, plus a margin of profit to make it worth their while. In this arrangement, all the risk is transferred from the supplier to the customer. The customer would not be thrilled of course - they could end up paying the supplier a great deal of money, and the Titanic may never be raised. But that's just the way it is, if you're some crazy billionaire who wants to raise an old boat.

But there is a third way in which prices may be determined, that is somewhere between the price of sugar and the price of raising the Titanic. It's the way in which the price of building a website may be calculated. An since, in my day job, I run a web design business, it's something that I'm painfully familiar with. It's a fixed price contract. The trouble is, that websites are not like bags of sugar - each site is different, and as such, each price is different. The price is also unpredictable, since programming tasks can sometimes turn out to be simpler than anticipated (in which case you come in under budget), or more commonly, you encounter an unexpected programming challenge, which results in the project taking longer than anticipated, and consequently going over budget. So the cost of building a website is more complicated than the price of sugar, but it's not as complicated as the cost of raising the Titanic (or at least, not quite that complicated).

Like raising the Titanic, however, neither customer, nor supplier, quite knows what the costs will be before the project is undertaken. However, since there are plenty of web design agencies out there for a customer to choose from, the customer has the upper hand. She can effectively say "I know that it's hard to calculate the price at this stage, but I have limited budgets, and I need to know how much it is going to cost. Therefore I require you to set a fixed price for building my website, which you must stick to regardless of what costs you incur during the development of the project." A lawyer would never be daft enough to enter into such an arrangement - they'll charge you by the hour, and it will cost you as long as it takes. But we web designers are suckers, I guess, and so we routinely enter into this kind of arrangement.

And that brings us back to the negotiations that I mentioned earlier. If the service (building a website) is to be undertaken for a fixed price, then getting the negotiation right is essential. Neither side, at this stage, knows what the costs will really be. But the supplier, having delivered similar services in the past, should be able to make a reasonable estimate. Likewise, the customer may have paid for similar services in the past, and have a preconception of how much they should cost. Usually, in fact, the prospective customer already has a set budget for the project. However, she's unlikely to reveal this budget figure to the supplier - at least not at this stage. So the supplier knows what they want to charge, and the customer knows what she wants to pay. But neither side wants to "go first" by revealing their figure. Why?

Presumably, both sides imagine that there is some advantage in going second. They want to hear a figure that they can respond to. From the customer's perspective, she fears that if she reveals her budget, the supplier will just say that that is what it will cost, even if they originally had a figure far lower in mind. Likewise, the supplier is concerned that their figure may be lower than the available budget, and that if they reveal their price before the customer reveals her budget, they might miss the opportunity to use up the entire budget. But are they right?

Of course, this is largely dependent on the figures that neither side has yet disclosed. Notice, that the assumptions stated above are that the customer assumes she could be paying less than budget, whilst the supplier assumes that they could be charging more - in other words, both sides are optimistic. In fact, the opposite is more likely to be the case. The customer wants to pay as little as possible, and so may already have set her budget too low, whereas the supplier wants to charge as much as possible, so has probably put in too large a contingency for the unexpected, and overly inflated their profit margins.

In the event that the customer's budget is greater than the suppliers quote, the customer would be right to keep this information to herself. However, if her budget is lower, it might be to her advantage to reveal it, since this might encourage the supplier to bring their quote down (by sacrificing some contingency and profit margin). If the supplier's quote is greater than the customer's budget, it's less clear whether it's in their interest to go first. From past experience, if the supplier's quote is substantially over the customer's budget, this can cause embarrassment so substantial that the customer walks away from the negotiation, before an agreement can be reached.

The advantage in going second, here, is clearly the opportunity to learn from the other side, who goes first, and in the process, discloses some useful information. It gets more complicated than this, however, since both sides may play games. One side might anticipate that the other side plans to bargain. If, for example, the supplier knows that the customer will always insist on a 10% discount, then the supplier might add that extra 10% into their initial quotation, in order to ensure that the compromise price is one that they perceive to be fair. Likewise, a customer may pretend that their budget is smaller than it really is, in order to encourage the supplier to submit their lowest possible quote.

So negotiating tricks can sometimes undermine the advantage of going second in a negotiation. Another factor to be aware of is a cognitive bias known as anchoring. Cognitive biases are predictable patterns in our behavior that indicate a consistent divergence between our expectations and reality. Anchoring was first proposed by Israeli psychologists Amos Tversky and Daniel Kahneman, who conducted a study where they asked subjects to guess what percentage of African states were members of the United Nations - more or less than 45%. They then repeated the experiment with another group, asking if it was more or less than 65%. The second group guessed higher values than the first. Tversky and Kahneman theorize that this was due a cognitive bias which leads us to excessively focus, or "anchor" on a single piece of information when making a decision. In the context of our negotiation, this tendency to anchor implies that once an initial figure has been proposed - whether it's the customer's budget or the supplier's estimate, negotiations from this point forwards will be skewed in relation to this figure. The scenario I gave previously, of the customer who always insists on a 10% discount is one example of this. Rather than focusing on the value of the service to him, he instead chooses to work from the figure quoted to him - he anchors on this, and then demands a figure adjusted from it. He imagines that by demanding a discount, he is in fact in control of the negotiation, when if fact, the opposite may be the case.

One reason why people have a tendency to anchor within a negotiation is because they don't actually know what the value of the service under discussion truly is to them. A website is a good example of this problem. Most organizations know that they need a website, but they don't know in advance how much value that it is going to deliver for them. If it delivers millions of sales, then they can justify a bigger investment than if it delivers only a handful. But until the service is delivered and the site is live, the customer has no means of knowing exactly what value it will deliver. And even after the site is live, a great deal of the value is often intangible - whilst with an online store it may be simple to estimate, since you can just count the sales, how do you quantify intangible benefits such as enhancing brand prestige, or influencing offline purchasing behavior? With so many imponderables, it's no wonder that customers have a tendency to anchor on something.

So, whilst negotiations provide us another example of the advantages of second place - one can learn from the leader, in the sense that one can respond to a price proposed by the other side, we must qualify this advantage with the risk of getting tricked into anchoring on the first figure to be quoted.

Whether you're leaving the bleeding edge to early adopters; allowing your opponent to make the first move in a game; or insisting that a supplier quotes on a project without knowledge of your budget; your are seeking to gain insight from your competitor by allowing him to go first. *Learning from the leader*, then, is not dissimilar from *Cover from threats ahead*. The difference is essentially that by observing the fortunes of the leader, we may modify our own behavior when we encounter the same obstacles or opportunities, in order to secure a better outcome for ourselves.

Chapter 8: Room for growth

In Chapter Two, we explored Enoch Powell's depressing assertion that all political careers end in failure. We found that this was in part due to a combination of the Peter Principle (everyone is ultimately promoted to their own level of incompetence), and the fact that once you reach the top, there's really nowhere to go but down - especially with the media, and their "build 'em up, knock 'em down" mentality, ready to help you on your way back to the bottom of the heap. The corollary to this is of course, that when you find yourself in second place, you can take some comfort in the fact that you still have a peak to climb.

At the time of writing, Google is one of the most successful IT companies in history, and certainly the most wealthy and powerful in Silicon Valley. The company has ascended to the top of its own particular peak. It's achieved this heady status in no small part as a result of the brilliant minds that the company employs. And yet, even now, at the height of its zenith, Google is starting to experience a brain drain. Of particular note are the number of high profile people switching from Google to Facebook, including Facebook's chief operating officer, director of platform product marketing and vice president of communications and public policy.

There are doubtless any number of reasons for Google staff to be making this switch, but one underlying reason probably has something to do with the difference between being part of an entrepreneurial, growing organization, as opposed to a large and established corporate entity.

Industry website AllThingsD claimed the motivation behind VP Elliot Schrage's move was:

> *"because [Facebook] was a company poised for explosive growth, much like Google in its early days. In addition, unlike Google, which has grown large, Schrage would have more of an ability to make an impact in arenas he favors."*

Of course, companies like Facebook, that are experiencing rapid growth can attract talent with promises of potentially lucrative share options. Stories of people making millions from the IPOs of companies such as Sun, Netscape and Google are legendary in the Valley, and so the best and brightest are always keen to make sure that they're part of the next big IPO.

Indeed, excitement with the potential millions to be made from big tech IPOs was the principle driver behind the "dotcom bubble" of the late 1990s, which Alan Greenspan, chairman of the Federal Reserve at the time, famously described as "irrational exuberance." When you're on your way to the top, the only limit to what might be possible is your imagination. The rewards for staff who join you along the way could be enormous, and there's also the possibility of revolutionizing the industry - really making a difference, or putting "a ding in the universe," as Apple's Steve Jobs once put it.

Once you reach the top, your potential suddenly becomes clear, defined, and somehow limited as a consequence. Athletic coaches refer to this as "anticlimactic depression." An athlete focuses so much upon achieving a goal, that when they ultimately succeed, after the initial euphoria has subsided, they sometimes struggle to come to terms with their success.

For most of us, it's all about the struggle, rather than the ultimate victory. When Leonard Cohen sings about "The Man," he's creating a faceless adversary with which we must perpetually battle in order to fight for our rights, and our freedom. How unsatisfying it would be if The Man finally acquiesced, and accepted our reasonable demands. As much as we may be able to see the wisdom in a fairly negotiated settlement, it doesn't always seem as sweet as a righteous fight.

THE ADVANTAGES OF SECOND

The gay scene in Belfast, is a another example of this. Whilst the city may remain divided along sectarian religious lines, there's one thing that both sides seem to agree on - they're very conservative when it comes to gay rights. I'm told that it can feel very oppressive, being openly gay in Belfast, and if you decided to go to a gay club in the city, don't be surprised to be accosted by protestors handing out leaflets filled with hateful sentiments about homosexuals. As a consequence of all this unwanted downtroddenness, the gay scene in Belfast enjoys an exuberant, hedonistic quality. People there really know how to party. By contrast, in those parts of the world blessed with a more tolerant attitude, the gay community tends to focus on more conservative aspirations, such as marriage and pension rights - and the club scene probably suffers as a consequence.

Consider, also, the devotion of Mac fans to their computer of choice. When Apple releases a new version of their operating system, these fans will queue at their local Apple Store for days in advance. Whereas, when Microsoft launches a new version of Windows, they're simultaneously met with moans of "what took you so long" combined with protestations of "don't expect me to upgrade any time soon." Why does Microsoft not enjoy the same obsessive following for Windows, that Apple receives for the Mac? Mac users feel passionate about their operating system of choice, precisely because they want to evangelize it - they want to see it's wider adoption. This keys into two previous points as well: Metcalfe's law indicates that a Mac user's computer will increase in value exponentially with each new user that adopts the platform; whilst Apple also benefits from the obvious allure afforded to those with underdog credentials. Windows doesn't enjoy that level of fanaticism primarily because it's already top dog, and there is therefore no reason to evangelize the platform.

And when you reach the top, what then? Have you heard of the sophomore slump? In Britain, we don't tend to use the word sophomore (since it's a term primarily used to describe the second year of college or high school in America.) That's one reason why I didn't call this book sophomoronics (but not the only reason, obviously.) The difference between second and sophomore is essentially that the latter means second in the sense of a followup, whereas in this book, we're concerned with the other meaning of second - being in second place. And whilst, as we have seen, second place can have plenty of upside, sophomore, in the sense of a followup, tends to have a big downside.

The sequel to a movie tends not to be as good as the original (whilst I'd argue that Aliens and Empire Strikes Back are superior to their progenitors, even I could not make a case for The Matrix Reloaded). And in music, followup "sophomore" albums have a bad reputation. Whilst a first album is usually developed over a number of years - often as the culmination of trying out a large number of songs in front of live audiences, and discovering which work and which do not - a followup album is usually written and recorded under tremendous time constraints. A record company will usually be keen to capitalize on a band's successful first album with a swift followup. As a result, the second album is notoriously a disappointment, failing to live up to the high standards set by the first.

Mathematics provides a technical term for the sophomore slump, called "regression to the mean." Essentially, regression to the mean tells us that when a statistic is extremely unusual (either higher or lower than average) we can expect it to head back towards the norm on subsequent measurements. So for example, if an athlete achieves a personal best, it's unlikely that they will do even better in a subsequent trial.

Another sophomore slump scenario provides us with an antidote to the 2.0 craze that we explored earlier. The Second-System Effect. Whilst millions of users are holding off from purchasing the first release of a software products to allow the early adopters to find the bugs, it's a sobering thought to consider that when the next release comes out, it may not be as good as the previous one. The Second-System Effect, is a term coined by computer scientist Fred Brooks in his highly regarded book on software development, *The Mythical Man Month*. In this book, Brooks explore the counterintuitive way in which, as you put more programmers onto a software development project, you somehow end up getting less done (this is a gross one-line simplification of a long and complex argument!) As a part of this argument, Brooks introduces the concept of the Second-System Effect - a phenomenon where the second release of a software product is not as good as the first, because it usually comes loaded with a lot of unnecessary additional features that add to the complexity of the product, but do not add to its value. And as any software developer will tell you, unnecessary complexity is always a bad thing.

So which is it to be? Is the second release of a software product better, or worse? Do vendors learn from previous mistakes and release a better product (as we found in the preceding chapter) or do they add more features, adding unnecessary complexity? The answer is usually a bit of both. When planning a second release of any software product, there will usually be developers pushing to fix problems under the hood, and marketing executives pushing to add more features. The marketing team want new features to differentiate the second release from the first. The trouble is, that this is the worst possible reason to add a new feature. A better reason would be to add a feature that was missing from the previous release, and for which there is genuine user demand. But consider the problem of the Microsoft Word marketing team. After all, there's only so many features that a word processor needs. After eleven major releases of Word (at the time of writing) what relevant new features could there possibly be to add? The perpetual addition of new features leads to a phenomenon known as "software bloat" where a package becomes overly cumbersome, and no longer suited to its original purpose. And all the time, the bugs persist.

The chances are, then, that after we have achieved our true potential, our followup is likely to disappoint. This is simple regression to the mean. Whilst, when we are in second place, we still have the peak to look forward to: somewhere left to ascend to. It is precisely this unrealized potential that makes growing companies more attractive than established ones, makes lines form outside the Apple store, and gives the gay scene in Belfast its hedonistic quality.

Chapter 9: Total cost of ownership

At the start of this book, I introduced the concept of leadership bias - our predisposition to accord exaggerated significance to first place, as evidenced by popular sentiments such as "the winner takes it all" and "no prize for second best." Whilst our conscious minds are aware that the winner does not always take it all, and there often are prizes for second best, I believe that our minds still trick us into miscalculating the value of leadership and, as a consequence, we over invest in order to attain it.

Perhaps evolution has caused our minds to be hard-wired in this way. The cost to our early ancestors in not winning a race could very well have been their lives, since they might get eaten by a perusing predator. Rather than pausing to weigh up all the available options and determine the optimal amount of energy to invest in victory, we instead, all to often decide to throw all the resources that we have into victory - no matter the cost. Indeed, it's telling that phrases like "no matter the cost" and "whatever it takes" have entered our psyche at all. These are hardly sentiments that an economist would understand.

As we explored in Chapter One, from a classical economics perspective, people act rationally in order to "maximize their utility". It would be rational, when entering into a competition, to calculate how much investment would be necessary in order to win, add an extra margin to allow for the unexpected, and then to make that level of investment, and no more. Investing any more would be wasteful, and economists don't tend to allow for wasteful behavior.

The trouble is, that economists can be wrong. In practice, we're wasteful all the time. According to a recent study, shoppers in the UK currently throw away 6.7 million tonnes of food a year - that's equivalent to one third of all the food that they buy. We can explain this behavior in economic terms on the basis that it suits consumers purposes to have extra food on hand, just in case they need it. Rather like the margin for the unexpected that I allowed for earlier in the calculation for how much one should invest in winning, consumers are buying more food than they think that they need, to ensure that they don't get caught short. No one wants to go to the refrigerator and find that it is empty. However, this extra allowance for the unexpected is clearly greater than required.

The effect is all the more pronounced in a competitive situation where we are trying to win. In many cases, we may not be thinking rationally at all. Instead, we choose to "throw everything we have at it" - expending all available resources in the pursuit of victory.

Psychologists have long been aware of these mental states where we temporarily cease to act based upon conscious rational thought, and instead allow more instinctive behavior to emerge. One such state is a "limbic hijacking", which Daniel Goleman lucidly describes in his book *Emotional Intelligence*. A limbic hijacking, Goleman explains, is a brief moment where our mind is not able to think rationally, and the emotional part of our brain temporarily seizes control. It is a "fight or flight" response - where our brain reacts to a perceived threat, and must determine how to deal with it. For our ancestors, presumably threatened by predators far more frequently that we are today, in our sanitized built environments, every millisecond counted as they hesitated whilst deciding between fight or flight.

The limbic system is a part of the brain that is involved in processing emotional responses. It is also an aspect of our brain's anatomy that we have in common other mammals and reptile species, indicating that from an evolutionary perspective, it's probably the oldest part of our brains. As such, it's not the part that makes us smart, but it does appear to be crucially important in helping us to make decisions - especially under pressure. Whilst other areas of the brain, such as the prefrontal cortex, are concerned with our conscious reasoning these processes are slower than the rapid responses of our limbic system. That may be why our conscious mind briefly surrenders control to the limbic system when we are threatened - allowing a more rapid kind of thinking to get us out of danger, before our normal mental state reasserts itself. Goleman, goes on to explain that the emotional part of our brain is involved in all decision making processes - not just those where we are under threat.

I suspect that a kind of mini limbic hijacking is taking place each and every time that we participate in competitive activity. We might not be surrendering conscious control of our actions, but we are entering into a realm of thought that rational economists struggle to model with their sensible sums. The trouble is that deep down we want to win. We REALLY want to win. No matter the cost. Whatever it takes. We want to win. We see people pushing themselves to extraordinary lengths in the pursuit of victory. We see grown men crying on the soccer pitch. We see Olympic athletes collapsing after a race. We see gamblers bankrupting themselves in pursuit of that illusive win.

It's completely irrational. Adam Smith would not be able to make any sense of it. But we do it nonetheless. In Chapter Two, when we were exploring the Winner's Curse, I pointed out that we should expect mobile phone operators to over-bid for a prize, if they perceive their very existence to be at stake. Where survival is threatened, we can expect a genuine fight of flight response - a true limbic hijacking. But I would argue that human beings today lack the same levels of stimulation from threatening situations that our ancestors evolved to withstand. As a result we contrive artificial threatening situations, in which we may behave as if a fight or flight response is required. Sporting endeavor is a perfect example of this simulated fight or flight behavior. There's no predator pursuing Olympic athletes as they compete in a 100 meter sprint, but they behave as if such a threat existed. Athletes often talk of the adrenaline rush that they experience in competition. A similar burst of adrenaline is symptomatic of a limbic hijacking.

It's amazing to watch as football players throw themselves at a ball. Certainly, they're wearing plenty of protective gear, and trained medics are standing by, but their ability to throw themselves at the ball with no seeming regard for their own personal safety is sobering. And of course, we know that these sports are not safe - sports injures are a fact of life. But these risks do not seem to act as much of a deterrent. Are these sportsmen weighing up the risks of injury against the payoff for victory and arriving at a rational choice to maximize their own utility? Probably not - it's more likely that they're just getting "absorbed in the game," to the point at which they're willing to do whatever it takes to win, no matter the cost. And there's that expression again.

So in a competitive situation, we seem to have an inclination to defy the economists, and make entirely irrational investments with a view to achieving victory, regardless of the cost, and with little consideration of the payoff. And even when we do consider the payoff, it may be substantially smaller than could be justified for the effort required to obtain it. To explain this, we can use a rationale with which Adam Smith would have been altogether more comfortable. It's a simple matter of supply and demand.

In any competitive scenario, we have multiple participants in contention for a single goal - first place. That equates to excessive demand, and constrained supply. Which, as everyone know, leads to inflated prices.

Way back in ancient history, when I was at school, I used to refuse to participate in competitions, or any kind of competitive sport. (I was a very annoying child!) My rationale for this subversive behavior was that I was a communist, and that I thought that any kind of competition was morally wrong. At the time, my arguments had some traction with the predominantly left-wing teachers at my school, and so it took me many years to realize the error of my ways. In retrospect, I wonder if my teachers would have been as indulgent if I'd explained to them that I was an advocate of neoclassical economics, and that I chose not to compete because I was a rational actor, and I had calculated that the effort required to compete did not justify the potential payoff if I was to win. Probably not.

But not all budding communists shun competition. Far from it. Take the cold war, for example. On March 23, 1983, President Ronald Reagan delivered a speech in which he announced the United States' plan to develop a ground and space-based system to prevent nuclear ballistic missiles from being used to attack America - the Strategic Defense Innitiative. The plan was breathtaking in its ambition, and always questionable in terms of feasibility. Indeed, it became known as "Star Wars' because it seemed more like science fiction than hard science.

But despite seeming far-fetched, the idea of Star Wars was extremely subversive. It threatened the notion of "Mutual Assured Destruction," or MAD, whereby if either side in the arms race - America or the USSR - were to launch a nuclear attack, both sides would certainly perish, since a devastating counter-attack would be inevitable. MAD was the invention of John Von Neumann, the mathematician and game theorist. It was Von Neumann's role in the United States Atomic Energy Commission that Peter Sellers is said to have been parodying in Stanley Kubrick's 1964 movie Dr Strangelove. If America had a shield to protect itself from nuclear attack, then it could safely attack the Soviet Union, whilst defending itself from the Soviet's response. This change in the balance of power was perceived by many to make the threat of global thermonuclear war significantly more likely.

THE ADVANTAGES OF SECOND

The Soviet Union took this new threat very seriously, and substantially increased its defense spending in response. This came at a difficult time for the Soviets, however, since the country was experiencing practically zero growth, and receipts from oil sales - a major source of income for the country, then as now, were down as a result of a drop in the price of crude oil. This dangerous combination of high military spending in combination with a struggling economy is cited by some as a serious contributing factor to the Soviet Union's collapse. Whilst the Soviet Union may well have collapse anyway under the weight of it's own oppressive inefficiency, it seems reasonable to suppose that their aggressive response to America's elevated military spending served to precipitate its collapse.

Where did the Soviets go wrong? I would argue that the Soviet leadership were suffering from leadership bias. Their mistake was to imagine that they could not allow the Americans to beat them. They were in the same mentality that we explored earlier - victory, no matter the cost. Since they believed that the arms race was a battle for survival, they were ultimately prepared to spend more on it than they could have afforded. The pertinent question to ask here is: would it have been so bad to have come second? Did the battle to have the most missiles really matter when both sides had already achieved MAD?

If, instead of perusing first place, the Soviets had pursued a Secondomics strategy of pursuing second place, and investing only as much as might be required in order to achieve this, and sustain MAD, that oppressive Soviet regime may have still been with us today. Of course, Star Wars was a game changer - threatening, as it did, the MAD principle. But few, even at the time, believed that Star Wars could be effective. Even supposing that the technology was feasible, it would only take one missile to get through the shield in order to undermine the entire purpose of the project. In other words, the system had to be 100% effective in order to be effective at all. Quite a tall order. The correct response to Star Wars from the Soviets, if indeed any response was required at all, was to investigate the feasibility of Star Wars, and explore the much less technically challenging task of penetrating the supposed shield. It was certainly not necessary to make any attempt to match US defense spending. Instead they could simply have sat back and enjoyed the show as Reagan undermined his country's own economy with a crippling budget deficit.

This "arms race" scenario is one that we also encounter in political campaigning, where a large war chest of funds is considered a prerequisite for victory. A large part of President Obama's success in securing the Democratic nomination for the 2008 presidential election was down to his record-breaking ability to raise funds for his campaign. With greater funds, comes more advertising, resulting in more exposure for the candidate - the oxygen of any campaign. Of course, your candidate's level exposure is only significant relative to that of his opponent, and as such, it's not the absolute size of your campaign fund that counts, but its size relative to that of your opponent. And that makes the battle of campaign funding another example of the Prisoner's Dilemma game we explored earlier. In this example, matching your opponent's funds, and not raising more, is cooperating, whereas raising more than your competitor is defecting. If both sides perpetually defect, then both sides loose out, in the sense that they need increasingly larger funds. In this situation, the guys who win are not the candidates, but rather, the media owners who charge for the advertising. This makes a particularly strong argument for targeting second place - once your opponent is satisfied that you will not defect, he's probably ease-up on fund raising too. And as the old saying goes - it's not size that matters - it's what you do with it. Investing money on exposing a bad candidate to the public will do more harm than good, after all.

The example of VHS versus Betamax is one often sited in this kind of book, so I've been hesitant in raising it. But in this context, we can explore the subject from a slightly different perspective. Traditionally, the battle between VHS and Betamax is cited as an illustration of how standards emerge. The point that is normally labored about these two competing standards for video cassette recorders is that whilst Betamax was arguably the superior format, VHS got an early advantage, which tipped things in its favor, and then Metcalfe's law kicked in - VHS players gained greater value with each additional player that was sold, and the rest is history. More recently, we've witnessed a similar situation in the battle between Blu-Ray and HDDVD.

Entering into this kind of industry leading platform game is a risky business. Once one platform gains an early lead (which might occur through random events), that lead will subsequently be magnified by Metcalfe's law. You may have the best platform, but random events could still conspire against its adoption. And here's the key - since random events have a large part to play, being the best is of limited value in this kind of competition. As a consequence, you are likely to invest too much in technological leadership, when this plays a fairly minor role in the outcome. Betamax may have been a bit better than VHS - perhaps it was even a lot better, but it didn't help. Blu-Ray was a bit better than HDDVD, and this time, the better platform arguably won. But that doesn't mean that Blu-Ray's superiority actually helped its adoption. The outcome of the battle rested on a knife's edge for months - the industry held its breath, but the great unwashed public did not seem to care. If anything, the commercial relationships between the movie studios and the platform backers seemed to have more to do with the outcome than the technical superiority of one platform over the other. But even in this regard, neither side should take too much comfort from this. It was such a close run battle, that luck surely played a large part in the outcome.

And luck, is of course a factor that we rarely allow for in planning how much we will invest in winning. We construct all kinds of post-rationalizations when we are successful, but when we fail, we've very willing to cite luck as a major component in our opponents victory over us. Of course, when you're a senior suit at a big corporation, and you're responsible for ensuring the success of a fledgling platform such as Blu-Ray, when your boss asks you what you're strategy will be, you can hardly say that you expect luck to play a large part in it. You'd probably get fired on the spot. But there are, of course, many occasions when people have sadly been fired for speaking truth unto power.

But what role, then, should luck play in determining our level of investment in competitive endeavor? The answer to this question depends largely upon the context. If you are fighting for your very survival, then clearly, you don't want to leave that to chance, and therefore almost any level of investment may be justified. But don't allow yourself to get tricked into over-investing in victory, simply because your limbic system is playing tricks on you. We should always question whether our response to a competitive threat is correctly calibrated - what is the real level of threat? What is the real potential payoff? To what extent will the outcome be random anyway? As Nassim Nicholas Taleb warns us in *The Black Swan*, we must always take care when we indulge in forecasting. The future is usually far less certain than we imagine. Nonetheless, we would be even more foolish to allow a quirk in our mental makeup trick us into assuming that any level of investment is justified in securing victory.

I'm advocating a careful calculation to assess the "total cost of ownership" of victory. In order to do this, we need to make a realistic determination of the value of the payoff associated with victory, being minded of the fact that we often perceive this to be of greater value than it truly is. We then need to consider what level of investment would be required in order to secure victory, making an allowance for the inevitable role that luck will play in the proceedings. How does the payoff measure up against the necessary investment? Then try running the numbers for targeting second place. How does that compare to targeting first?

The tragedy here is that most people who achieve second place have payed over the odds for it because they were actually trying to attain first place. However, if they had done the calculation that I'm advocating, they may have determined that second place offered greater overall value anyway, in which case they could achieved that result with substantially less investment. After all, if you target second place, you only need to invest enough to beat 3rd place, rather than compete with first. And there can often be an enormous gulf in the cost between the two.

Every competitive situation will be unique, and doubtless in some scenarios, even allowing for the necessary investment and the uncertainties of luck, first place may well represent better value than second. All I'm advocating here - and indeed, it's the gist of this entire book - is to be aware of the fact that first is not necessarily best, and second may on some occasions be a better place to be, provided that's were you set out to get to.

Chapter 10: Supporting the underdog

The trouble with rolls of toilet paper is that they run out... and usually at the least opportune moment, leaving you high and dry - or rather - not dry at all. What to do. This bothersome problem introduces us to another advantage of second place - everyone loves an underdog, if you will allow, for a moment, that we might think of a toilet roll as an underdog.

The problem of toilet rolls running out has been occupying the best and brightest minds of computer science for many years now. Yes, I said computer science. Way back in 1984, the renowned Donald Knuth, Professor Emeritus of the Art of Computer Programming at Stanford University, wrote a seminal paper on the subject: "The Toilet Paper Problem." Twenty years later, usability guru Don Norman raised the problem again, with an essay on his website entitled: "Toilet Paper Algorithms: I didn't know you had to be a computer scientist to use toilet paper." Apparently you do.

The problem that both Donalds were grappling with is as follows. Since toilet paper running out presents a problem for anyone on who finds themselves in need of more paper, and indisposed to go find some, the ideal solution is to have a second "backup" role to hand. But rather than having the backup roll lying around somewhere, making your bathroom look untidy, you decide to invest in a dual roll holder. Now you can have both rolls sitting tidily side by side, and be confident that when one roll runs out, there will always be a back up roll.

The trouble is that this turns out not to be the case. There are four pos-

THE ADVANTAGES OF SECOND

sible ways in which one might choose which role to select from:

- **Random** - you select from either roll
- **Closest to hand** - you take which ever is easiest to reach (like our magazine browsers, earlier)
- **"Big Chooser*"** - you take from which ever roll is largest
- **"Little Chooser*"** - you take from which ever roll is smallest

* Knuth's technical term

If everyone was a little chooser, there would be no problem - one roll would be used up, and then everyone would start on the next. The trouble is, very few people (if any) are little choosers in practice. Quite the opposite, in fact. Most of us seem to be Big Choosers - we prefer to take from whichever roll looks largest. As humans, perhaps we have evolved to be hard-wired to seek out abundance. Perhaps that larger role looks more attractive somehow - we just can't resist it. And so, there that second role sits - neglected, until the larger role becomes the smaller role, and allegiances switch. Suddenly everyone begins to take from the other roll, and things start to even up.

Ultimately, our predilection towards larger rolls results in both rolls running out at the same time - defeating the entire purpose of having a backup roll to begin with. Norman points out that the solution was discovered some time ago in the commercial toilet paper dispensing industry, with the introduction of a serial constraint enforcement mechanism - in layman's terms, a device that prevents you from getting at the second roll until you've finished the first. Problem solved. When the first roll is finished, it is discarded, and the backup roll drops down to take it's place - allowing some time for a friendly janitor to come along and replenish the backup. To Norman's frustration, however, such a solution is not yet available in domestic toilet roll dispensers. But then, usability experts are a funny sort.

What does this have to tell us about everyone loving an underdog? I would argue that our smaller toilet roll is, in this context, the underdog, having less sheets remaining than its plumper sibling. Perhaps we are drawn to take from the larger roll because we're driven by an instinctive sense of fair play, and we're seeking to even things up. Far from favoring the larger roll, we're punishing it in order to even the score.

Our taste for the underdog has an ancient pedigree. In the bible, consider David's unlikely victory over the mighty giant Goliath. We all instinctively support David, because he's an attractive young man (or so Michelangelo would have had us believe). And we all imagine Goliath to be brutish and evil, because of his strength advantage over David. But it turns out that David had the advantage after all - after knocking out his opponent with a lucky shot from a catapult, he later severs poor Goliath's head, and takes it back to present to the king. A few bloody wars later, and he gets to be the king himself - conquering many other countries along the way. He later sleeps with one of his soldier's wives, and then arranges for that soldier to be killed in order to cover up his indiscretion. Not an innocent underdog any more, then.

Today, our culture is dominated the underdog. It's a theme particularly favored by Hollywood, with Sylvester Stallone's Rocky being the archetype. In sporting events too, our taste for the underdog emerges, as crowds cheer on weaker competitors in the Olympics, who valiantly battle against the odds. Joseph A.Vandello, Nadav P.Goldschmied and David A.R.Richards from the University of South Florida have conducted some very interested experiments in their study of support for the underdog. In one experiment, students were asked to read a short essay outlining the Israeli-Palestinian conflict, from the perspectives of both sides. With the essay, two groups were also presented a map. For one group, the map focused on Israel, whilst for the other, it showed the entire middle eastern region. On the first map, Israel appears large, with the Palestinian areas relatively small. On the second map, Israel appears small, surrounded by much larger Arab neighbors. A third control group was shown neither map. After reading the essay, and carefully studying the map, the students were asked which side they considered to be the underdog, and which they felt more supportive to. The map appears to have had a significant influence upon their views. When Israel was portrayed as large, 70% perceived the Palestinians as the underdogs, and 53.3% were more supportive toward them, whilst, when Israel was portrayed as small on the map, 62.1% saw Israel as the underdog, and 76.7% were more supportive toward them.

It shouldn't come as a surprise in these types of conflicts if the parties involved go to great lengths in order to portray themselves as the underdogs, since this perception may engender more support from parties external to the conflict.

And so it goes - sympathy for the underdog translates into support, to the point where the tables may even turn, and the roles are switched. This predilection for underdogs is, in almost every case, a misreading of the situation. Rather than focusing on a fair and reasonable negotiated settlement, interfering third parties try to impose order from outside, by addressing perceived imbalances. The result is often to benefit the weaker side - regardless of the rights or wrongs of the situation.

But where does this insight leave our toilet rolls? It simply means that in selecting which roll to use, we unconsciously misread the situation - imaging we must redress an imbalance, and in the process missing the point that the two rolls should be used one after the other, not in parallel. This bias in favor of the underdog provides us with another benefit of second place.

To see this effect in practice, let's turn our attention to Sweden. Sweden is a very large country, relative to the size of it's population. As a consequence, communication is a sensitive topic. Without government intervention, there's a risk that people in outlying areas could become cutoff from modern communication technologies. The Swedish government has taken some innovative steps over the years to ensure that this does not happen. Their visionary approach to the roll out of broadband internet services has resulted in Sweden being one of the best connected countries in the world, despite their far-flung populace. Newspaper production and distribution is another area to benefit from state subsidy. Presstödsnämnden is the government body tasked with supporting Swedish newspapers. Way back in the early seventies, without the obvious benefit of being able to read this book, Presstödsnämnden had already devised a secondomics solution to the problem of monopolistic media ownership that was becoming so prevalent in other countries. They subsidize the production of 'second' newspaper - those with a larger competitor. They're effectively punishing the leader - a Big Chooser strategy - leveling the playing field for the smaller player. In Sweden, coming second truly has its rewards.

Summarizing our eight advantages of second place

We've covered a lot of ground in this chapter. In my attempt to illustrate the advantages of second place, we've explored everything from toilet paper rolls to fighter pilots. I've used these disparate examples to illustrate eight different advantages of second place. We can categorize these eight advantages into two groups - contextual advantages and behavioral advantages:

Contextual advantages:

- Coasting in the slipstream
- Cover from threats ahead
- Enemy in your sights
- Learning from the leader
- Disproportionate share of payoff

Behavioral advantages:

- Room for growth
- Total cost of ownership
- Everyone loves an underdog

Behavioral advantages occur as a result of our (sometimes flawed) interpretation of a situation, and the way in which we react to it. So the *Total Cost of Ownership* of first place is so much greater than second, because we have a tendency to overestimate its worth, and over-bid for it as a result. Whilst peoples' tendency to *favor an underdog* means that they will frequently intervene to help even the score when they see us in second place. And *Room for Growth* is concerned with the positive motivational impact that having a competitor to beat may have on our behavior, as opposed to the natural complacency that tends to accompany a leadership position.

Contextual advantages arise from the structural constraints of a given situation. By simple virtue of being behind someone, rather than in front of them, we may be a wheel sucker, coasting in their slipstream; we may avoid a bullet, since they provide us cover; and we may fire at them or stab them in the back, before they get a chance to return fire. These contextual advantages are often unavoidable - Gordon Brown and our protein molecules are not being heroic when they provide a layer of protection - it's just an inevitable consequence of their context in a given situation, and we will just as inevitably reap the benefits of being in the number two spot, behind them. And the tendency for second place to get a disproportionally higher payoff, is a simple matter of power curves and feedback loops - it's just the way things tend to turn out. After all - no one ever said that life was fair.

What can we learn from all this? In the case of behavioral advantages, we must take care to ensure that we don't allow our inherent biases to color our perception of a situation. We must not allow our innate competitive desire to

THE ADVANTAGES OF SECOND

win to make us overlook the possible benefits of coming second, or the fate of the Soviet Union may await us. So the behavioral advantages illustrate mistakes that we should avoid in ourselves, and look for in others - where they may represent an opportunity. Contextual advantages are opportunities scattered all around us, that all too frequently go overlooked - is there someone passing you, whose slipstream you could coast in? Opportunities may be passing you by all the time. By becoming aware of them, you increase your chances of seizing these opportunities as they arise. You may even be able to engineer these situations - if you are uncertain of what lies on the other side of the door, be chivalrous - let the other guy go through first.

We'll explore secondomics in practice in greater detail later. But before we do, there are a couple of other matters to attend to. Is being second always such a great thing, and if so, why doesn't everyone already know about it?

Part 4 - The disadvantages of second

It's not nice to kick a man when he's down. But, by design or otherwise, those in second place, like those in first, can sometimes come in for more than their fair share of slings and arrows.

Whilst this book is largely concerned with ferreting out those oft-overlooked advantages of second place, I would be remiss in my duties, if I did not also explore the flip-side of the coin. Second place is not always such a great place to be, and not just for the obvious reasons.

Indeed, some of the mechanics that we explored in the previous chapter - that frequently work to the advantage of second, may also, in some circumstances, conspire against us. As such, whilst they are negative proofs, we may also consider some of them as exceptions that prove the rule. Second place is special, but although this specialness is frequently reflected by some kind of advantage, it may at times result in second place being singled out for more than its fair share of flack.

So lets turn our attention now to those examples of where second place turns ugly

Chapter 11: Sometimes the winner does take it all - that Abba song again

In my introduction, I questioned the veracity of Benny and Björn's claim that "the winner takes it all," pointing out that in practice, this is rarely the case - payoffs tend to be distributed between multiple actors, rather than reserved exclusively for a single winner. However, there remain a minority of occasions where Abba are, in fact, correct. In some specific instances, the winner actually does take it all. One example that immediately springs to mind is *the pitch* - a scenario well known to anyone involved in the sales, marketing and advertising industries.

As I have already confessed, in my day job, I work in advertising, where a *creative pitch* is the typical process for winning new business. A creative pitch represents an enormous investment for an advertising agency - and also a huge risk. When clients are seeking to appoint a new agency, they will typically invite

THE DISADVANTAGES OF SECOND

a number of companies to participate in a pitch process - usually between two and five companies, but sometimes many more. For the invited agencies, the pitch represents a huge opportunity - winning a new client could bring substantial long term income. They will therefore be willing to make a big investment in order to win the business - typically up to $10,000, but sometimes significantly more. Occasionally, the client will make some contribution towards these pitch costs, although this is rare, and usually does not come close to covering the true costs.

The trouble is, that most pitches are an all or nothing game. The winning agency will be appointed, and the others will walk away with nothing but an art bag filled with unwanted concept boards. It's true that on some occasions, agencies are pitching to form a roster of agencies, and in this case, there may be multiple winners. But for the most part, in this game the winner really does take it all, and the payoff for second place looks very different as a result.

The level of investment that an agency makes in a pitch tends to have a big impact in the ultimate result. From a prospective client's perspective, level of investment is a key indicator of how much a agency "wants" the business. Equally, if you have a creative team working on concepts for a pitch, the more of their time you pay for, the greater their chances of coming up with a pitch-winning concept. So the advertising agency that has come second in a pitch will often have made the largest investment after the winner, but will have received nothing in return. The process is a little like an auction, except for the fact that all the bidders must pay for their bids, regardless of whether they win the item that they are bidding for.

Whilst you won't find this type of auction conducted at Sotherby's or Christies, it's a common scenario in the natural world, where resources are invariably limited, and organisms must compete for these resources for their very survival.

I was watching a group of pigeons the other day, on my way back from a pitch. The pigeons were fighting for a crust of bread which had been discarded on the sidewalk. It was a fairly large crust of bread, which could have afforded an ample meal for all of the pigeons present. However, it was pretty stale, which made the lump impossible to divide into smaller pieces, even supposing that this is what the pigeons were minded to do.

So instead, the pigeons played an all or nothing game - where only one victorious pigeon would claim the prize. The competition rules appeared to be simple. The pigeons would walk towards each other in a menacing manner, attempting to drive each other away from the bread. They would puff up their feathers in an attempt to exaggerate their size. The advantage of this kind of non-contact posturing is that it has the potential to resolve the dispute without resorting to violence. That's a very efficient solution, since no damage need be done to any of the birds - victor or otherwise. It's easy to see how this kind of non-violent behavior may have been selected through evolution, since it is to the advantage of all of the birds.

Sadly, however, the battle for the bread was not resolved by non-violent posturing alone. On occasion, where two birds attempt to intimidate each other, and neither chooses to submit, the situation escalates to a violent resolution. A pecking attack ensures, which can be costly to both sides.

During this battle, control of the bread lump temporarily transferred from one bird to another - which did afford the occasional opportunity for multiple birds to take small bites out of it. But a hierarchy swiftly emerged, where one bird dominated the others in the group, who eventually lost interest and departed.

It's sad to consider that despite our many evolutionary advantages, and all of the sophistication and intellect that underlies an advertising agency's creative pitch, our behavior is little different to that of pigeons, who do not possess our capacity for reasoning and abstract thought.

But if we did apply our big human-brains to the problem, what solution would we arrive at? How could we make the pitch process, and similar games more efficient? As discussed, evolution itself has already hit upon one solution - ritualized non-violent posturing. But as we have seen, that does not always suffice. We can do better than this, anyway. Looking at the pitch from a game theory perspective, it turns out to be yet another example of the Prisoner's Dilemma, that we briefly explored in the previous chapter.

From a Prisoner's Dilemma perspective, we have two choices. We can decide to make a greater, or lesser investment in the pitch - the former is to defect, whilst the latter is to cooperate, since if all participants spend less on their pitch, it has no impact on the overall result, and the client will still pick the best pitch from those available. Defecting involves breaking ranks from the other agencies, by increasing your level of investment. But such an action inevitably results in a continuing spiral of tit-for-tat additional investment, unnecessarily inflating the required pitch investment as a result. It is true that in any given pitch, each agency is unlikely to know how much its competitors are investing, but since agencies get involved in multiple pitches, the game is iterated over time, and the required market norm becomes clear.

THE DISADVANTAGES OF SECOND

Most economists would argue that the principles of supply and demand will kick in over time. Since its unsustainable for agencies to invest more in pitches than they're worth, agencies that over-invest will be punished, and ultimately become insolvent. In other words, market forces will determine the appropriate pitch investment over time. And this is arguably what happens in practice.

But consider, for a moment, the Prisoners Dilemma again. If we were able to break down the cell walls, and allow the prisoners to communicate, we could agree upon a cooperative scenario, where all agencies agree to voluntarily limit their investment, and consequently improve the efficiency and profitability of the entire industry as a result. In the battle for the bread, the equivalent would perhaps be for the pigeons to agree to not use their beaks in combat - the damage incurred from the battle would be lessened as a result.

Such industry cooperation does occur from time to time - union block negotiations and trade organizations such as OPEC are examples. For the most part, however, such collusion is regarded as a bad thing, described as anti-competitive, and damaging to the consumer. And it's certainly true that if all the agencies in a pitch colluded to reduce their level of investment, the prospective client would have less pretty pictures to look at as a result.

So, whilst both evolution and rational thought provides us with methods of reducing waste in these scenarios, there are both practical and legal obstacles in the way, which mean that second place is still liked to be punished in these "every bidder pays" wasteful scenarios.

As I walked away from that particular pitch (which we lost), I couldn't help feeling empathy for the pigeon who had fought most valiantly for the lump of bread, but had it pecked from his beak by a more aggressive bird. He walked away with nothing but some nasty peck wounds and ruffled feathers, whilst I had some hefty pitch costs to write off.

Chapter 12: Tripping over the fallen leader

In Chapter Three, we explored the complex intricacies of the cycling peloton. The advantage of being behind the leader in cycling is the opportunity to wheel-suck - gaining an energy efficiency by cycling in the area of lower air pressure created in the wake of the cyclist in front. Whilst you're cycling along, enjoying what is, essentially, a free ride, you should, perhaps consider the extent to which you are placing your trust in the leader. As a wheel sucker, you're cycling in very close formation. If, for any reason, the guy in front comes off his bike, you probably will do too. In a split second, you'll find your bicycle about to crash into his, and you won't have enough time to react.

Suddenly, wheel-sucking doesn't seem such a free ride after all, coming, as it does, at the cost of you entwining your fate with that of the guy in front. You've elected to undertake a greater risk in exchange for an optimization in your energy efficiency. Perhaps this wouldn't matter so much if you were cycling behind Lance Armstrong, but could you even keep up with him anyway? It's more likely that you're cycling behind someone of a similar skill level to yourself - someone who is just as likely to come off his bike as you are off yours - and so the lowest common denominator principle is important. Since you're encountering obstacles in parallel (if one falls off, you both fall off), you have a far greater risk of an accident.

You haven't increased the number of potential obstacles in the road ahead, however, and if the lead cyclist successfully negotiates the obstacles, there's a chance that you will too - simply by following his lead, as the two of you navigate your way around pot holes, hedgehogs and other fallen cyclists. Since you're directly behind the bike in front, it obscures much of your view of the road, making you largely dependent on the leader's navigational skills. You've not only accepted greater risk in return for energy efficiency, but you've sacrificed some control of the situation as well.

People often struggle with the concept of surrendering control. Of course, there are many situations in life in which we have little option but to do so. I remember when I was undergoing chemotherapy, every month I would hope that the doctors would tell me that I could finish the treatment. But each month they would tell me that it was continuing to be effective, and so I should continue. I really wanted to stop the treatment, since it was making me very ill, and I discussed this with my doctors. Ultimately they said that it was my choice, but they recommended that I continued. What option did I really have but to surrender control to my doctors in this situation? After all, I'm not an oncologist. (I'm very glad that I did surrender control in this situation, since I went on to beat my cancer, with their help).

Every time we wait at a bus stop for a bus, mail a letter, or enter a web address into our computer, we make a similar decision to surrender some control - putting our faith in the ability of someone else, whom we hope will be better able to serve our interests. In a sophisticated, technologically advanced society like ours, we are all interdependent. We can't possibly know everything about everything. If we were never willing to surrender control, we would be forced to return to some kind of hunter-gatherer lifestyle, picking berries and catching fish - and abandoning thousands of years of civilization in the process.

Perhaps to some hard-core environmentalists, abandoning civilization as we know it might seem an attractive process, but most of us would struggle to surrender the comforts of our daily lives. And so we accept that we must surrender some control to those around us. As our technology has become increasingly sophisticated, our scientists, medics and technologists have become increasingly specialized, resulting in an intellectual balkanization. Take your computer, for example. You might not know everything about how it works - but the truth is that no one else does either. By that, I mean no *one person*. The design and production of a computer involves so many different disciplines, that it would be impossible for one person to know everything about it. In fact, it's unlikely that any one company would posses the skills in isolation either. Rather, it takes the combined effort of a huge team of specialists, from many different companies in many different countries. Each of these people and groups of people are entirely interdependent.

It's as if all of humanity forms one giant peloton, where we're all wheel-sucking each other in enormous circles that encompass the entire planet. We have no option but to continually surrender control. And as a result, in any given hierarchy, there's almost inevitably someone ahead of us - another wheel that we need to suck - another leader upon whom we are dependent. And in such an environment, a single slip-up by a single individual, can have significant and substantial implications.

Not everyone is comfortable with this loss of control. And hence we encounter the frustrating character traits of the back seat driver, who reluctantly cedes control, but still attempts to exert it from their secondary position. Back seat drivers are not limited to motoring - you can find them in almost all fields of human endeavor. From the expectant father urging the mother in labor to "push!" to the customer at the hair salon, who wants to ensure that her fringe is cut "just right".

In chapter two, we explored the rise and fall of UK prime minister Gordon Brown, and how he became so powerful in the number two position, as Chancellor, but somehow lost all that power when he claimed his prize as leader. In his job as chancellor, he was able to steadily build his power base, benefiting from both good and bad news for the government. Whilst good news benefited the entire Labour party, including Gordon Brown, bad news weakened Prime Minister Blair's position, and consequentially strengthened Brown's bid to wrest leadership from Blair.

But this cosy arrangement could only be tested so far. If things got so bad for the Labour party that they lost their majority in parliament and were no longer able to form a government, Blair would certainly have lost his job as Prime Minister, but Brown would also have lost his opportunity to take it. It's as if Brown was wheel sucking Blair - if Blair had come of his bike, Brown would inevitably come off his as well.

We must take care, therefore, when choosing whose wheels to suck - since their mistakes and misfortunes are likely to become our own. Nonetheless, we derive such great benefits from wheel sucking our way through live, that we're unlikely to stop any time soon.

Chapter 13: Decoys and fall guys

It's interesting to note that hunters know a thing or two about secondomics. They have been successfully exploiting the instinctual secondomic behavior of birds for centuries, without even the assistance of reading this book. In the introduction, we explored how no hungry penguin wants to be the first into the sea, since the first is most likely to get picked off by a predatory leopard seal. If these seals had big brains, capable of abstract thought, they might hit upon a strategy to coax the reluctant birds into the water. This new breed of über-seals might create a robotic replica-penguin, that appears to be a real penguin, already in the water, happily guzzling fish. Upon sight of this robo-impostor, the real penguins might then be lulled into a false sense of security, and all dive in at once - making dinnertime come early for our hypothetical seal.

Of course, leopard seals are not capable of abstract thought - and even if they were, it would be tough for them to assemble a robot with their stubby flippers. We humans, on the other hand, are perfectly capable of making such an automaton - and that's exactly what some humans do. A human hunter will place a decoy duck onto the water, and then conceal himself nearby. It seems that many birds have evolved to instinctively judge it safe to land on water when they see another bird already paddling safely around. In effect, they choose to be the second bird. However, a decoy changes the game - the bird that believes itself to be second is in fact the first real bird, and worse than that, the presence of the decoy does not indicate that the water is safe to land in, as they instinctively assume, but quite the opposite instead.

So the use of a decoy is a strategy specifically designed to exploit secondomic behavior. Interestingly, this is not limited to hunting. Behavioral economists have a term for it as well: decoy pricing. As Dan Ariely explains in, *Predictably Irrational*, decoy pricing is a technique used to influence the purchasing

THE DISADVANTAGES OF SECOND

behavior of consumers.

Imagine two items are for sale - you're only going to buy one of these items, and each has its own pros and cons. Say, for example, it's arm chairs. One chair is ugly but comfortable. The other is stylish but uncomfortable. Which do you choose? Supposing that you get equal utility from looks and comfort, the decision seems impossible. Until along comes a crafty salesman to make things easier for you. The salesman points out a third chair. It's just as stylish as the other stylish chair, but a little less comfortable. Now you have three chairs to choose from. Two are stylish, one is comfortable. But you want both style and comfort. The odds are that at this point you'll choose the slightly more comfortable of the two stylish chairs. Superficially, this behavior may seem rational, but how can the introduction of a third, less favorable options possibly have influence you decision between the other two chairs?

The answer is, of course, that it shouldn't influence you at all. The salesman could just as easily have shown you another comfortable chair that was slightly less stylish than the one that you were considering. You'd then have been more likely to select the comfortable chair over the stylish one.

The introduction of a second option, which is similar to one of the choices already available, but slightly inferior in some way, makes the original option seem more appealing as a result. It's like the proverbial big fish in a small pond, and visa-versa. The fish may be the same size, whilst the pond size is changing - but our perception of the size of the fish is relative to the size of the pond. Consider the dating games that we explored in Chapter Two. There, we found that satellite toads would gather around the best croaker in order to intercept the females that he attracted, in order to mate with them. Decoy pricing is effectively this strategy in reverse. If you're an average-looking high school girl who wants to be asked to the prom by a good looking guy, you'd be well advised to ensure that your best friend, who you hang around with at school, is slightly less good looking that you are - making you look all the more attractive by comparison. You don't want her to be excessively ugly, mind, since this will unnecessarily bring down your overall team score, discouraging boys from approaching you in the first place. You are using your pal as your decoy - she may not get a date for the prom, but she's significantly increasing your chances. In this situation, first is deliberately positioning herself in proximity to second, in order to enhance her attractiveness, at the expense of second.

"Second cheapest bottle syndrome" provides us with another illustration of the role of the decoy in influencing our behavior. In the introduction, I raised the distasteful topic of cheap wine, and the tendency of those who care little for fine wine, but do not wish to appear cheap in a restaurant, to select the second from cheapest bottle on the menu. This is a quintessential seondomics behavior, where we regard cheaper as better, and in this sense, the cheapest is the first. The disadvantage of being first in this particular ranking is the appearance of being cheap. When someone selects the second from cheapest, they're effectively determining that the negative utility associated with appearing cheap is greater than the price difference between the cheapest and second cheapest bottle.

The problem arises in the fact that so many people routinely make the same calculation, and arrive at the same conclusion, as a recent survey in the UK revealed. And the results are all to evident for the canny restauranteur to observe in his sales figures. The second from cheapest bottle tends to be one of the best sellers on the menu, and as we explored in the introduction, armed with this knowledge, restauranteurs may deliberately select an inferior wine for second place, thus allowing themselves a greater margin on every sale. But what has this to do with decoys? Simply that the cheapest bottle on the menu is in fact acting as a decoy in this scenario. To fulfill this role, the cheapest bottle must be similar in price to the second - making it feel very affordable to trade up and avoid the stigma associated with the cheapest. By setting the prices so closely, the restauranteur can maximize his chances of catching the wine ignoramus out, by ensuring that the price utility associated with the cost saving in buying the cheapest is entirely offset by the utility associated with the prestige of not buying the cheapest.

So the cheapest bottle on the menu is performing the same function as the hunter's wooden duck. The latter tricks the unsuspecting bird into mistakenly judging the water to be safe to land on, whilst the former tricks the unsuspecting diner into thinking that the inferior, yet slightly more expensive bottle represents better value.

In the Star Wars prequel movies, the character Queen Amidala, played by Natelie Portman, employs a decoy - her "handmaiden" Padmé. The latter has the misfortune of looking exactly like her employer (both characters are, played by Portman). The role of the decoy is to swap places with the queen when her life is at risk - a somewhat thankless task. Disaster ultimately strikes in *Episode II: Attack of the Clones*, where Padmé is killed whilst performing her decoy duties. In this scenario, the value of one individual's life is deemed of less worth than the other's. This kind of devotion to duty may seem the stuff of fiction, but there are many instances, throughout history of it happening. Most recently,

THE DISADVANTAGES OF SECOND

the former leader of Iraq, Saddam Hussein, was widely reported to have employed the services of decoys. These decoys were intended to massively increase the risk to any individual who attempted to make an assassination attempt, since anyone who made such an attempt and inadvertently killed a decoy, rather than Saddam Hussein himself, would not only have failed in his mission, but would have made their intentions clear, and would inevitably suffer the consequences.

It's worth pausing, at this point, to consider the incentives from the decoy's perspective. In Star Wars, we are expected to believe that the decoy Padmé's desire to put her life at risk is motivated entirely by the desire to serve her queen, whom she both admires and respects. But a decoy's incentives needn't been so altruistic. Potential decoys may be incentivized to undertake great risks with equally substantial rewards. In a dictatorship, such as Saddam Hussein's Iraq, of course methods of coercion may also be possible. In all cases, however, where a decoy's vocation results in a negative payoff that outweighs his or her remuneration for undertaking that role (death), we may reasonably conclude that the individual involved miscalculated the net payoff.

So, what do decoys tell us about secondomics? The first duck on the lake, that is in fact a wooden replica. The cheapest wine, that is in fact worth more than the second cheapest. The politician who is in fact a bodyguard in disguise. In each case, a kind of substitution has taken place, with the intention of deceiving others in order to influence their behavior. The duck that is tricked by the decoy thinks that it will be the second duck on the lake, when it will in fact be the first. The guy in the restaurant thinks he's ordering the second cheapest wine on the menu, when he's actually buying the cheapest (in terms of cost the the restauranteur). The would-be assassin who thinks he's killing the leader, is in fact only killing a bodyguard.

In the case of the duck and the wine, the duped party is targeting second, but is tricked into selecting first. In the case of the bodyguard, the opposite is happening. The duped party targets the leader, but is tricked into targeting a substitute. Here the bodyguard is the secondary party, to whom the leader deputizes the negative payoff of leadership. In all cases, a decoy is used to blur the boundaries between first and second place - and the technique is frequently used to turn the tables on those targeting second place. And when you find yourself performing the role of decoy, you can expect to receive the leader's negative payoff, even though you don't get the leader's benefits.

A close relation to the decoy is the fall guy - an equally high risk occupation, but without the potential rewards that are offered to a decoy. Both decoys and fall guys receive another parties' negative utility - the difference is that a decoy does so willingly (or unknowingly in the case of a wooden duck, or a bottle of wine), whilst a fall guy is made a victim. Take care not to be too close to a leader when they're in trouble, or you may find that they attempt to deputize their negative payoff onto you.

In British politics, it's traditional for a minister to resign when something goes wrong. Once the media have claimed their scalp, they start to settle down, and things can go back to normal. This kind of self-sacrifice on the part of the resigning minister provides protection for the government, and ultimately the leader. The minister involved may not even have been directly responsible - their resignation may be motivated by the fact that whatever events precipitated the resignation happen "on their watch," rather than as a result of their actions. Of course, this means that it also happened on the Prime Minister's watch. But leaders are usually not expected to resign, providing that they've deputized the disgrace to the resigning minister instead - thus containing the damage inflicted to party. This is presumably because it wouldn't be practical to have the kind of revolving door politics for the leader of the country, that tends to happen at the offices of his subordinate ministers. The resignation of a senior minister is perceived as an effective way of punishing a prime minister without the inconvenience of perpetual changes in leadership. One may treat a disease with drastic surgery, but not with head amputation.

Returning, briefly, to the case of Gordon Brown and Tony Blair, we find an alternative perspective. We explored the way in which Brown was more powerful in the secondary role of Chancellor, than he became as prime minister. This was only the case because he never fell victim to the decoy/fall-guy scenario. Brown was extremely fortunate to occupy the role of Chancellor, responsible for the fate of the British economy, for a period in which the global economy in general, and the UK economy in particular, was maintaining consistent, healthy levels of growth. As a result of this good fortune, he was never called upon by his leader to fall upon his sword to save his party.

The role of the decoy, illustrates one special circumstance where being in second place confers a specific disadvantage. Interestingly, however, it also provides us with a useful illustration of secondomics principles in practice, since it is a strategy for an individual in first place to transfer some of the negative utility associated with that rank to second place.

The introduction of decoys complicates matters greatly. The presence of a decoy may trick us into believing that we're second, when in fact we're first - resulting in us incurring the winner's penalty that we were trying to avoid.

And on other occasions, we ourselves may be used as the unknowing decoy - increasing someone else's chances of success, at our own expense.

Chapter 14: Punishing losers

We've already explored the Cold War arms race between the United States and the Soviet Union. In this scenario, I argued that it may have served the Soviet's interests better to have pursued a strategy of second place rather than first place, since destruction was mutually assured anyway, and so in this sense, the assumption was that neither side would use their weapons.

But this is not always the case. In some circumstances, we must assume that the opponent certainly will use the weapon, once acquired. Scenarios such as the good old-fashioned western style gunfight at the O.K Corral. The first to draw his gun will shoot the other guy. There's not much benefit to second place in these circumstances, certainly. But is this just the stuff of movies, or do these situations actually arise in real life?

Sadly they do, although perhaps not as frequently in this day and age. *Gunfight at the O.K. Corral* is based upon a true story. Another famous example in American history concerns the duel in 1804 between Alexander Hamilton, America's first finance minister, and Aaron Burr, America's second vice president. The two men were long standing political rivals. Oddly, their animosity in part originated from an irregularity in the fledgling constitution that left Hamilton, as leader of the House of Representatives, determining which of his two political opponents - Burr and Thomas Jefferson - was to be president, and vice president. Whilst Hamilton supported neither, he judged Jefferson to be the preferable candidate, making an enemy of Burr in the process. Matters came to the head upon the unfortunate publication of a letter in which one of Hamilton's relatives indicated that he had expressed a "despicable opinion" of Burr.

When Burr demanded that Hamilton withdraw these privately expressed views, and Hamilton refused, one thing lead to another, and the two concluded that honor could only be satisfied by a duel. An unfortunate conclusion, to be sure, but one that was not uncommon in that day and age.

A duel is, in essence, a zero sum game. One gets to live, whilst the other must die. In some situations, where neither side successfully kills the other, a draw may be declared. But in these circumstances, whilst honor may have been served, neither side has achieved "satisfaction". The concept of a duel emerged in fifteenth century Italy as a means of limiting the brutal violence that allowed disputes between families to develop into *Romeo and Juliet*-style family feuds, with the consequential Shakespearean body-count. The rules of the duel were set out in the *code duello*, which prescribed how a duel was to be fought in order to preserve honor whilst minimizing unnecessary injury. This code proved to be popular, and remained essentially unchanged four centuries later, when our two founding fathers sought to settle their differences. However, whilst the code may not have changed, technology had moved on a pace, with dueling pistols replacing swords as the weapon of choice.

Dueling with pistols is a brutal and pretty random business. Gun shot wounds have a tendency to be fatal, and when fired at fairly close range (typically twenty paces), a mortal wound is not only possible, but it is actually quite likely. Typically, in this scenario, the winner will be the one to fire first, if he is able to kill the other guy before he can return fire. Once the duel has commenced, it's therefore rather dangerous to attempt a truce. Nonetheless, a tradition of *deloping* emerged, where one of the duelists would fire his weapon in the air, rather than at his opponent - indicating his desire to draw a line under the dispute, now that honor had, in some symbolic way, been served. The deloper is in effect surrendering his power to the second duelist, who must then decide whether to acquiesce, or to shoot at his conciliatory foe.

The precise circumstances surrounding the duel between Hamilton and Burr remain a mystery. All we know for certain is that both men travelled across the Hudson River from Manhattan to New Jersey to a pre-ordained spot (dueling was, in those days, illegal in New York, but not in New Jersey). Two shots were fired in quick succession, and Hamilton was mortally wounded, whilst Burr walked away - to later cause all kinds of trouble in Texas.

In *Founding Brothers*, Joseph Ellis concludes, after careful analysis of the available evidence, that Hamilton fired first, with the intention of deloping, but that this gesture was misinterpreted by Burr, who believed that Hamilton, on discharging his weapon, had attempted to kill him. It seems that only a few seconds passed between the first and second shot - and it all comes down to what went through the minds of those two gentlemen in that brief moment, two centuries ago. There's no way to be certain whether Burr truly fired first or second, but it's interesting to consider that if Ellis's conclusions are correct, then whilst the second to fire is normally at a disadvantage in a duel, this would be a famous example of where the duelist firing second "won" the duel.

The code duello may seem brutal by today's standards, but by codifying a measured solution to conflicts, it arguably saved the lives of friends and family who may otherwise have become entangled in a feud. As a result, it kept the casualty list to a minimum. Sadly, global conflicts are rarely resolved in such controlled and measured arenas. Imagine how many lives may be spared if world leaders were forced to resolved their differences in hand-to-hand combat, rather than using huge armies and weapons of mass destruction, with the inevitable collateral damage in civilian casualties.

In duels, then, it pays to fire first, since there may not be a chance to return fire if you are wounded. In a nuclear arms race, however, there is an important difference: unlike bullets, intercontinental ballistic missiles take a longer time to reach their target. Time enough for the opposing side to detect them and respond accordingly, and hence both sides enjoy the protection of mutually assured destruction. (If the code duello specified that both parties should die, it is unlikely to have enjoyed the such enduring popularity).

Whilst the prospect of mutually assured destruction almost certainly helped to save us from nuclear armageddon during the cold war, no such protection existed *prior* to the discovery of nuclear weapons. During the second world war, the Allies established *The Manhattan Project*, a multinational initiative to develop a nuclear bomb, in response to fears that the Nazi's *Uranverein* (Uranium Club) might develop one first. Clearly, the first side to achieve a nuclear bomb, would have a decisive advantage over the other. As it turned out, Allied fears that the Axis may develop a nuclear bomb first were unfounded. Japan and Germany were not close to developing such a technology. Nonetheless, America's advantage in this area did not prompt her leaders to practice restraint. Much like Burr, who seized his advantage when Hamilton's shot (for whatever reason) missed its target, America did not hesitate to use its new nuclear arsenal against its enemy, once acquired. The result was the bombing of Hiroshima and Nagasaki, with the resulting deaths of over 200,000 people. Unlike the Hamilton-Burr duel, however, Japan had not deloped. (They had instead made the deadly mistake of rejecting the Potsdam ultimatum.)

It seems reasonable to assume that, had the Japanese developed the nuclear bomb first, rather than the Americans, they might have taken a similar action - with equally destructive consequences in terms of loss of life. Of course, this is just speculation. What is certain, is that without the protection afforded by mutually assured destruction, the cost of coming second in an arms race is just as fatal as in a duel.

Essentially, these situations are a special instance of the *Winner Takes It All* example, we previously explored. The difference is that the winner not only claims all of the payoff (in this case weapons), but he goes on to use that payoff against his opponent, inflicting a consequential negative payoff. A classic Hollywood example of this is the *Single White Female* scenario, where our heroine invites a seemingly friendly stranger into her home, only to later discover that she's a homicidal maniac, and in the ensuing struggle, every household object becomes a potential weapon. You know the score - Jennifer Jason Leigh has you pinned down, and she's reaching for that mantel piece ornament, and so are you. Whoever grabs the porcelain figurine first will bash the other over the head with it.

In a more elemental sense, this same scenario is played out by the ape tribes in Stanley Kubrick's "2001: A Space Odyssey", where the apes are competing for control of a watering hole (not unlike our wildebeest). Upon the arrival of the mysterious monolith, one of the apes discovers how to bash another ape over the head with a bone, and the rest is cinematic history.

In a commercial context similar situations may arise. Companies get locked in combat to acquire an asset that will enable them to dominate a market at the expense of their competitor - this asset may be a key employee with unrivaled expertise in a particular field, or an exclusive contract with a supplier who makes a critical component that both companies require. By signing an exclusive contract, you not only create value for your own business, but you do substantial harm to your competitor. Whilst in this scenario, unlike Burr, you may not kill your rival, the damage you inflict may nonetheless put them out of business. In these situations, coming second means making the second most attractive offer - and it may be every bit as deadly as being slow on the draw at the O.K. Corral.

Chapter 15: Becoming predictable & learning the wrong lessons

As we've seen, one advantage afforded to second place lies in being able to learn from whomever goes first. The trouble is, that others may also learn from the leader, and as a consequence, they may anticipate the behavior of second place, based upon their observation of the behavior of first.

For example, consider our flock of birds from chapter three, only this time they're flying in a less tight formation, and some chap with a gun is hiding in a bush on the ground, hoping for dinner to fall out of the sky. The first bird to fly past catches the hunter's attention, but it is gone before he can shoot. As he is looking up at the sky, a second bird follows behind. The hunter is now primed and ready to fire - and sure enough, bird number two will be feeding his family tonight. In other words, when birds fly past in a line, the second

THE DISADVANTAGES OF SECOND

bird makes an easier target than the first.

The difference here is, of course, the element of surprise. I went out of my way in chapter two to highlight how often the concept of "first mover advantage" is overstated. But this does not mean that there isn't a grain of truth to it. Whilst it certainly does not follow that the first company to market in a particular product category will be the one that goes on to dominate that category, there are many circumstances where the element of surprise gives the first mover a distinct advantage over those who follow.

We can find many references to this phenomenon in culture, such as the truisms: "fool me once, shame on you, fool me twice, shame on me," or "once bitten, twice shy." Where we observe a behavior for the first time, we learn from it, and are therefore prepared on the next occasions. Our immune system also works this way - developing antibodies to combat the viruses to which we are exposed, which may afford us some degree of protection on a second exposure to the same pathogen. Indeed, the very fact that our brains evolved to possess such a sophisticated faculty for memory is probably due to the advantages associated with this elemental learning from experience.

Computer security provides another illustration of this. With the kind of complex, networked software that we use today, it's inevitable that the code will contain flaws. Programmers are, after all, only human, and everyone makes mistakes now and then. (Apart from my partner, that is, who tells me that he's never written a line of bad code). Flaws in software represent potential vulnerabilities. But a potential vulnerability only becomes a security breach when it is exploited. And once it has been exploited, the victim of the breech will likely fix the flaw, or report it to the software vendor, who should issue a security advisory, and over time, will deliver a patch to correct the flaw.

In other words, if you're a malicious hacker (sometimes referred to as a "black hat" hacker), and you discover a security vulnerability that you intend to exploit, you should pick your first target carefully. Your second target may not be so easy to attack.

The 9/11 attacks on the World Trade Center and the Pentagon were so devastatingly effective because they were largely unanticipated. Before September 11, 2001, few people seriously believed that commercial jumbo jets could be hijacked and converted into missiles to attack large office buildings. After 9/11, the threat was all too well understood. As such, inflicting such a devastating attack was much easier before 9/11 than is was after the event. Today, the security services are keenly aware of such a threat, making a repeat of this type of attack much less likely. In the same way that our immune system learns from exposure to a pathogen, our security services learn from a terrorist attack. Those behind the 9/11 attacks would naturally plan on the grandest possible scale, since they would anticipate that a similar strategy would be unlikely to succeed on a second occasion.

In his book, *The Political Brain*, psychologist Drew Westin describes the way in which our memory is structured into networks of associations. Trigger a memory, and a network of associations to that memory are also activated, even if we're not consciously aware of it. These networks are a property of the way in which we process memory, physically storing it in, and recalling it from parts of our brain. So, for example, if we hear the sound of a mosquito buzzing, it's very likely that this sound has close associations with mosquito bites in our network of associations. We might not even be consciously aware of the sound, but it could still activate the "mosquito" node in our memory. The first mosquito may get away with scoring a heomo-smoothie at our expense. But the second is more likely to get squished, since all of the ideas that we have associated with the sound of the first mosquito are activated, making us far more sensitized to the threat upon its second occurrence.

All of this teaches us that we should take care not to become too predictable. And here again, second has a special status. It takes two points in space in order to plot a vector - or in other words, knowing where something is now, gives us no means of anticipating where it is going. Whereas if we know where something has been *and* where it currently is, we might be tempted to infer from this the direction in which that thing is heading. Of course, two values in a data set could be very misleading indeed, especially if you don't know anything about the processes involved in generating the data. Nonetheless, a single point gives us not indication of direction - either historically, or in the future. In this sense, a second point changes what we know significantly.

Consider the seemingly simple game of Rock, Paper, Scissors. This is the game of making shapes with your hands, beloved in playgrounds the world over. It's a two player game. In each round, the two players must simultaneously choose one of the three hand shapes - rock, paper or scissors. Scissors beats paper, paper beats rock, and rock beats scissors. This is a strangely circular scenario, and seemingly contradictory. The game cannot be solved by thinking about utility points, since if scissors has greater utility than paper, and paper has greater utility than rock, then rock cannot logically have greater utility than scissors. There's a technical term for this kind of apparent contradiction - it's said to be intransitive. (As opposed to something which is transitive - for example, I prefer bananas to apples, and I prefer apples to oranges, therefore I prefer bananas to oranges). The introduction of metaphorical verbs into the game: scissors *cutting* paper, paper *wrapping* rock and rock *blunting* scissors, helps us to comprehend a real-world intransitive scenario. In practice, much to the bewilderment of many economists, some peoples tastes may also be intransitive - as illogical as it may seem, we may find an individual who prefers bananas to apples, and apples to oranges, but prefers oranges to bananas. Quite literally, there's no accounting for taste.

...But I digress, as fascinating as the intransitive nature of Rock, Paper, Scissors may be, that's not the reason I brought it up. What's interesting about this game in the context of the disadvantages of second, are the risks inherent in allowing your strategy to become apparent, by inadvertently revealing discernible patterns in your behavior. Because, contrary to first appearances, Rock, Paper, Scissors is far from a random game of chance. The game can be rich in nuance, as each player attempts to anticipate their opponent's next play based upon past patterns of behavior and other subtle indicators such as body language. It's widely believed, for example, that women have a tendency to play scissors first, whilst men have a tendency to play rock. Despite the fact that all three symbols have equal value (each can beat one symbol, whilst being beaten by the other), they still have metaphorical significance, which may lead players to favor one over another.

What is interesting about the game Rock, Paper, Scissors, is that in selecting your symbol, you must address two questions - what symbol will your opponent guess that you will play next, and on the basis of this, what symbol do you anticipate that your opponent will play next. In order to win, you must not only consider what your opponent's strategy might be, but in doing so, you must consider how your opponent will interpret your strategy. And in attempting to infer a strategy, both sides will look for patterns in each others behavior.

In order for a pattern to emerge, a strategy must be repeated, and as such, using a particular strategy a second time confers substantially more risk than the first. For example, a very poor strategy in Rock, Paper, Scissors, would be to never repeat the same symbol twice in succession, since in so doing, you increase the odds of your opponent guessing your next move correctly from 33% to 50%. The solution to this is to ensure that you are perpetually altering your strategy - never play the same strategy twice, rather than never playing the same symbol twice.

So we must take care when repeating our strategies not to become predicable in ways that will give our competitors an advantage. And if, like the ducks flying in a line at the start of this chapter, we're the second to fly past the hunter's gun, then that strategy (following the leader) has just become a lot more risky.

Whilst the dangers of repeating a strategy in this way do indeed illustrate a potential disadvantage of second place, it's interesting to note that these situations do still follow the basic principles of secondomics, and by changing the circumstances, we can quite easily illustrate how this mechanic may instead favor second place. For example, imagine that the birds flying over have a disease, and that the hunter is in fact a veterinarian who has developed a cure - his gun fires a tranquilizer dart - the second bird falls into a safety net, where it receives the cure and is then released. The first bird later dies of the disease, whilst the second goes on to live the rewarding life of a duck, into old age. A far fetched scenario, perhaps, but it does illustrate that what is happening here is that number two is being singled out, and that whether this is good or bad news for second place is entirely dependent of the intent of those responsible.

Finally, whilst we are considering the disadvantages of learning from the leader, a word on who is learning what. We've explored how a third party may anticipate our behavior based upon observation of the behavior of those we follow (hunters and ducks). We've also explored how our competitors may learn from our behavior and anticipate it, if we repeat it. In Chapter Seven, we also looked at how learning from the leader may work to our own advantage (for example, the leader trips over the banana skin, saving those who follow from the same mishap). But this requires that we take the correct learning from the leader. Sometimes we may misinterpret the circumstances, or decide upon a poor course of action, based upon these learnings. This kind of fallibility may turn a potential advantage of second into a disadvantage - snatching defeat from the jaws of victory.

Imagine that you're in a restaurant with a group of friends, and together you're deciding what to order. It's very likely that you'll each be influenced by the choices that the others make. It's common to hear diners in a restaurant saying things like "well if you're going to order X, then perhaps I'll order Y". These efforts to coordinate who is ordering what are presumably supposed to result in a more enjoyable dining experience. But behavioral economist Dan Ariely, expert in all kinds of irrational behavior, thinks otherwise. In his book *Predictably Irrational* he describes an experiment that he and Jonathan Levav (a professor at Columbia) conducted at a bar in Chapel Hill, North Carolina. In the experiment, they tested two different methods by which groups of friends could order beer: one was the traditional method, where each friend states their order to the waiter, for all the others to hear; whilst the other was in private, where each friend marks their order secretly on a piece of paper. After the drinks were consumed, they then conducted a satisfaction questionnaire, to see which group enjoyed their beer more.

Intriguingly, it turns out that the groups of friends who ordered secretly enjoyed their beer more than those who order in public - with the significant exception of the friend who ordered first, who enjoyed his beer equally well, regardless of how it was ordered. The conclusion that Ariely draws from this is that when people know what each other are ordering, they can be irrationally influenced by these decisions - rather than ordering the beer that they prefer, they may instead choose to order the beer that they think will impress their peers. Specifically, Airely suggest that in societies where individuality is highly regarded, people may choose to order beers that differentiate them from the group - and if in fact they all tend to actually prefer similar beers, then this will be to the detriment of their drinking experience. The reason that the first person to order does not succumb to this irrationality is because he has not heard what the others are ordering, and as such, he is not influenced by their choices. As a result, he orders the beer he prefers, rather than the beer that he thinks might differentiate him from the group.

In this scenario, where each friend orders in sequence, only the first to order has no knowledge of what his friends will order, which appears to give him a significant advantage. Strangely, this is one of those counter-intuitive situations where it can be to one's disadvantage to posses more information. If the person in front of you falls over a banana skin, you may learn the location of that obstacle and contrive to avoid a similar error, and as a result, you have processed the information correctly, and to your advantage. But this same secondomics scenario can work against you, if you process the information incorrectly - choosing to order a beer that is different to that of your peers, rather than one that you like the taste of.

Chapter 16: No time for cheats

Even before this book was published, the advantages of second place were well know to many. In my humble way, I aim only to bring this insight to a wider audience. Our hungry penguins, for example, know all too well the risks of being first into the water, combined with the advantages of being the early bird, and catching the fish. And armed with this valuable information, smart penguins and people alike are inclined to take advantage. Hence our penguins all attempt to linger at the edge of the water, waiting for someone else to go first.

But what happens when someone over-plays their hand? Might we not choose to always go second, ensuring that we always get the benefits of being towards the front, without the disadvantages of leadership? In many cases, of course, this is precisely what happens. But if too much cheating takes place, it upsets the natural balance, and the cheating behavior inevitably becomes unsustainable.

For example, imagine that you live in a city which is blessed with a low crime rate - or better still, you work in a city where there is no crime at all. In this situation, where there are no cheats, and assuming you have an economically liberal government, the incentive to work hard is at its greatest, since you can be confident that you will be able to retain the proceeds of your work. You'll also be happy to spend your money, since you know that what you buy will not be stolen. The low crime rate will result in people becoming complacent about crime prevention, whilst filling their properties with valuable items. As the incentives for criminals rises, so the crime rate rises.

Now imagine the other end of the spectrum, where you live in a city with a high crime rate and no rule of law. Property is continually looted. In this situation, there is little incentive to work hard, or buy possessions, since your money and property will be stolen. In this extreme scenario, the criminals will ultimately run out of things to steal, and the crime rate will inevitably fall.

So as the crime rate falls, the incentives for crime will rise, and visa versa. As a result, the crime rate will ultimately arrive at an equilibrium point, where the incentives and disincentives for crime are balanced. In practice, this usually means that there is a certain amount of crime that a city can tolerate before the crime level becomes so damaging to the city's wealth that crime begins to fall again. The actual crime rate will then oscillate around this level, pushed a little in one direction or the other as events take their course - whether as a result of a government sponsored an anti-crime offensive, or the emergence of a particularly successful crime gang.

In terms of evolutionary biology, this kind of equilibrium point, where the levels of crime are in balance, is referred to as an *evolutionarily stable state*. And as the hungry penguins illustrate, there are many different ways in which such a state can be achieved. In the case of the penguins, if no individual bird ever went into the sea first, then the entire colony of birds would fail to feed. As we saw, the best solution to maximize the payoff whilst minimizing the risk of getting caught by a leopard seal was to share the risk by taking it in turns to

THE DISADVANTAGES OF SECOND

go first (a Nash equilibrium). This is not achieved by the penguins keeping a record and calling names - "Big Beak, it's your turn to go first, Little Flippers went first last time!" Penguins can't keep lists because the ink gets frozen in their pens.

Instead, the cooperative strategy emerges seemingly by chance. The penguins all crowd around the water's edge, trying to avoid falling in, until, during the jostling, one of them gets pushed, and then the others all dive in afterwards. The fact that this outcome looks a lot like the optimal cooperative solution is unlikely to be chance. It's far more likely that this solution has been arrived as over thousands of years of evolution, as different combinations of bird behavior have emerged until the right balance is achieved - an evolutionarily stable state, where no small changes in the mix of strategies can deliver a better outcome. Much like our example of crime in cities, however, it may be possible in such a scenario for some cheating penguins to emerge. The naughty family of penguins I described in the introduction. If this family of cheats gets too large, the whole fabric of penguin society will start to break down, as the penguins no longer feed sufficiently. But a certain number may be sustained in penguin society without the others being sufficiently impacted to notice.

Whether it's crime bosses or penguins who hate going first, we don't have much time for cheats. Indeed, our innate sense of fair play makes us humans willing to punish cheats, even at our own expense. It probably comes as no surprise that games theorists have come up with a game to test this kind of punishing behavior. It's called *Ultimatum*, and despite its simple rules, the results are enlightening. It's a two player game. The first player is offered a sum of money, which he must choose how to share with the second player. The choice is entirely his, and the second player has absolutely no say in the matter, beyond deciding whether or not to accept the share that is offered to him by the first player. There are not multiple rounds to this game - it's a once only thing. So unlike the iterated Prisoners Dilemma game that we explored earlier, there's no opportunity in Ultimatum for each side to punish the other in order to encourage them to cooperate on subsequent rounds, since there are no subsequent rounds. Player one gets to chose how to divide the sum, and player two gets to decide whether to accept what is offered to him, or not. The one catch is that if player two does not accept, then player one does not get any money either.

Rationally speaking, player two should accept however much money he is offered, since any amount of money is better than nothing, and by punishing player one, player two achieves nothing, and must sacrifice his own share in the process. But in tests, over and over again, around the world, with all kinds of different subjects, player two tends to punish player one if he is offered significantly less than 50% of the overall sum - even though player two should rationally be happy with whatever he can get.

Why are we willing to punish those who do not conform to our own notions of what is fair, even at our own personal expense? It is as if we have an innate tendency towards vigilanteism, taking the world's problems onto our shoulders, and trying to right wrongs. Since this tendency to punish cheats is so widespread, we should look for evolutionary explanations to account for it. From an evolutionary perspective, we must look for ways in which this behavior helps the individual, rather than the group. Altruistic behavior only has evolutionary advantages in very specific circumstances, such as kin altruism. Whilst it is easy to see that the altruistic act of punishing cheats is to the advantage of the group, how does the individual vigilante benefit from his behavior? It is, perhaps an example of the opposite of criminal behavior. Vigilantes help their society, and as members of that society, they derive some benefit. However, they would derive more benefit by cheating - not being a vigilante themselves, whilst allowing others to police society on their behalf. An example of this behavior would be a strikebreaker, "scab" or "knobstick." These are people who work during a strike. By breaking ranks with their union, they continue to receive an income, and don't risk getting into trouble with their employers. However, they still stand to benefit if the union successfully negotiates better terms with their employer.

In just the same way that a city can only tolerate so much crime, a union can only tolerate so many strikebreakers. If the majority of workers are not willing to strike, then the union has no power to force a reluctant employer to negotiate. So ultimately, an equilibrium point will be reached where the population of vigilantes and strikebreakers are in balance. But how do the vigilante moral majority feel about the minority who follow a secondomic strategy, willfully persisting in going second - even at the expense of the rest of the group. Do vigilante penguins punish the family of naughty penguins who never go first?

In the case of the penguins, since they're not consciously taking it in turns, there's no role for vigilanteism. The penguins all jostle at the waters edge until one falls in. It's a kind of competition, and if one family of penguins are better at holding their ground, then good luck to them. Others may also learn their trick over time, raising the stakes in the competition not to be first in.

Consider instead the case of vampire bats. In *The Selfish Gene*, Richard

THE DISADVANTAGES OF SECOND

Dawkins describes the behavior of a colony of bats, in order to illustrate how reciprocal altruism provides evolutionary advantages to the individual. Each night, the bats go out in search of food. Some will get lucky, and gorge themselves with blood, whilst others may not be lucky, and return to the roost without having fed. That's just life - sometimes you win, sometimes you don't. But vampire bats have arrived at a system of cooperation that benefits them all over time. Bats that return with bellies full of blood will regurgitate some of their feast for the less fortunate bats to consume. Its not as much as they would have received had they succeeded in feeding themselves, but it's usually just enough sustenance to keep them going. This generosity is repaid over time because the roles will eventually be reversed, and the giver becomes the recipient.

Dawkins explains that in order for this type of *reciprocal altruism* to emerge, the species must have the capacity to recognize individuals, and withhold feeding from those bats that do not share their own food in return. Without this key ability, the population would become dominated by cheats - who receive food from others without ever giving food to the needy. Dawkins outlines a variety of tests that have demonstrated this ability within bats.

Humans are, also notable in this regard. In fact, we are so good at recognizing each other, that we even give each other names, social security numbers, finger prints, passports and these days, biometric identity cards. And in so doing, we've dramatically reduced the opportunities for cheating within human society.

Whilst adelie penguins may not use recognition to punish those who refuse to go first, it turns out that other birds do just that. We've already considered the example of migratory birds flying in a v-formation, where those birds following the leader receive a benefit from the wing vortex of the bird in front. In some cases a parent may fly at the front - an example of Hamilton's rule, where parents improve the chances of their genes being replicated by helping their offspring, even at their own expense. But the scenario where parents lead their children is not the only one in which birds fly in a v-formation.

Malte Andersson and Johan Wallander, zoologists from Göteborg University, speculate that birds may also cooperate - taking it in turns to lead the flock. This arrangement once again raises the possibility for cheating, where a naughty bird may choose to always fly in second place - taking advantage of the wing vortex of the other birds, whilst never undertaking their fair share of the leadership role. If this cheating strategy were allowed to succeed, it would soon dominate the entire flock, and as a result, the birds could not fly in the v-formation and gain from the efficiency benefits.

It is a problem not limited to bird populations. It's been with us for thousands of years in human society as well. In Plato's Crito, Socrates is in prison, awaiting the death sentence. His wealthy friends visit him and try to persuade him to escape - back in those days this was a more realistic prospect that it is today.

Socrates, famously provides a number of rationales for why he should not attempt his escape. One of these arguments essentially boils down to "what if everyone did that?" The answer is, of course, that if everyone evades their punishment, then the entire rule of law breaks down, and society will cease to operate. Much like our birds, who can no longer fly in a v-formation if everyone insists on cheating.

The relative luxury of ancient Greek society required that its citizens obeyed the rule of law - indeed this luxury was only afforded by the judicious implementation of these laws. And thus, since Socrates had benefited from these laws, he was duty bound to obey them.

If Socrates was a migratory bird, there's no doubt that he would have taken his turn at the front of the v-formation. But not all birds are this noble. Where an individual bird consistently violates the cooperative rules of the flock, Andersson and Wallander suggest that they may become the victim of a mobbing attack whilst in the air, or perhaps more likely whilst at stop-over sites. Punishment of bad behavior, combined with the threat of future punishment for further transgressions is usually enough to keep the laziest bird in line (or rather, at the front of the line).

So, one important disadvantage of consistently coming second, at the expense of others in your society, is that you may be punished by others - even at their own expense. However, a certain degree of cheating seems to be both sustainable and tolerated by others. In human groups such as the cycling peloton, we tend to be pretty intolerant of persistent wheel-suckers, who do not do their fair share at the front. On many occasions in competitive cycling, where an individual is perceived to not be following the rules of the peloton, they will be ostracized. The solution for a crafty cheat in these situations would be to cheat as much as possible, without being spotted, coming second as often as you can without drawing unwanted attention to yourself. This kind of invisible wheel-sucking happens the world over - take a look behind you right now. Is someone wheel-sucking you? Is it time that you punished them for their repeated transgressions?

Chapter 17: Knowing when to follow, and when to lead

In chapter three, we considered how throughout history, talented women such as Abigail Adams, had little option but to associate themselves with powerful men if they wished to put their talents to good use. Two hundred years ago, there was no opportunity for Abigail Adams to become president of the United Sates - it was considered an exclusively male domain. So instead, she made do with her role as first lady and most trusted advisor to President John Adams. We will never know whether Abigail Adams would have stood for the presidency herself, if she had the opportunity.

John Adams was not the most capable of the founding fathers, and his wife often seems to have possessed a sharper intellect. He did not take well to the number two position of vice president. As he once wrote his wife:

"My country has in its wisdom contrived for me the most insignificant office that ever the invention of man contrived or his imagination conceived."

Of course, Adams didn't settle for this "insignificant" office, and went on to become the second president. The importance of John Adams' role in American history is not concerned with his intellect, which was consistently eclipsed by those of his brilliant colleagues such as Franklin and Jefferson. Rather, his pivotal role was to be the second president, and thus establish the first smooth transition in executive power. Washington may have been America's first president, but it was not until executive powers were transferred by democratic process that the constitutional democracy of the nation was truly established. Adam's character and approach to duty played an integral role in this historic landmark - one of the first instances in recorded history of a peaceful handover of power from one living head of state to another. And it was this event, perhaps more than any other, which cemented the path of the fledgling United States to becoming the world's first truly democratic republic.

Whilst many claim to want power, and claim to be frustrated by the incompetence of those in power above them, Adams remained consistently loyal to his leader, George Washington, whilst being ready to take the responsibility of the top job, when the time came. This ability to loyally follow a leader whilst being ready to assume leadership when the time comes is a surprisingly rare commodity. It's more common for people to either seek leadership at all costs, or to act as if they could do better than the leader, whilst choosing instead (consciously or otherwise) to heckle from the sidelines in a secondary position - like a rebellious teenager.

This type of heckling behavior is indicative of some kind of inner conflict - a frustration with the powers that be, combined with an inability or reluctance to take over responsibility. There are many legitimate reasons for targeting second place, but fear of taking responsibility for one's own actions is not one of them. One may quite legitimately conclude that one is not yet ready for leadership, and therefore willingly choose to follow the leadership of someone else. And one may legitimately conclude that he is never ready for leadership. There's a clear positive payoff to second place if we honestly believe that someone else will do a better job of leading that we could ourselves. After all, we will then get the benefit of their good leadership. But if we avoid leadership simply because we're too fearful of taking responsibility for our own actions, then we have no one but ourselves to blame when things go wrong.

Hecklers are frequently unaware of their inner conflict. When we bitch about our boss over the water cooler with a colleague, we may not even realize how fearful we are about taking that responsibility for ourselves. We may convince ourselves that our disempowered state leaves us no option but to heckle, when in fact we have unconsciously chosen to perform a secondary role, because we are fearful of the responsibility and accountability associated with a leadership role.

A heckler, in secondomics terms, is the inverse of a sidekick. Whilst sidekicks position themselves in proximity to leadership in order to exert a positive influence, a heckler does the same, but with negative intent. Of course, it is important for us to listen to the hecklers in our society. Often they are the only voices of reason, such as those of the civil rights movement in America, or the anti-apartheid movement in South Africa. But when the opportunity to put ones ideas into practice arises, to leave the comfortable security of second place behind and adopt a position of leadership, we should be ready to take responsibility for what we believe in.

Like America's second president, we must learn the time to be a loyal follower, and the time to step up and take responsibility as a leader in our own right. There's no advantage to second place if what we really want first place, but we're afraid to claim our prize.

Chapter 18: When two is one too many

As we saw in Chapter 10, people often have a tendency to try to even the score - whether they're depleting two rolls of toilet paper, or supporting the un-

THE DISADVANTAGES OF SECOND

derdog in a sports event. But we are not always so even-handed. There are three circumstances in which we're more likely to punish the underdog, rather than support it:

- **second is ignored** - leadership bias
- **second is redundant** - two is one too many
- **second is expendable** - sacrifice second to save first

1. Second is ignored

We keep returning to that Abba refrain, "the winner takes it all". I've already argued that this is, in practice, rarely the case - the winner may take the biggest prize, but there is usually more than one prize on offer. However, if this mantra is repeated often enough, it has a tendency to become a self fulfilling prophecy.

In the 2008 Beijing Olympics, the United Kingdom achieved its highest number of gold medals in living memory. Within the UK, there was much discussion about who could claim the credit for this remarkable achievement. As is so typically the case, few were willing to consider the possibility that it might just be random luck. In the same year that Gordon Brown has been held accountable for a global downturn in the economy that was beyond his control, there also seemed to be a consensus in the media that someone must be credited with this remarkable Olympic success. No one was willing to accept that it could simply be down to a fortuitous confluence of events.

Personally, I believe that luck played a large part of it, and the psychological advantage of knowing that the next Olympics would be held in their home country probably helped the British athletes as well. But the popular explanation was that it must have something to do with the National Lottery Fund, which had been launched in 1994, providing, amongst other things, funding for UK sports organizations.

Britain ranked fourth in the medal league table at the 2008 Olympics - winning a total of 19 gold medals. As a result, a kind of gold fever hooked the nation, and all eyes focused on repeating or even exceeding this achievement in the 2012 London Olympics. *The Economist* argued:

> "*The way public cash is awarded, using a formula gauging past and potential performance against targets, has sharpened the incentives to take a more professional approach. Underperforming sports risk losing financial support.*"

This quasi-market-based solution would naturally appeal to a free-market oriented newspaper like The Economist. And there is certainly a ruthless logic to the idea of rewarding success and punishing failure. Rather than supporting the underdog, and redressing perceived imbalances, this policy is more concerned with creating the right incentives for success. Looked at in terms of incentives, the idea of supporting the underdog starts to look like incentivizing failure.

The trouble with this kind of quasi-market-based solution is that it is not really market-based at all. It's actually a government intervention designed to increase the differential in sponsorship between the rich and poor sports, with a view to focusing funding on a small number of successful sports. The idea underlying this type of policy is that more value can be achieve from government expenditure if it is focused in a small number of areas, as opposed to being spread too thinly to have a meaningful impact anywhere.

There's doubtless some merit to this argument, if winning is the only success criteria for government spending. But since optimization, consolidation and market domination are things that markets seems to be very effective at achieving by themselves, a better argument may be that government funds should be used to correct market imbalances, rather than to reinforce them.

Olympic funding is just one example of this type of market-magnifying policy - the UK takes a similar approach in punishing failing schools and hospitals. And it is not only governments that pursue this strategy. As we saw in Chapter 2, parents tend to invest more in their older children. And favoring the leader is hard-wired into all manner of other game mechanics - for example, the player in Monopoly who achieves an early lead has a built in advantage, since he is then able to start charging his opponent rent, and use the proceeds to further advance his lead. In these situations, second place is certainly not a very comfortable place to be.

In games such as Monopoly, where rules contrive to reward success with further success, this is essentially a gearing mechanism in the game to accelerate game play towards a conclusion. Without these mechanisms to compound the lead player's advantage, games could last for ever, with the balance of power switching perpetually between one side and another - oscillating between an equilibrium point. Rewarding success with further success tips the balance in favor of the first leader, helping to bring the game to a close, with a decisive winner and loser. This is the same outcome that the UK's government hopes to achieve, by creating decisive winning and losing sports.

In all such scenarios, where third parties intervene with the view that

THE DISADVANTAGES OF SECOND

winning is all that matters, they will inevitably put second place at an exaggerated disadvantage.

2. Second is redundant

The second scenario where we tend to punish the underdog, is where we perceive second to be redundant. Since this book is concerned with competition, we have focussed on second in the sense of "second place", where second means coming after or achieving a lesser payoff than first. But second can also mean "in addition to first." These two separate definitions may be simultaneously applied to the same subject - in particular, when we consider the ways in which people choose to reward or punish second place. If I choose to award a second prize, then by definition, I'm rewarding second *in addition to* first.

When judging a competition, we may struggle to decide who should get first and second prize, since the standard of the two leading entries is so close. We may decide to award a joint first prize, or make a special commendation for a particular runner up. Whilst some may congratulate us for our fair-minded judgement, others may argue that two winners is one too many, and we that have failed in our responsibilities to adjudicate. Again, popular culture provides a pointer to people's preferences in this area - consider the enduring popularity of the phrase "there can be only one," famously used in the movie *The Highlander*. It is a popular phrase in sports events the world over. It seems we have an innate desire to see an unambiguous, decisive victory arising from competition. Interestingly, this is precisely the outcome that the code duello is designed to ensure - since this clarity of outcome helped to reduce the risk of deadly family feuds. Perhaps we have evolved to favor decisive single-victor outcomes for precisely this reason - it reduces the risks of an isolated conflict escalating into a larger dispute, involving multiple parties, resulting in significantly more damage. Perhaps we're programmed to favor the security of the balance of power, even if this means that our preferred candidate does not end up as top dog.

In some decisions, where we struggle to decide between two options, we may be tempted to go for both. And in many cases, this equivocation is considered as intolerable by others. One such example is marriage. Imagine that you're struggling to choose between two possible partners, both of whom, you feel, offer you equal utility. In most cultures, if you decide to bring both home together to meet the family, your parents will not be delighted. Whilst they may have their own personal preference in terms of which future son or daughter-in-law they favor, the odds are that they'd prefer that you pick one, whichever that may be. This reticence on the part of your parents is doubtless due, in no small part, to the fact that in most western countries, the practice of polygamy is illegal. But this is simply the proximate cause of their antipathy. We should instead consider why these laws exist at all. Why, when in so many situations, second place receives a generous second prize, second (concurrent) wives or husbands are instead frowned upon?

Since the practice of monogamy is so widespread, and is observed in the behavior of several species, we can infer that in some situations it has an evolutionary benefit. In species with a long gestation and child-rearing period, such as humans, the advantages of monogamy to the female are obvious. Her chances of procreation are increased if she seeks out a loyal mate, who will assist her in raising children. From a male's perspective, monogamy appears less advantageous. He may maximize his opportunities for procreation by inseminating as many females as possible, and leaving them to raise the children on his behalf. The solution to this is typically that females seek out males that seem loyal, through elaborate courtship rituals. Males will inevitably develop cheating strategies, where they attempt to trick the female into believing that they will be loyal, only to leave the female after procreation to raise the children by herself. We've already explored how societies handle the punishment and toleration of cheats, and it is quite easy to imagine that society will arrive at an equilibrium point for this kind of cheating as well. A certain amount of cheating is tolerated, but for the most part, monogamy is enforced.

So if you are a female, competing for the most attractive mate in your community, there will be no prize for second best. Even if your man is struggling to decide between you and the other woman, he cannot choose both of you, since society is unlikely to tolerate it.

Another example of intolerance of choosing two is second homes. In the late 20th century, as house prices in the West began to rise rapidly, and credit became cheaper, the acquisition of second homes became very popular. Legislators, however, have a tendency to punish second home owners. This is in part simply because a second home is a luxury, and luxuries tend to come in for more than their fair share of taxation. It's also due to the fact that second homes are left vacant for the majority of the time (since, by definition, the owners will spend most of their time in their primary residence). As a consequence, governments tend to perceive second homes as having a negative impact on economic activity in an area, whilst driving up local house prices at the expense of local first time buyers.

The key to this difference in fiscal approach is luxury. Where the term "second" is used to describe the recipient of a lesser payoff, legislators tend to reward, as in the case of the Swedish media laws. Conversely, where second means supplemental, (in additional to first,) legislators are more likely to punish. This is in part due to redistributive policies which intend to reduce the difference between rich and poor. Since owning a second home, or for that matter, a second car, may to some extent be an indicator of wealth, legislators often take the opportunity to extract further taxation.

It's all just a part of the perennial battle between liberty and equality - two concepts that, whilst frequently lumped together into a single agenda, have a tricky tendency to be mutually exclusive concepts. The history of the French Revolution, during which the national motto, "liberté, egalité, fraternité," (liberty, equality, brotherhood) was coined, provides a fine illustration of the problem. It all boils down to how we define equality. In chapter one, we explored the irony of wealthy Virginian slave owner, Thomas Jefferson, declaring "all men are created equal". Clearly, in his own mind at least, Jefferson was able to resolve the seeming paradox that all men are equal, and yet some men were at the time able to own other men as if they were property. Jefferson was also famously sympathetic to the French Revolution, believing that it represented similar values to those that he had so eloquently expressed in 1776.

If, by "equality," we mean simply that all men should be treated equally under the law (which is presumably the sense in which Jefferson mean it), then we should find little difficulty in reconciling this aim with liberty, since together we have a concept of equal freedom for all. However, in Jacobin France, equality rapidly developed a new meaning, concerning equality of wealth, rather than equality under the law. As the Austrian/British economist, Friedrich August von Hayek explained in his famous libertarian essay *The Road to Serfdom*, this sense of equality is entirely incompatible with liberty. Redistributive policies may serve to reduce differentials in wealth, and as a result, promote this type of equality. But this is achieved at the expense of liberty, since governments must curtail the freedom of their subjects to acquire wealth. It is also incompatible with the original meaning of equality, since by definition, the law will be applied differently to different individuals - the wealthy are treated differently to the poor.

By exploring this paradox, I do not mean to comment on the rights or wrongs of these different legislative agendas. But rather, by understanding the paradoxical ideological positions in which governments find themselves, we may better understand how government policy may reward or punish second

SECONDOMICS

place. Governments may use ownership of a second property as a signifier of wealth for their redistributive policies. They may also use it as a signifier of antisocial wastefulness or profligacy, and punish it in order to provide a disincentive that would otherwise not exist in a free market. Identifying an individual's behavior as profligate, and punishing it accordingly, may be illiberal, but it is sometimes motivated on the basis that protecting the majority from the antisocial behavior of the individual can be justified as a means of advancing equality.

So, are second homes and second cars an example of a particular category that bucks the secondomics trend? Where "second" indicates abundance, the underdog principle does have a tendency to kick in. As we have seen, governments have a tendency to push ostentatious displays of wealth as a result of their redistributive policies. Certainly, in this sense, second carries a unique disadvantage over first. But if we explore second homes from another perspective, the more familiar principles of secondomics still apply. Since a second home is inhabited less than a first home, it incurs less wear and tear, less accidents happen in the home, and it is therefore less likely to burn to the ground as the result of a kitchen fire. Likewise, a second car is driven less that a first car, and is therefore less likely to be involved in an accident.

In this sense, second represents a redundant backup. Whilst regulators may not perceive the need for a second home, it can certainly come in handy when your first home burns down. And whilst a second car may seem to be a rich man's play-thing, it comes into its own, when your first car makes an unplanned trip to the mechanics. Certainly, backup may not be the intention of those fortune individuals who own second homes or cars, but it is an intrinsic advantage well known in the IT industry. In data storage for example, RAID 1 (which stands for "Redundant Array of Independent Disks"), is a system whereby identical data is written simultaneously to two separate hard drives. In this context, we should expect governments to be less likely to punish us for owning a frivolous excess of disks. There are a couple of interesting points to note about RAID 1. Firstly, whilst RAID 1 can be used with more than two disks, this is normally considered sufficient redundancy, since the odds of two disks simultaneously failing are considered to be sufficiently low as to negate the value of adding additional disks. But whilst there are typically two disks in such a system, there is arguably no second disk, since there is no primary disk. The point of a RAID 1 solution is that each disk acts as a backup for the other.

Consider, for a moment, the comparison between a RAID array and the toilet paper algorithm from the previous chapter. In that context, we wanted to force the user to use the two rolls in a serial fashion - exhausting the first roll before moving on to the second, backup roll. In a RAID array, however, quite the reverse is the case - here we want the two disks to be used in parallel. The difference is, of course, that toilet rolls are exhaustible - the paper from the roll cannot be re-used, for obvious reasons. In contrast, hard drives can be re-written - when you erase a file from your hard disk, you can use the reclaimed space to save something else. So, whilst a backup toilet roll protects against resource exhaustion, a RAID array protects against failure. And since either disk may fail, the optimal solution is that each provides backup for the other.

Second homes and second cars may also, in practice, be used in serial or parallel fashion. Whilst in the UK, your accountant may need to know which home is your primary residence, in order to determine whether it qualifies for relief from capital gains tax, in practice, you may not make such a clear distinction. Your lifestyle may, in fact, dictate that you share your time equally between your two homes. A scenario that the legislators may not have anticipated. In this case, your are likely to designate the more valuable of your two residences as your primary residence, in order to maximize your potential tax relief. In this kind of special case, where an individual owns multiple parallel redundant assets, he may choose which to designate first and second, to his own advantage - in this case, at the tax payer's expense.

So, in many ways, society encourages us to rank our options and select the top-ranking candidate. "You can't have everything" as the saying goes. We may want to pick first and second, but our peers will sometimes discourage us, and may even punish us if we do. Whilst most people support the principle of equality, they have differing definitions of what equality means. Some mean equality of opportunity, in which case having more than others may be tolerated, whilst others mean equality of wealth, in which case everyone must have the same quantity - which means second home, cars, wives or husbands may be frowned upon, as excess.

3. Second is expendable

The third area in which the behavior of others may act to the detriment of second place is where second is perceived as expendable. Something I like to describe as "Best China Syndrome." Around the world, many households have a set of china that is reserved for special occasions. This china is perceived as so special and valuable that it is rarely used, and in some households, it literally is never used. In these situations, the people involved probably don't in-

SECONDOMICS

tend to never use their china - it's just that as each potential opportunity to bring out the best china arises, they somehow feel that they should defer use of it for an occasion of even greater import. As a result, the best china goes unused, and accumulates dust, whilst the second-best china gets worn out very quickly indeed. In this sense the second-best "everyday" china is sacrificed in order to protect the best.

Best China Syndrome is not limited to china - the same principles apply in a wide range of situations. As we've already seen in a military context, the commander will often be considered non-expendable, and so will normally command operations from well behind the front line, whereas the second in command will often be expected to risk his or her life in order to protect the commander.

Star Trek provides a good illustration of this. In the original series, it seems somewhat unrealistic that Captain Kirk would always lead away missions - leaving command of his ship and overall operations to whomever was available - often his chief engineer, or some other unknown character (but notably, never Lieutenant Uhura). The creators of the show realized their error, and sought to correct it in Star Trek: The Next Generation. In the new show, Captain Picard would typical remain in overall control, commanding operations from the bridge of his ship, whilst delegating away missions to his second in command - Will Riker. In this role of second in command, Riker was exposed to far greater danger than Picard.

Coming second - weighing up the pros and cons

Winners, by definition, tend to achieve more than runners up, and this book does not attempt the fools errand of proving otherwise. It is only to be expected that in most situations in life, winners will receive the largest payoff. In that sense, this section could have been very long indeed, if I had attempted to comprehensively catalogue the innumerable ways in which second place may afford a lesser payoff than first.

Instead, this section has focused on those situations where the mechanics of secondomics work in reverse, serving to punish second place, rather than to reward it. As such, we have explored situations where second place not only has a lower payoff than first, but in most cases, secondomics contrives to deliver a lower payoff than third as well. For example, when a minister resigns to save the job of a prime minister, he tends to protect the jobs of his subordinates as well, by taking the responsibility on his own shoulders.

This chapter has, in turn, taken each of the principles of secondomics from the previous chapter, and turned them on their heads. Rather than negative proofs, this illustrates that many aspects of secondomics are to some extend reversible. As the table below illustrates, the first four sections of this book, where we have in turn explored the advantages and disadvantages of first and second place, have each followed the same structure.

Rather than simply eight advantages of second, we can now think in terms of eight generalised principles of second place:

Contextual:

	Advantages of first	Disadvantages of first	Advantages of second	Disadvantages of second
Payoff distribution	Largest payoff	Winner doesn't always take it all	Disproportionate share of payoff	Winner actually takes it all
Encountering what's ahead	Getting there first	Breaking new ground is harder	Coasting in the slipstream	Tripping over a fallen leader
Encountering threats	Clear line of sight	No cover from threats ahead	Cover from threats ahead	Decoys and fall guys
Competitive rivalry	Outrunning a predator	Back-stabbing from behind	Enemy in your sights	Winner punishes loser
Exchanging information	Getting the news first	Setting an example	Learning from the leader	Becoming predictable

Behavioral:

	Advantages of first	Disadvantages of first	Advantages of second	Disadvantages of second
Attitudes to ranking	Savoring victory	Nowhere to go but down	Room for growth	Punishing cheats
Planning investment	Windfalls from suprise victories	Over-investing in winning	Lower total cost of ownership	Leadership anxiety
3rd party intervention	Rewarding the winner	Punishing pride & arrogance	Supporting the underdog	When two is one too many

But where does this leave us? In this book, I have promised to demonstrate that coming second can be a winning strategy. I can appreciate that at this point, if you paid good money for this book, you may feel a little short-changed. How can I now be saying that secondomics is a pretty complicated thing, and sometimes it's better not to come second?

The answer is that I never claimed that coming second is always a winning strategy - merely that it *can* be. The trick is, of course, to learn how to identify when this is the case. And that it precisely the subject of part seven, where we will be exploring secondomics in action. But before we get there, we still have some more ground to cover.

Part 5 - Secondomics over time

"Nearly all of humanity share your predicament. When you can't get what you want, you suffer. And even when you get exactly what you want, you still suffer, because you can't hang on to it forever."

The Way of the Peaceful Warrior, Dan Millman

Now that we have explored the pros and cons of coming first and second, we're ready to look at how these principles operate in practice. When we think about real-life examples of competitive scenarios, we tend to frame them in terms of stories, with a beginning, a middle and an end. In a story about competition, the beginning tends to be some kind of challenge, the middle is concerned with an interaction of some kind - perhaps a fight or a race - and the end is concerned with the result: who won, who lost and what the consequences were.

Real life is, of course, not self-contained in this way. Only the most contrived of competitions has a beginning, a middle and an end. In practice, competition tends to be an ongoing state of endless iterative interaction. In this context, seeking out a beginning and an end is an arbitrary determination. In the case of story-telling, defining a beginning and end is more of an aesthetic decision than anything else. When a tale begins with the immortal words "it all started when...," what the narrator actually means is that he is going to frame the events that he's concerned with in relation to this arbitrary starting point. After all, from a scientific perspective, to the best of our knowledge it actually all started with the big bang - and very few narrators take that as the beginning of their story.

But there is a point after the big bang, and before now, which we may identify as the definitive starting point of the particular competition with which much of this book is concerned. When we think about the evolution of life on earth, we may, with some confidence, identify the primordial soup, over 2.4 billion years ago, as the point in time at which it really all started. In effect, any story about competition between organisms on earth that starts after this point, is framing events from an arbitrary starting point. So let's begin this section about time with a bit of time travel, back to the moment when it all began.

When organic, self-replicating molecules formed in the primordial soup, our planet's nascent economy was born. In those early days, the economy got off to a great start with a boom - there was a lot of soup, and a small number of replicating molecules to consume it. In effect, that was the free lunch which economists have been looking for ever since. But as the molecules multiplied, they gobbled up the available nutrients in the soup, resulting in the first global economic crash, as the supply of nutrients became constrained. Inevitably, the molecules began to turn on each other in search of further food to fuel their replication. That's where competition began, and ever since we evolved from those early self-replicating molecules, we've been participating in that competition for the world's limited resources.

Whilst there's only one organism on earth with a central nervous system that is sophisticated enough to be consciously aware of the principles of secondomics, that hasn't stopped other creatures from getting in on the act. Like our hungry penguins and satellite toads, they get the benefit of secondomics through phenotypic behaviors that have evolved over thousands of years. (Phenotype refers to the expression of a genetically influenced trait). In those special cases where coming second offers the greatest payoff, we may expect natural selection to favor those genetic replicators that produce phenotypes that have a tendency to come second.

So in situations where secondomics applies, natural selection favors those that take advantage of it. Once again, for the record, I'm not saying that secondomics *always* applies - simply that secondomic situations are more common than we often realize, since our perception is so often skewed by leadership bias. Evolutionary adaptation, however, is blind to such biases, and will ineluctably stumble upon secondomic opportunities as the occur.

But we can't all be second all the time. How do we resolve situations where many find themselves in contention to come second? Imagine the hypothetical (fantasy) scenario where this book becomes an international best seller. As more people read the book and discover the benefits of second place, it will become increasingly hard to be second, because it is suddenly such a popular place to be. In just the same way, where genes for second place are selected over time, they come to dominate, reducing the chances of any one organism possessing those genes from ever coming second. How are such situations resolved?

Clearly, once a strategy becomes over exploited, its value reduces for those organisms employing it, and consequently, over time alternative phenotypic behaviors will be selected instead. Ultimately, we may expect the penetration of secondomic behavior in a population to reach an equilibrium point, where any greater use of the strategy will be to the disadvantage of all, and any less use will present an opportunity for individuals to exploit by increasing their use of that strategy.

This equilibrium point need not be reached by changes in the population numbers of secondomic versus non-secondomic individuals. The selective use of this strategy may occur within individual organisms. These organisms may begin to take it in turns to come second, and that's essentially what this part of the book is about. Selectively using secondomic strategies in order to take it in turns is an example of what John Nash (subject of the movie *A Beautiful Mind*) would term a *mixed strategy*.

In game theory terminology, the word "strategy" describes the actions that a player will take in a game, often dependent on the actions of the opposing player or players. A "pure" strategy is one that is consistently pursued in all situations. For example, in a game where the players bet on the outcome of a coin toss, a pure strategy would be to always bet "heads." A "mixed" strategy would combine various strategies, usually played in random combination, according to predetermined probabilities. For example, betting "heads" sixty percent of the time, and "tails" for forty percent would be a mixed strategy.

At the start of this book, I argued that, on the long journey to my parents' house, I could maximize my speed whilst minimizing my risk of getting caught by the traffic police, if I and a fellow motorist took it in turns to be fastest and second fastest on the road. This is a good example of a mixed strategy, so let's examine how it works.

If we think of this problem in terms of a game, and imagine for the sake of simplicity that there are only two motorist on the road, me and one other boy-racer, then the two of us are effectively the "players" (or as a game theorist would say, "actors"). The prize we're playing for is to travel as fast as possible, without getting caught by the police. So let the game begin, and let's start awarding points.

How should we award these points? Well there are two things we're playing for here - speed and risk reduction. So, for the sake of argument, let's say that every ten mile per hour above the speed limit is worth one point. And let's also say that reducing (or eliminating) the risk of getting caught by the police is worth two points. On this basis, how fast should we travel in order to maximize the points that we can win? (For the purpose of this game, we should think of points as a good thing, as opposed to points on our license, which is the more likely outcome in a real world scenario!)

From a secondomics perspective, the best strategy would be to reduce my speed in order to ensure at all times that another motorist within close

SECONDOMICS

proximity to me is traveling faster, or if no other speed violators are around, I should stick to the speed limit. That's all well and good, until we factor in that this is a game, and that my opponent also knows the rules. If he follows the same strategy as me, we'll both end up sticking to the speed limit. Good news for a lazy police officer, but not such great news for me or my opponent, who are not getting home any sooner.

In this situation, my opponent and I are both vying for second place. In order for us both to gain the maximum possible points from the game, we must learn to cooperate - literally, we must take it in turns to be in second place. That way we share the risk of getting caught equally, whilst maximizing our possible speed. This is what Nash would describe as a symmetrical non-zero sum game with pure and mixed strategy equilibria.

A zero-sum game is how game theorists refer to win-lose situations, where one person's gain always comes at the equivalent cost to someone else. So these situations may be "zero-sum" if, when you add all the gains, and subtract all the losses of the people involved, the total amounts to zero. Whilst a "non-zero sum game", would be a situation where the sum of gains and losses does not necessarily add up to zero, and the overall "value" of the game varies depending on the actions of the individuals participants. Non-zero sum games may represent potential win-win opportunities.

	70mph (him)	80mph (him)	90mph (him)
70mph (me)	2, 2 points	2, 1 points	2, 2 points
80mph (me)	1, 2 points	1, 1 points	3, 2 points
90mph (me)	2, 2 points	2, 3 points	2, 2 points

This table illustrates three possible speeds at which my opponent and I may travel. In each of the nine boxes, the number of points we would win are indicated - first mine, and then my opponents, after the comma. If I stick to the 70mph speed limit, I get 2 points regardless of what our opponent does, (2 points for risk protection, no points for speed). Equally, if we both drive at 90mph, we also both get two points, (2 points for speed, no points for risk protection). But as you can see from the highlighted boxes - if I drive at 80mph, whilst my opponent drives at 90, I could get even more points (one for speed, two for risk protection). But if we were both to drive at 80mph, hoping to get 3 points, we'd actually only get 1 point each, (1 point for speed, no points for risk protection). You might conclude that you have no option but to travel at

90mph, and accept a sub-optimal payoff. This is certainly one solution: it's known as a *pure strategy Nash equilibrium*.

But in this situation, Nash's *mixed strategy* (as opposed to pure strategy) offers us a potentially better alternative. A mixed strategy in this context means alternating between 80mph and 90mph. So that, for 50% of the time, I'm travelling at 80mph, and for the other 50%, I'm travelling at 90mph. If I do this, then the worst payoff my opponent can get is an average of 2 points, and the best that he can get is 2.5 points, if he starts to alternate between 80mph and 90mph in coordination with me. There is the risk to me that he might choose a pure strategy of always sticking to 80mph, which would give me an average of 1.5 points - but since he would still only get an average of 2 points, there's no incentive for him to do so. Instead, his only incentive is to collaborate with me.

If both my opponent and I alternate between 80mph and 90mph in co-ordination, such that when he's at 80mph, I'm at 90mph and visa-versa, we achieving an average payoff of 2.5 points each. This is a greater payoff than we can get by any other strategy.

Of course, this is all hypothetical anyway, since I would never be so reckless as to deliberately break a speed limit. Nonetheless, in a situation where everyone has read this book and wants to come second, a pure strategy of always seeking second place may fail, because we can't all come second, all the time. Whereas, a mixed strategy of seeking second place for a certain proportion of the time may prove to be more effective, if it becomes prevalent in a population.

Chapter 19: Anticipating competitor behavior

To come second in a competition, we must predict the investment that our competitors are going to make in order to determine what level of investment we should make. Too much investment, and we may come first, whilst not enough may result in us coming third. The task is further complicated by the fact that our level of investment, and that of our competitors, may change over time as the competition progresses, and they are covariant. A change in the investment level of one competitor may naturally have an impact on the investment levels of the others.

So, as we participate in competition, we must constantly evaluate the situation, analyzing our opponents' strategies and considering how best to respond. In order to perform this task, our brains are equipped with faculties for anticipating competitor behavior. It's easy to envisage situations where natural selection would favor organisms with an ability to anticipate the behavior of their predators, since this will presumably enable them to evade those predators and thus make them fitter to prosper in their environment. But this process of selection will only favor those whose prognostication skills are good enough - it will not continue to optimize these abilities beyond the point at which they offer a survival/reproduction benefit. Since any optimization in one area comes at a cost, when incremental improvement no longer offers benefits to outweigh those costs, further optimization will cease.

As a result, our brains are good enough for predicting some aspects of competitor behavior. But much of this evolutionary adaptation took place a very long time ago in human history, where we tended to be engaged in very different forms of competition from those that occupy us today. As a result, we're better at anticipating when a dog is about to bite us, or a horse is about to kick, than we are at anticipating when a foreign power is about to invade, or a corporate raider is about to launch a hostile takeover bid.

In game theory terms, the effects of time can be introduced in the form of iteration. An iterated game is one played in multiple, repetitive rounds. In Prisoner's Dilemma, as we have seen, a single game is unlikely to result in both sides cooperating, since there is no means for the two parties to communicate. However, where the game is played in multiple rounds, such that in each round the players may decide whether to cooperate or defect, in full knowledge of the decisions that their opponent made in previous rounds, more sophisticated strategies can emerge. As we've already explored, in these scenarios, strategies that are *nice, provokable and forgiving* tend to dominate. Or in other words - "I'll play nice with people that play nice with me, but I'll punish those that don't."

So over time, we can establish dialogue with our competitors, that facilitates both cooperative strategies and the opportunity to punish non-cooperation. As we discover more about our competitor's strategies, we may come to anticipate their behavior. Whilst this will often be to our advantage, it can also benefit our opponents on occasion. Competitors may deliberately mislead us by build up our trust only to subsequently betray us. We are all too inclined to assume that because someone has always cooperated in the past, they will also cooperate in the future. But if we don't have insight into the underlying motivation of their cooperative strategy, our method of prediction is flawed. In effect, we're attempting to establish empirical laws based upon insufficient evidence. Because our opponent has always used strategy x in the past, we anticipate that they will continue to use strategy x. When in fact, they may be using a conditional mixed strategy, and since we don't know the conditions under which they will switch from strategy x to strategy y, it will come as a complete surprise to us when such a switch occurs.

Chapter 20: Anticipating change

Whilst anticipating competitor behavior is essential, more skills are required in order to maximize our chances of achieving second place. We must also seek to anticipate how the course of the competition will progress over time, and this task is complicated by the unreliability associated with any predictions of the future, combined with our ingrained biases and fallacies that may conspire to cloud our judgement.

The aphorism "win some, lose some," is often invoked to express the view we should not allow ourselves to become too hung up upon short term defeat, since we cannot expect to win every time. Another popular phrase "the best of three" is a logical extension of this premise. When participating in a game, the loser may propose the best of three - questioning who will win two out of three rounds. In other words, this player does not judge the initial result to necessarily be indicative of all subsequent results. This idea, that winning a battle is not the same as winning a war, is well understood. And with it comes an assumption and acceptance of change. No one can stay top dog forever - as we saw in Chapter Two with Enoch Powell's law, all political careers end in failure.

How strange then, given this popular understanding, that in so many situations, change seems to be exactly what we don't anticipate or plan for. We tend to focus so much on competing for victory that we rarely plan for what will follow that victory - such that when we lose the subsequent battle, it all too often comes as a surprise. Likewise, when we are deciding what to invest our money in, we tend to over-rely on past performance as a guide. Even to the extent that financial services advertisements referring to past performance are required to remind prospective investors that this is not necessarily an indicator of future success. Such statements, typically buried somewhere in the small print, are intended to disabused people of the notion that, simply because something has done well in the past, it will necessarily also do well in the future. This fallacy is in fact diametrically at odds with the "best of three" sentiment, where it is assumed that a change in fortunes is likely.

This is just one example of cognitive dissonance - our remarkable ability to simultaneously hold diametrically opposing views, determined entirely by context. The "best of three" sentiment is invoked when we are in a playful mindset, where change is exciting and fun. The "past performance" fallacy is invoked when we are planning for the future, and change indicates the unknown, which is threatening, and therefore undesirable. Where we perceive an appearance of consistency in past events, we anticipate that events will continue in a similar manner in the future, and as a result, we underestimate the possibility of change. Conversely, when events have been disruptive in the past, we anticipate that they will continue to be disruptive, and we consequently underestimate the possibility that things may settle down. By basing our expectations for the future upon our superficial observations of the past, without an understanding of the underlying causes, we will inevitably underestimate endogenous potential for change.

Another supposed truism also perfectly illustrates this fallacy: "if you do what you always did, you'll get what you always got." Whilst this is presumably intended to encourage change as a part of personal development, it is based upon an assumption that there will be no external change. As a result, it encourages dangerously lazy causal thinking. For example, we might infer from it that "I always brush my hair in the morning, and my train always arrives on time. Therefore, if I always brush my hair, *then* the train will always arrive on time." In other words, the truism implies that what we get is due entirely to what we do, and does not allow for the possibility of external or unknown factors that may change. Furthermore, it implies causal relationships exist universally - an interesting philosophical perspective, but not one borne out by empirical science. We may continue to do what we always did, but *not* get what we always got. In competitive scenarios, we may pursue strategies and frequently win or come second - but those strategies may not be the reason for our ranking. The performance of other competitors, for example, will surely also have a big impact.

In competition, it's notable how superstitious sportsmen can be - attributing tiny changes in their preparation ritual with success or failure in competition, no matter how tenuous or downright irrational the argument for causality may be. Tennis star Goran Ivanisevic, for example, is known to eat lucky foods during tennis tournaments, and take care to always use the same lucky shower cubicle. This is another example of unreliable causal thinking. In these situations, sportsmen attempt to infer causal relationships between their actions prior to victory, and the victory itself. By attempting to ritualize these actions, repeating them before each new contest, they seek to recreate the circumstances that previously led to victory. Sports coaches, versed in Neuro-linguistic programming (NLP), may inadvertently (or on occasion deliberately) encourage this type of wrong-thinking in their attempts to "model excellence". In seeking to determine the "difference that makes a difference," NLP encourages a focus on the smallest of details, which may seem to be of no consequence, but may in fact be an essential ingredient in achieving peak performance. Whilst, in principle, there's nothing wrong with this approach, inevitable failures in the modeling process can result in this kind of fetishization of unproductive behaviors.

In these circumstances, a skilled coach may do better by encouraging his client to prepare for the unexpected, and accept change as inevitable, rather than creating a fallacy of control, by ritualizing behavior in the run-up to an event, in an attempt to make change seem impossible.

So, typically, we will draw on our past experiences in order to anticipate what the future has in store. And those aspects of our experience that are easiest to recall will exert the greatest influence upon our judgement. This is an aspect of the cognitive bias described by psychologists Daniel Kahneman and Amos Tversky as the *availability heuristic* - our tendency to judge the likelihood of a future event based upon the ease with which we can recall similar events that have occurred in the past. If we recall a particular strategy having been successful in the past, we're inclined to believe that it will also be successful in the future. In competition, we must temper this inclination with a careful analysis of our competitors behavior, and the impact of other external factors.

Chapter 21: What's the frequency?

We've seen that it is not always possible or prudent to target second place, when our competitors are doing the same. Instead we must employ a mixed strategy, targeting second place for a certain proportion of the time. In order to determine what proportion that should be, we must attempt to anticipate the behavior of our competitors, whilst taking care not to allow our judgement to become clouded by the availability heuristic. With all this in mind, we must seek to arrive at the right frequency for targeting second place.

It's very easy to get an accurate sense of frequency when we're looking at a nice spreadsheet, with all the data plotted on a graph for us to view. But the reality of a situation feels very different. We don't experience events simultaneously, with the ability to compare their relative impact and significance. In the real world, we experience events one at a time. In order to compare these events, we must cast our minds back into the past - and the further back we go, the murkier and more unreliable our memory tends to become. This unreliability is further skewed by our flawed perception of the passage of time. We're all familiar with the truism "time flies by when you're having fun." It's more than just an expression. We genuinely experience time passing faster when we are engaged in a meaningful task, (what psychologists term a "flow state"), whilst time seems to pass more slowly when our brains are under-stimulated. Hence the phrase "a watched pot never boils." We tend to commit these subjective perspectives on the passage of time to memory automatically, and when we recall past events, our memories are skewed by this subjectivity.

As an example, take my train journey to work. I used to work in Wimbledon, and now instead I work in Richmond. Both commutes start from the same station - Earls Court. When I used to wait for Wimbledon trains, I would get very frustrated that all the trains seemed to be Richmond trains. I was relieved when I switch jobs, because I would have to spend less time waiting on the platform. However, I found to my surprise that the Richmond trains we very infrequent, and Wimbledon trains seemed to arrive all the time instead. Of course, what was actually happening was that both trains were arriving with a similar frequency. I was simply remembering all the long waits for trains, whilst forgetting about the short waits. As a consequence I was led to believe that the frequency was never in my favor.

I would speculate that such a bias may be selected through evolution because it will encourage greed on the part of those individuals who posses it. If you believe that you are getting less than your fair share, you may feel entitled to fight for more. The perceived injustice of others receiving more of a particular resource than you can be a great motivator. Inevitably, as a consequence, if everyone in a group suffers from this particular bias, they'll fight even harder for a greater share of a resource in contention. If second place is where everyone wants to be, they'll begrudge every moment that you spend in the number two spot, considering it more than you deserve.

As we compete for our favored rank, we are engaging in a subtle but complex dance with our rivals, because we can't directly control the ranking process. We may want to be second, but our rank will ultimately be assigned to us as a result of the combined behavior of the overall group, of which we are but one component part. What's more, the performance of each individual is likely to influence the performance of others in the group. So, for example, where a leopard is pursuing a gazelle, the speed with which the leopard makes chase will to a large extent be influenced by the speed of the gazelle. As the gazelle increases its pace, so its predator matches or exceeds that new velocity.

So, neither we, nor our competitors, are necessary employing our full resources in the competition. We may be inadvertently, or deliberately holding back. Like a pool hustler, for example, who allows his opponent to imagine that he is an inferior player, by deliberately losing the first game. Or a competitor may be deliberately reducing his performance in order to achieve a desired rank, such as R2D2 in *Star Wars* who is advised by his robot buddy C3PO to "let the wookie win." As Richard Dawkins explains in *The Extended Phenotype*, the amount of effort an individual will exert in a particular competitive encounter is determined by how much they have riding on the outcome. In our example of the leopard and the gazelle, the leopard is running for his lunch, whilst the gazelle is running for his life. In this situation, the gazelle clearly has more riding on the outcome, and will employ all of his resources to escape, whilst the leopard is more likely to hold back, depending on how hungry he is at the time.

In evolutionary terms, Dawkins describes "*arms races*" where tit-for-tat changes in strategy are selected. As prey evolves to run faster in order to evade a predator, so the predator will evolve to run faster in order to catch his prey. With this in mind, it is easy to understand why leopards and gazelles run so fast.

In order to come second, we must anticipate the performance of our competitors, and moderate our performance accordingly, whilst taking care to factor in the influence that our changes in performance will have upon that of our competitors. It's as if we're piloting a plane where our destination moves each time we make a course correction to head towards it. Suddenly, winning begins to seem easier than coming second. In order to win, we tend employ a simple (but arguably wasteful) strategy of "*giving it our best shot.*" In this sense, whilst we may employ a *pure strategy* in our attempt to win, aiming at second place is more of a challenge, because it is a moving target, and we must therefore employ a *mixed strategy*.

Coming second at being second

We have seen that rankings inevitably change over time, that the behavior of our competitors will have a material impact upon our own ranking, and that we have limited ability to anticipate how our competitors will behave. All of this leads us to reluctantly conclude that we can't stay in second place for ever. In this chapter, I want to take the argument a step further. Not only can we not be in second place for ever, but usually, we shouldn't even seek to be.

SECONDOMICS

For one thing, second place is not always the best place to be - we should only seek it in those special instances where secondomics applies. And even when we find just such an instance, we shouldn't assume that circumstances won't change. Remember that if you do what you always did, you *won't necessarily* get what you always got. Windows of secondomic opportunity open and close all the time - we must seize these opportunities when they arise, and be ready to accept when they come to an end.

Since rankings inevitably change over time, when we think about future rankings, we should consider what proportion of the time we can reasonably expect to occupy any one rank. We've already seen that perpetual wheel-suckers in a peloton will get punished if they don't do their fair share at the front. Likewise, if you're a bird that never leads the v-formation, you may become the victim of a pecking attack. So when planning in what rank you expect to be, you would be wise to assume that you'll only be in second place for a certain proportion of the time. If there are ten birds in your flock, and only one position available directly behind the leader (this would be a single skein, rather than v-formation), you can perhaps expect to occupy that position for 10% of the time (one in ten). If you achieve more than 10%, you have done so at the expense of the other birds in your group - and providing that they don't notice, you may well get away with it.

Intriguingly, secondomics very much applies in this situation as well. How much should you exceed the 10% equal allocation of time in the spot behind the leader, in order to maximize your allocation without incurring punishment? The answer is that you should exceed it by as much as you possibly can, whilst ensuring that there's always someone being more greedy than yourself. In other words, you should ensure that you are in second place, the second most frequently of all those in your group. So, although you can't always be in second place, you may be able to be second the second most frequently. Coming second at being second, is in effect a compound implementation of the secondomics doctrine.

This way, your competitor who comes second with greatest frequency, draws the attention, and thereby retribution, of the group, whilst your lesser transgression (a somewhat less excessive occupation of the number two spot,) will likely go unnoticed and therefore unpunished.

If this all sounds rather selfish, let me add the caveat that this is merely how you should behave if you wish to maximize your own individual fitness/utility, without giving consideration to your fellow man. Human's may make the abstract decision not to cheat, but the process of evolution knows no such luxury - adaptations that offer advantages will be selected, even if we may think of these adaptations as sneaky, cheating or unethical.

Seeking second place in frequency rather than rank may be applied more generally than simply in scenarios where we seek second rank. In any situation where we wish to monopolize a resource that must be shared over time, and where excessive use will incur punishment, this technique may be used. In other words, this strategy is for situations where one must "take it in turns", and its use may frequently be observed in children's play. A classic example would be children fighting over a computer game, where they must take it in turns to play the game. The following exchange would be typical of how children would negotiate relative time-slots at the controls:

> Tom whines: "Dick, you've been playing it for ages"
> Dick protests: "But I haven't had half as long as Harry!"

Dick probably *has* been having more than his fare share, but he excuses his actions on the basis that he's not the worst transgressor. He feels that if Tom is going to attempt to enforce more equal time slots, he should focus his retribution on Harry, since he is a greater transgressor. Adults are, of course, equally capable of employing the same self-serving reasoning. Whenever police crack down on minor transgressions such as traffic offenses, those motorists who wish to drive fast, tend to protest that the police should have more important things to do, such as tackling violent crime. If we were to apply the reductio ad absurdum test to this argument, we would be forced to conclude that since it would be impossible to ever eliminate all violent crime, then motorists should always be allow to commit traffic offenses, since the police will inevitably always have something more important to do.

The flaw in this reasoning is, of course, that the policing needn't be reduced to a binary decision in terms of budget allocation - a police force may maximize its law enforcement potential by a proportionate allocation of budget to various areas, determined by policing priorities. The fact that on occasion, the police may enact a "crack down" on petty crime does not not mean that the majority of their resources are not allocated to more serious crimes.

If we apply this reasoning to our secondomic scenarios, such as the cycling pelaton and the birds in v-formation, we can clearly see that the enforcement mechanisms of these groups need not be focused exclusively upon the greatest violator. Why should our birds limit their pecking attacks to the single worst offending bird? Why not attack all of the birds that take more than their fair share of time in second place? Equally, should we expect a cycling pelaton to turn on a single individual who is the worst cheat, or punish all cyclists who fail to do their fair share at the front? And if this is the case, then surely my argument for the benefits of second-frequency break down.

This is where the law of diminishing returns comes to my rescue. Let's take the example of our 10 birds, each of whom should occupy the second place spot for 10% of the time, if every bird was to have an equal share. Before we factor in cheating, we can assume that no bird will have exactly 10% of the time-allocation, since, in the real world, things are never this accurate. Instead, we can assume that some will have slightly more, whilst others will have slightly less. If we allow for cheating, we can expect this variance to consequently increase. But however much cheating is going on, there will always be some birds that are getting more than their fair share, and others that are getting less. Over time, *the law of large numbers* tells us that if we take a sufficiently large sample of data, perpetual cheats will become evident. If we assume that whatever cheating going on is reasonably subtle, we can expect that in whatever data sample we take, roughly 50% of the birds will get more than their fair share, and roughly 50% will get less. We must therefore find a way to determine the difference between random variance and cheating. Whilst statisticians have plenty of tools for doing this, birds (or indeed cyclists on the move) do not. They must use simple heuristics in order to spot the cheats.

Heuristics are essentially "rules of thumb". They are methods of decision making based upon a simple set of rules, derived from past experience. Whilst these rules won't necessarily elicit the *optimal* solution to a problem, they may offer an *adequate* solution, arrived at with reasonable efficiency. One example of a possible heuristic would be be to say that the individual that is spending the most time in second place is probably a cheat. Since identifying this individual is a relatively easy task, it is more efficient than attempting to statistically identify *all* those who are cheating. Birds are not capable of doing complex calculations, and cyclists can hardly get out a laptop and crunch some numbers in a spreadsheet whilst they're on the move, so heuristics provide an alternative.

The difference between cyclists and birds is that cyclists' brains are capable of learning new heuristics during a single lifetime, whereas birds' less capable brains may not be. Animals with more limited mental capacity may acquire heuristic strategies through evolution. As we've already explored, evolution has a tendency to select genes that are "good enough," rather than optimal (such as our ability to anticipate competitor behavior). These *good enough* strategies have a tendency to be heuristic in nature. So for the behavior of a v-formation to evolve, it is necessary for birds to acquire the ability to recognize each other, and be able to punish cheats with pecking attacks in order to enforce cooperative strategies within the group. But it is not essential to punish all of the cheats - only the worst transgressors, since, as we have seen, a certain amount of cheating may be tolerated in a population, when an equilibrium point is found. After a heuristic enforcement mechanism such as punishing the bird in second place most frequently has emerged, the benefit of identifying and punishing lesser cheats may be outweighed by the evolutionary cost in doing so. Resources expended in this task may be more optimally applied elsewhere.

My proposed heuristic of punishing the individual most frequently in second place is merely hypothetical, for the purposes of illustration. I've found no research to indicate that this is the case, for birds, cyclists or any other competitive group. But this kind of evidence, whilst it would be very interesting, is not necessary for the purposes of my argument. Whatever heuristic may be applied in each secondomics scenario, the individuals participating may be expected to use *some* kind of heuristic in their enforcement behavior. And the law of diminishing returns indicates that the biggest single cheat will be statistically far more likely to be singled out for punishment that other lesser cheats.

Heuristics come into play in situations where any reasonable decision is better than no decision at all, and once this decision has been made, it must be decisively enforced. But how is this enforcement to be coordinated? In the case of a heuristic that has been selected through evolution, we may expect a majority within the group to posses the necessary genes for this behavior, and therefore a consensus is likely to exist without any communication within the group. Each individual may arrive at the same conclusion independently, by observing the same cheat-like behavior, and applying the same heuristic. So with birds engaging in a pecking attack, what appears to be group behavior, may theoretically be individual behavior, undertaken spontaneously and simultaneously. (In practice, it is perhaps more likely to be a complex interaction of individual *and* group behaviors).

But where the heuristic is acquired during an individual lifetime, by a brain capable of learning such things, other individuals may not posses this same heuristic, and therefore may not identify the same individual as a cheat. And yet, a consensus decision will be better for each individual in the group than no decision at all (with the obvious exception of those individuals on the receiving end of the punishment). So we may expect other methods to emerge, to enable the conflicting views of the group to coalesce into a single view of whom must be punished. And this application of group-think to turn upon an individual or minority within the group is known as *pack mentality*.

A group decision may be arrived at through a hierarchical social structure, where the views of an alpha male are enforced within the population. In some human societies, this role is performed by a big man, or tribal leader - in others the role may be performed by a monarch, judge, jury or politician. In a cycling peloton, there also tends to be an informal hierarchy, where the opinions of the cyclists with the greatest prowess may have an exaggerated influence upon the others, helping the group to arrive at a consensus. Once a consensus starts to coalesce around the leader, it becomes in the interests of all within the group to join that consensus, even if their individual judgement differs, providing that they are themselves not the individuals singled out for punishment.

Are there really alpha males in competitive cycling? In French, the patriarch of the peloton is known as *Le Patron*, and one of the most remarkable patrons is Lance Armstrong. An inspirational figure, Armstrong famously beat cancer, going on to win the Tour De France, cycling's most prestigious event, on five consecutive occasions. His remarkable achievement, and athletic prowess singled him out as the patron of the peloton - the individual to whom others will defer judgement.

And Armstrong has proved willing to use his influence, when he argues that it is in the interests of the group to do so. In the 2004 Tour de France, when Italian cyclist Filippo Simeoni attempted to escape from the peloton, in the hope of winning the 18th stage, Armstrong used his influence over the other cyclists in order to bring Simeoni back into line. He pursued Simeoni as he broke away, and continued to follow him as he joined a breakaway group at the front. Armstrong warned Simeoni, and others in the breakaway group that if Simeoni did not return, to join the rest of the pack, the entire peloton would overtake the breakaway group. Simeoni reluctantly relinquished his hard-earned lead. Under normal circumstances, Simeoni's actions would not incite the disapprobation of the group. But Armstrong and Simeoni had history, concerning a court case, and allegations of drug abuse in the sport. Armstrong argued that "I was protecting the interests of the peloton... All Simeoni wants to do is to destroy cycling...to destroy the sport that pays him. The other riders were very grateful."

The enforcement of peloton etiquette takes place routinely, normally in far less remarkable circumstances. Patrons need not be world-class athletes such as Armstrong - group leaders will emerge in all competitions, over every class, in just the same way that every group of apes will have its alpha-male. And this individual acts as a point of focus, where the views of the majority may coalesce into a course of punitive action against transgressors to enforce the benefit of cooperation for the entire group, by preventing cheats from prospering. But regardless of whether its an Armstrong or a collection of independently acting birds making the decision, the nature of the decision is ultimately the same. Identifying cheats from non-cheats within the group is a difficult task - the group's judgement will likely be imperfect, relying on heuristics that may be blind to secondary transgressors. And as a result, wheel sucking in moderation will likely go unpunished.

So, being in second place, with second greatest frequency may well deliver significant advantages, but it is not a simple thing to achieve. As we have seen, second place is, in itself, a moving target. Likewise, second frequency is also a moving target. When the two are combined, the uncertainly is compounded. Attempting to control both our rank, and our frequency at that rank is a very complex task, requiring conditional mixed strategies. A conditional mixed strategy, is one where your choice of strategy will be determined by external factors. For example, if your competitor defends, you attack, and visa versa.

Simplistically, a conditional mixed strategy for achieving second place is as follows:

> *if you're ranking is less than 2, increase your effort, whilst if your ranking greater than 2, reduce your effort.*

But if you wish to target second place with second highest frequency, you will need to introduce an additional rule:

> *if, over n period of time, your frequency in 2nd place has been greater than your competitors', reduce your effort until a competitor has been in 2nd place for longer than you*

The extent to which you will need to adjust your effort in each of these conditions will be determined by your competitors' behavior - your corrections must be calibrated relative to theirs.

But what happens if your competitors are following exactly the same conditional mixed strategy? You will find that the adjustments that you make in your effort must become increasingly precise in order to achieve second ranking, and the duration of contiguous lengths of time in which you occupy second place reduces. Indeed, if the group of competitors is large enough, and your skill in making adjustments is not good enough, you will find that you are never able to achieve second place.

Endgame

Finally, in this chapter, we must consider our endgame. What happens when the resource in contention becomes entirely depleted, or when the competition itself comes to an end? In our examples of birds and pelotons, the individuals involved, whilst acting as a group, have a selfish ultimate objective in mind. In the case of migratory birds, it may be the optimal breeding grounds, whilst in the case of cyclists, it's the coveted yellow jersey. The sad fact is that there's no yellow jersey for coming second, and the second bird to arrive may have to make-do with the second-best nesting site. So as the game comes to an end, the optimal strategy switches from being in second place with the second greatest frequency to coming first.

Similarly, in iterated games, there's often an advantage in switching strategies for the final round, since you know that there will be no further opportunities for your opponent to punish your defection. So, for example, in Prisoners Dilemma, two players may have arrived at a stable pattern of mutual cooperation, choosing to never defect, since they've discovered that their opponents are likely to punish them for this in subsequent rounds. But when it come to the final round, you can expect this situation to change. Since there's no possibility for further retribution, both players are likely to switch from a cooperate to defect strategy.

So, in a competition where our ultimate goal is to come first, but where occupying second place during the competition is advantageous, we have to identify the optimal point at which to make the switch in strategy. This is essentially the point at which the overall utility of first place becomes greater than that of second. Identifying when this point occurs takes a great deal of skill and judgement. It's the point at which the sprinter in a cycling team will break away from the peloton to approach the finishing line alone. For a pool hustler, it's the point at which you stop hustling and reveal your true prowess. For the ambitious politician, it's the moment when you stop plotting in the shadows, and publicly stake your claim for the leadership. Act too soon, and you'll fail without the the support that second place afforded you. Act too late, and you'll miss your opportunity altogether.

In Appendix III, I explore how the secondomics formula can be applied to end games, taking competitive cycling as an example.

Chapter 22: Resource depletion

When a game comes to an end, the situation materially changes, and the players are likely to adapt their strategies accordingly. In other contexts, whilst the game itself may not come to an end, the resources for which the players compete may become depleted. After all, second place is not necessarily an unlimited resource. We've already explored the newsstand owner's curse, where people at a newsstand browse the top copy of a magazine in a stack, whilst purchasing the second from the top. In this case, browsing the magazine results in wear and tear - the magazine on top becomes increasingly dog-eared to the point at which not only will people not purchase it, but they're also unwilling to browse it. And so the secondomic phenomenon begins to work its way down the stack. People browse the second from top, and purchase one beneath that. And since different people have different standards in terms of the level of dogearedness that they are willing to tolerate for browsing and buying, over time, a incremental dogearedness occurs, with the magazine on top being the most dogeared, whilst the one at the bottom being the least. Ultimately, the process will restart when the remaining copies of a particular issue are sent off to be pulped, and the next months pristine copies are substituted.

Some have objected to my use of dogeared magazine as an illustration of secondomics, arguing that, far from illustrating coming second, the newsstand example is about being first. In this situation, people seek to be the first to read a virgin magazine - one untouched by human hand. And of course, they're right. There's no denying that this is one valid way of framing the situation. But there is another way in which we may think about it. For much of this book, we've looked at secondomics from a competitor's-eye-view. This is only natural, since much of what there is to learn from secondomics concerns the strategies that we may wish to employ when we are ourselves engaged in competition. But if you'll allow me, for a moment, to explore the principles of secondomics from a resource's-eye-view, we find many other situations where the principles of secondomics apply.

Whilst a person may be buying the first pristine magazine in the stack, from the magazine's-eye-view it is the second magazine in the stack. The fashion industry operates on a similar principle to our magazine stack. Fashion shoppers have an insatiable appetite for new styles. Once a new style becomes too popular, and is mass produced and sold in malls across the country, it loses its caché, in just the same way that our magazine at the top of the stack becomes dog-eared. The fashion elite will soon abandon this style in favor of something new and unsullied by the mass market retailers. From the person's perspective, they are simply picking the latest, most fashionable style. But from the style's perspective, if we imagine a continuum of future fashions stretching out ahead of us, those favoring the very latest styles are in effect, picking the next-but-one, or second style on the list. Skip the mainstream, and go for the avant-garde. The gentrification of urban areas follows a similar pattern. In New York today, SoHo is a high-rent neighborhood, with exclusive shops, fancy hotels and luxury apartments. But this popularity arose from its adoption as a hip, affordable location for artists' studios and galleries. Whilst many of these original inhabitants have long since moved on to new studios, the area's popularity remains, albeit now in the more mainstream form of retailers such as Prada, Apple and DKNY. This process, the "SoHo Effect," happens the world over. The area of London in which I live, Earls Court, was once known as the poor man's Chelsea. These days, Fulham is the poor man's Earls Court, and so the process continues.

Whether the demand is for an un-thumbed magazine, a brand new look or an affordable neighborhood, there will always be those willing to skip a generation in order to find what they are looking for. Whilst they may be the first to exploit a new resource, their appetite for the new, new thing leads them to consume the second in line. They may not themselves be second, but the forces of secondomics are nonetheless very much at work. Wether it is magazines, fashion or real estate, as the resource becomes depleted, so the situation changes, and people's behavior changes accordingly.

And change is essentially what this entire section has been about. You can't win them all, and neither can you be in second place all of the time. Competition is a complex, dynamic, perpetually changing state. Sometimes second place will afford the greatest payoff, sometimes it won't. Sometimes we'll get second place all to ourselves, whilst on other occasions, we may find that everyone is fighting for the number two spot, and we'll get punished if we occupy it for longer than our fair share. And even when we're the only one actively trying to come second, it may still be very difficult to judge the precise amount of effort necessary in order to secure us that elusive rank.

Part 6 - Leadership Bias

"The trouble with competitions is that somebody wins them."

George Orwell

Throughout this book, we've explored the many ways in which coming second may, in some situations, be better than coming first. As we've evaluated the evidence, examined the examples, and crunched the numbers, I hope this fact has become increasingly evident. If I've constructed my argument well enough, the point may not just be conceded, but it may even seem obvious. Or perhaps you accepted the secondomics argument right from the start, in which case, I hope that the book thus far has served to entertain, rather than merely state the obvious!

If secondomics *does* seem obvious to you, you may well ask "why does it matter?" And that is precisely what this section is all about. Secondomics matters because people tend to behave as if it didn't.

"Stand clear, the doors are closing. Please stand back and allow the train to depart, there's another train right behind this one."

This frustrated refrain will be familiar to commuters on urban mass transit systems the world over, from the New York Subway, to the London Underground or Paris Metro. Commuters jam themselves into packed train carriages, pressing their faces up against the sweaty body parts of their fellow passengers. And yet, all too often, right behind the crowded train is another halcyon vehicle, blessed with bountiful space, and a small sprinkling of savvy travelers. Why do most of us insist on piling onto the first train, rather than waiting on the platform for the second train, right behind it? Does the minute saved in our journey time truly represent greater utility to us than the extra comfort afforded by the additional space. Probably not. So are we acting irrationally, and if so, why?

To be fair, there are some rational arguments to support the choice of the first train over the second. The strongest argument could best be characterized as "the bird in the hand is worth two in the bush." We only have the train driver's word for it that there's "another train right behind this one." Why should we believe him? Mass transit systems are notoriously unreliable, so perhaps we should not. Perhaps the driver is only *saying* that there is another train because he wants passengers to stop trying to cram themselves into his, already overcrowded train. Another rational argument would be that you are in such a hurry that the time saved in taking the first train genuinely does outweigh the utility of a less crowded train. A further argument may be that the train system is so busy at present that there's no guarantee that the second train will be any less crowded than the first.

Having allowed for the fact that there are *some* legitimate arguments in favor of boarding the first train, I'm not convinced that these are genuinely sufficient to account for the behavior observed on train platforms in these situations. It's certainly been my experience that when the driver announces that there's another train "right behind this one," this usually turns out to be the case, and it is usually substantially less crowded. It seems to me that a majority of my fellow passengers do not know this because they have never waited to find out. As such, the arguments in favor of the first train are largely excuses for what is, in effect, antisocial behavior (overcrowding the train), rather than a rational account of the maximization of individual utility.

So what is at work here? Why do so few passengers ever wait to see if the promised second train, with its less crowded carriages, will arrive? I would argue that the answer to this question is leadership bias. And it is leadership bias that makes secondomics so very interesting. Leadership bias occludes what might otherwise be the obvious fact that second place is sometimes better than first.

Leadership bias, simply put, is an exaggerated perception of the utility of coming first. Typically, this bias is coupled with a blindness to the utility afforded to every other rank. Or in other words, leadership bias turns the popular aphorism "it's not the winning, it's the taking part that counts" on its head. Instead, we may say "it's the winning that counts." Does leadership bias really exist? Do people think this way? The truth is that, if they didn't, it wouldn't have been necessary to come up with the "taking part" aphorism in the first place, because it would have been self evident.

Of course we have a tendency towards leadership bias. This bias, that unreasonably favors outright victory over all other outcomes, is expressed in behavioral terms as competition. Through millions of years of evolution, our brains are hard-wired to be competitive - once again, it all goes back to the birth of our planet's competition for survival in the primordial soup. In an evolutionary context, competition between predator and prey is often a life or death duality. Eat lunch or be lunch. In this type of situation, we must genuinely attempt to win at all costs. But even in evolutionary terms, competition is not always so cut and dried. If a gazelle does not escape a predatory cheetah, the gazelle will certainly be killed. But in a forest, where trees are competing with each other for sunlight, by growing to increase height relative to the other trees, the cost of failure will probably be to get less sunlight, rather than to be deprived of sunlight altogether. If trees were perpetually locked in mortal combat with each other, then forestry would surely not be so dense. So, when we focus exclusively upon victory, we are framing competition in terms of polarized win-lose scenarios (as is we think we're at risk of becoming lunch), whilst in many cases, we may actually be competing for how much lunch we get (like the trees and their share of sunlight).

Haggling in a souk with a market trader is a battle of wills between buyer and seller for the best possible price. From the seller's perspective, higher is better, and from the buyer's perspective, lower is better. The difference between the seller's starting price, and the cost to him in not selling is the margin, and this is what is in play. If the buyer is a poor haggler, the sale price may be close to the starting price, and the seller will make a good margin. If the buyer is a good haggler, the price may be close to the cost of not selling. So, in this game of haggling, there will be a ultimate winner. But regardless of who the ultimate winner is, it is still effectively a win-win situation. The buyer gets the item for a reasonable price, and the seller makes some money on the deal. This is nothing like the zero-sum competition between cheetah and gazelle, where one *gets* lunch whilst the other *gets to be* lunch.

And yet, so often, in haggling situations, tempers can become frayed in the heat of the moment. Either party may come away from the deal feeling cheated by the other, despite the fact that both sides have entered into a mutually consenting transaction. In these situations, where a negotiation ends up with an aggrieved party, somehow a potential win-win situation has become incorrectly characterized as a predator-prey situation.

It could be argued that the entire communist manifesto is built upon a mis-reading of potential win-win situations as predator-prey conflict. The philosophers Karl Marx and Frederick Engels, in their Communist Manifesto, wrote that "the written history of all hitherto existing society is the history of class struggle." In Marxist terms, "class" refers to one's relationship with the means of production, so, employer and employee are seen as differing class status. The idea that, throughout history employers and employees have been struggling with each other is to assume that employment is a game of winners and losers. That the employer by definition exploits the employee, and that there is no possibility of a mutually agreeable contract of gainful employment. The winner (in this case the employer) takes all (from the long suffering employee). Given the popularity of Marxism around the world, to this day, Karl Marx is arguably one of the world's greatest promoters of leadership bias.

In my business, an internet strategy agency, I have the good fortune of employing many extremely talented individuals. As with any consultancy, this is a people-based business. We sell people's time by the hour. And the value of an hour is entirely dependent on the skills and intellect of the people concerned. The more talented our staff, the more we can charge for an hour of their time. In this business, staff costs are by far the greatest of all our costs. Overheads and capital are incidental by comparison. We may invest in training, in order to develop staff skills, and thereby increase the value of our product. This also has the effect of increasing the value of our staff, who will, in turn, expect higher salary, since their market value will have increased as a result. And if they do subsequently decide to leave the company to work elsewhere, they effectively take the "means of production" (their brains) with them. My key job, as the manager of the business, therefore, is to develop and retain skilled and talented staff. Far from an exploiter/exploited relationship, we have an equitable relationship. In order for the staff to wish to remain with the company, we must make it in their interest to do so, or we lose the means of production. Equally, by enticing them to remain, we get the best talent in the business.

Whilst, like our example of the souk, there may be mild conflict between employer and employee over the margin - how profitable should the business be, relative to how much should the staff earn - this is negotiated between two parties with effectively equal power in the relationship. Besides which, the distinction is further blurred by staff profit sharing and share option schemes.

This kind of situation is far from unique in the workplace today. In part, it reflects a shift to a post-industrial, "information economy," where knowledge and skills have greater value than expensive capital expenditure in physical things like factory equipment - the original "means of production" to which Marx referred. But it seems unlikely that such mutually beneficial relationships *never* existed in Marx's day, or in "all hitherto existing society." What seems more likely is that something was driving Marx to interpret history in this adversarial way. Some bias was occluding his view. And, oddly, it is exactly the same bias that results in commuters cramming onto the first busy train to come along, rather than waiting for the quieter second train that is "right behind" the first.

In both the example of the trains, and Marx's class struggle, the value of the leader is exaggerated, at the expense of the rest. How are crowded trains and evil capitalists similar? The commuters overestimate the advantage of taking the first train in the same way that Marx overestimates the advantage of the employer. (Of course, there are plenty of historical and current examples of bad employers exploiting their employees, but remember that Marxism does not just assert this to be true in many, or even most cases, but rather that it is true in all cases throughout recorded history!) The employer is assumed to have the advantage because he is bourgeoisie. The busy train is assumed to have the advantage because it is the first to arrive. But, as we have seen, in the case of my business, I don't have any advantage over my employees. And in the case of our trains, the second train has an advantage over the first in that it is substantially less crowded. But both our commuters and Marx are blind to these advantages, as a result of their leadership bias.

Chapter 23: Dualism and zero-sum fallacy

So what is leadership bias, and what are the cognitive processes that lead to it? There are essentially two underlying cognitive characteristics: dualism and zero-sum fallacy. Dualism is our tendency to frame complex situations in excessively simplistic terms, with dual opposing interests. We all too often seek to resolve conflict by determining who is in the right, and who is in the wrong, for example. When in fact, it may not be that clear cut - the fact that a dispute exists does not necessarily indicate that one party is right and the other wrong. It equally doesn't follow that there are only two possible outcomes - one or the other party getting what they want. This is the second aspect of leadership bias - zero-sum fallacy. Like Marx, we're irresistibly drawn to the intuitive but frequently wrong assumption that one man's happiness must inevitably come at the expense of another's.

Are there really just winners and losers in life? It's a beguiling concept, which casts a menacing and distorting shadow across the history of human behavior. Despite our unique position on this planet as the only species capable of abstract thought, we sometimes seem incapable of escaping from this misleadingly binary way of framing the world around us, as if there can be only two outcomes to competitive engagement.

The number two has long captured the imagination of us humans. Left and right. Day and night. Yin and Yang. Mind and body. Spiritual and physical. Right and wrong. 1 and 0. We have an innate desire to perceive our world in terms of binary absolutes. In some cases, this seems superficially reasonable - our left hand is something quite separate and distinct from our right hand. We are not constructing an arbitrary framing of reality when we think of ourselves as possessing two hands. But our two hands are not identical. We tend to be right-handed or left-handed, so one hand offers us far greater utility than the other. Day and night is another example of the unsatisfactory nature of dualistic framing. There is surely not a clear cutoff when day ends and night begins - rather, there is twilight - a fuzzy inbetweenness that blurs our binary boundaries.

Framing our world in terms of duality may help us to resolve issues that trouble us. Descartes gave us mind-body dualism as a means of protecting religion from the emerging scientific method. How better to inoculate the superstitions of ancient religions than to argue that they operate on an entirely separate plane of existence to the physical world around us. Just like the fuzziness of twilight, which makes it difficult to discern day from night, modern science makes us increasingly suspect that the mind has a very physical relationship with the body. We can begin to map cognitive processes in physical space using fMRI scanning techniques, even as we may still accept that abstract thought is something quite separate from the physical world. With this in mind, dualism starts to look like an over simplified model for understanding the interaction between mind and body.

Perhaps our predilection for arbitrary dualist framing of complex problems stems from the fact that we are, ourselves, sexually reproducing diploid organisms - or in other words, we have two genders. In order for us to reproduce, one genetic parent is not sufficient, there must be a second, of the opposite sex. We are "diploid" in the sense that we get a set of genes from one parent, and a second set from the other. So for example, you might have two genes for eye color - one from your mother (brown), and the other from your father (blue). Since brown-eyed genes tend to be dominant, whilst blue-eyed genes are recessive, in this instance, we may expect you to inherit brown eyes. But things are not always this simple. For starters, there aren't just two eye colors - there are many shades of brown, ranging from hazel to near-black. And blues may be so undersaturated as to appear practically grey. And that's before we get into considering green eyes, or multi-hued eyes.

So phenotypic outcomes for diploid organisms may be more complex than simple binary resolutions. When we have *heterozygous alleles* (conflicting genes), the outcome is not necessarily resolved by reconciling dominance and recessiveness. In some cases, conflicting genes may result in a blended outcome, known as *incomplete dominance* - so, for example, a certain breed of flower possessing both red and white genes might appear pink. In other cases, alleles may get to express their phenotypes fully, even when they conflict - our blood types being the obvious example of this. If you're of the blood group AB, this means that you possess both A and B alleles. This is called *co-dominance*.

Incomplete dominance and co-dominance certainly illustrate that in nature, dualist competition does not necessarily result in binary outcomes. Indeed, it provides a useful model with which we may characterize many of the competitive outcomes that we have already explored. Incomplete dominance effectively means prizes for second best, whilst co-dominance means sharing first prize.

But does this also offer us evidence that in the world of genetics, the winner doesn't necessarily take it all? Not quite. It certainly illustrates yet another situation where the most dominant entity does not monopolize the payoff, but we have explored many such examples already. In order to determine if the winner takes it all in our genetics, we must look at the situation from the gene's point of view, and determine what constitutes "winning". We, as human beings, have ambitions and desires, but our genes are not thinking, living, breathing organisms like ourselves, they're nothing more than elaborate, self-replicating molecules. Genes don't *want* anything. They just keep on replicating, and we may infer that the more ubiquitous the gene, the more successful it has been at replicating in the past.

So, for the sake of metaphor, let us say that genes want to replicate, on the basis that this is what they tend to do. One might then say that winning, for a gene, is not about expressing itself phenotypically at all. A gene for blue eyes might be recessive to its brown eyed allele, but the blue-eyed gene doesn't mind at all, since it still gets to come along for the ride, and has a 50% chance of getting passed on to each of that brown-eyed individual's offspring. If its dominant allele's phenotype is fitter than its own, it will actually be better off not expressing itself, and just coming along for the ride. And, interestingly, brown eyes do appear to be more resistant to certain eye diseases than blue eyes, so perhaps, all things being equal, a blue-eyed gene *may* have a better chance of replicating from within a brown-eyed body.

Genes do not appear to have any problem with non-zero sum games, fully exploiting the fact that phenotypic expression is a complex interaction of multiple genes, and even, in the case of incomplete dominance, between alleles.

So whilst human sexual reproduction seems to be a perfect example of dualist competition, with diploid alleles fighting it out for dominance, there appears to be a more elaborate game of *coopertition* taking place.

The fact that we have two genders, may well be a significant contributing factor to our tendency to frame situations in dualistic terms. After all, we have a tendency to regard the battle between the sexes in depressingly zero-sum terms. The women's rights movement has all too often been characterized as threatening to emasculate men. Divorce courts have a tendency to award higher settlements to women than man, implying that the man is more typically the guilty party in a breakup. But the advancement of the interests of one gender needn't come at the expense of the other, and the notion of two opposing forces in perpetual combat to claim a prize is hardly an accurate portrayal of the interaction between our two genders. As we have seen, at a genetic level, no such binary battle exists. The genes passed down by mother and father are all in it together, and whilst they occupy that same body, their interests are closely aligned in promoting their host's opportunities to procreate. Whether a gene comes from the mother or father, is no longer relevant, and as we have seen genes from both parents, whilst they may compete for phenotypic expression, also collaborate to create a host organism, much like the ingredients coming together to bake a cake. When we look at a child, we may say "he takes after his father," but we don't seriously imagine that he *exclusively* takes after one parent. It's inconceivable that one parent's genes are entirely dominant in this way. Whilst the battle of the sexes may lead us to favor dualist interpretations, sexual reproduction is far from a two-player zero-sum game.

So, what do we mean by these zero-sum games, which seem to capture our imagination and attention far more than they merit? Have you ever been frustrated by a childish game of hypothetical dichotomy? You know the sort of thing - where a child might ask "if you could only rescue one person from a burning building, your mom or your dad, which would it be?" These childish thought-experiments are frustrating, since they attempt to force upon us an impossible choice. But they are also frustrating for another reason. They feel counterintuitive - the scenario is so contrived that we can't believe we would ever be required to make such as choice. We suspect that in practice there must be some third way, not present in the binary choices that the questioner allows us. Maybe mom could rescue herself, whilst dad would need more help because of his bad back... Maybe you'd find some way to help mom and dad at once.... But no, the questioner disallows these options.

This is a rare example of a situation where we have a tendency to doubt the veracity of zero-sum outcomes, and insist that there must be some third-way to a win-win situation. Would that we were always so resourceful. In most cases, we are all too willing to frame a situation in zero-sum terms. But what do we mean by zero-sum? In the case of rescuing mom or dad, let us assume that both afford us equal utility (we like our mom and dad equally), and that in the two possible outcomes, one will be lost, and the other saved. On this basis, we may award the survival of each parent 1 utility point, which provides us with two identical potential payoffs:

```
Save mom(+1), lose dad (-1) 1-1=0
Lose mom (-1), save dad (+1) 1-1=0
```

In either possible outcome, the sum adds up to a zero payoff. It is therefore a zero-sum game. However, in this particular game, there is only one player - the individual who must choose between their mom or dad. In most cases, when we talk about a zero-sum game, we mean a game of two players, were victory for one player comes with a consequential equivalent loss for the other.

Such zero-sum situations certainly exist, but they're not as common as we tend to think that they are. As with our genetic examples, whilst there may be two actors involved, that needn't limit us to two equally unprofitable outcomes, involving one winner and one loser. And yet, we tend to imagine that we are competing for a fixed, finite resource. A bit like slicing a cake. If we wish to slice a cake into eight slices for eight people, we may try to divide the cake as evenly as possible, in order to ensure that everyone gets a relatively similar portion. But if one slice is accidently larger, that inevitably comes at the expense of another slice or slices, since the overall size of the cake remains the same, however we cut it. Because the size of the cake remains the same, the slicing game is, by definition, zero-sum. (As an aside, we might consider more complex cake slicing games, where different parts of the cake are different - some with more frosting, some with more chocolate chips - and different people prefer different parts of the cake. This would then become a non-zero sum game).

In our zero-sum cake slicing game, the size of the cake is the finite resource, and the objective of the game is to divide it as evenly as possible, such that everyone gets their fair share. This "finite cake" view of economics is popularly held. If we imagine that economics is concerned with finite cakes, it's easy to see that in any transaction, there's a winner and a loser. An evil employer exploiting a downtrodden employee. A wasteful government charging excessive tax. A foreign immigrant taking one of "our" jobs.

This tendency to erroneously view economic problems as "finite cake" problems is commonly referred to as *zero-sum fallacy*. In practice, many economic problems are more like a cake that changes in size depending on how you slice it. The real debate is not over whether the cake changes size, but on how best to slice it. At this stage, with our cake metaphor little more that a pile of crumbs, let's consider instead some real world examples.

In 2000, president Jacque Chirac's government introduced new laws to limit the number of hours that French employees were allow to work each week to 35 hours. The idea was that there would be a double benefit to this - it would create more jobs, and it would improve quality of life. The latter may well be true, since substituting work hours for leisure hours may, within reason, be a formula for greater happiness. But the former claim proved not to be the case. Unemployment in France remained stuck at the 10% mark. The idea had been that if the current workforce reduced the number of hours that they worked, then employers would have no option but to employ more people in order to make up the shortfall. In effect, all of the benefit of this measure would come at the expense of employers, or in other words, this was to be a zero-sum game.

Employers, however, clearly did not respond to the new laws in the way in which the legislators had anticipated. Since unemployment remained unchanged, it seems that new jobs were not created. So what happened to the missing hours, the difference between the longer days that employees used to work, compared with their new shorter working week? Employers in this situation had three options in order to make up for the missing hours:
recruit additional staff
work the existing staff harder in the shorter allotted time
accept the drop in productivity (no doubt with a gallic "c'est la vie" shrug)

The government was banking on a lot of employers taking the first option. In practice, it seems that more preferred option two or three - probably reasoning that the administrative costs of additional staff made the first option look less favorable than the others. So if the "cake" we were slicing in this scenario was hours of work, it turns out that the size of the cake did indeed change as we changed the way we sliced it. A shorter working week was the equivalent of giving everyone a smaller slice, in the hope that there would be some more left over. But instead, the cake shrank with the size of the slices, so the anticipated leftovers never materialized.

Economists sometimes call this the "lump of labor" fallacy - the idea that the amount of work available remains constant. A similar example would be the argument that immigrant workers take jobs from local workers, or that increasing worker productivity reduces the number of available jobs. Whilst to some extent, there may be truth to these assertions, they are be no means always the case. Immigrant workers increase the size of the local economy, meaning that they will both take and create jobs - the questions is, what is the net payoff: more or less jobs? Likewise, automation may mean less factory workers, but it also means more affordable products - so, for example, new jobs in retail may be created to sell these products. Again, the question should be, what is the overall affect of the change? What is certain, is that the we're not dealing with a constant "lump of labor," and policies enacted by governments and employers alike, will result in changes in our employment "cake."

The lump of labor fallacy perfectly illustrates our inclination towards interpreting situations in zero-sum terms, regardless of the facts of the situation. This, combined with our innate tendency towards dualistic interpretations, can make the payoffs afforded to second place seem all but invisible, as we increasingly fixate on first prize.

The impact of this fixation is compounded by the fact that it is something that we all substantially share. We find ourselves perpetually in combat for a top prize that few of us can ever hope to claim. And when we can't be the best ourselves, then we seek comfort in *having* the best - vicariously living the victory of others by consuming the artifacts of their success.

Chapter 24: Leadership bias in groups

Naturally, we all want the best in life - for our children, and for ourselves. We may have finite means, but we seek to have the best we can from that which is available, and that we can afford. Economists call this *maximizing utility*. For example, in the supermarket, when we're buying fruit, we may not be able to afford the fancy exotic varieties, in which case, we must satisfy ourselves with cheaper, more mundane options, such as apples. Nonetheless, we may still seek out the best apple available. We may check for color, size and absence of blemishes. After all, we pay for apples by the pound. We certainly don't want to pay for bad apples.

The trouble is, of course, that we're not apple experts. We may know something about apples, since we've been buying and eating them our entire lives, but we're probably not selecting the very best apples on the shelves. We're selecting the best we can find, given our limited ability to judge. Furthermore, each apple is unique. We may learn more about them with each purchase we make. Red ones may be sweeter. Larger ones may be juicier. Blemished ones may be bruised. But these are ultimately just heuristics - helpful guides, certainly - but nothing more. Since each apple is unique, the only way to be certain of how much we will enjoy a particular apple, is to eat it. And even then, our pleasure in eating the apple will not be determined by the apple alone, but it will also be influence by our mood at the time, and how our palette may have been tainted by other things that we have recently eaten.

But in our age of mass production, not everything is as unique as an apple. Take books, for example. Whilst no two books are the same, in the sense that there will be inevitable imperfections in the production process resulting in them being trimmed differently, or that they may be slightly damaged, the corners dog-eared or whatever, the actual text of a given book will be identical from one copy to the next. So if you've read the latest Harry Potter book, you've read exactly the same text as millions of other people, who have read exactly the same book.

So books, in this sense, may be identical, whilst apples can never be. Which means that whilst no two people can eat the same apple, millions of people can read the same book. When we consume an apple - that unique apple is gone. The experience of eating it will never be repeated. When we read a book, the text of that book is not exhausted. There is no limit to the number of times that it can be read. We may lend our copy to someone else, or other copies may be purchased. And when the book is sold out, there may be reprints. A popular book need never go out of print. As Thomas Jefferson once said,

> *"He who receives an idea from me, receives instruction himself without lessening mine - as he who lights his taper at mine, receives light without darkening me."*

We can't all eat the same apple, then, but we *can* all read the same book. So whilst only one shopper in the supermarket will be lucky enough to purchase the tastiest apple, we may all enjoy the good fortune of buying the best book in the bookshop. And superficially, that seems to be exactly what happens. In a bookshop, the Pareto principle (sometimes known as the 80/20 rule) applies. A small number of best sellers account for the vast majority of sales. But this fact does not necessarily indicate that everyone is choosing to buy the best books. It's actually indicative of the method in which book shoppers choose which book to purchase. Whilst with apples, our choice is largely determined by heuristics, with books we may also be guided by the recommendation or choices of others. So, when a shopper choses to buy the latest Harry Potter book, rather than a classic like J. R. R. Tolkein's The Hobbit, this decision is not necessarily based upon a carefully reasoned analysis of the relative merits of the two works. It may instead simply be an act of herding - choosing the book that everyone else is choosing. This is, in itself, a heuristic method of decision making - based upon reasoning such as "I tend to like the best selling books". But it is a very different kind of heuristic to our apple shopper's heuristics of "I tend to like red apples". The apple heuristics are based upon properties that are intrinsic to the apple itself, such as its color, size, or blemishes. The best seller heuristic is based upon the behavior of others - which is not directly related to the intrinsic merits of the book itself.

The significance of choosing a book based upon the behavior of others rather than the intrinsic properties of the book itself are huge. If people bought books the way they buy apples, there would probably be no best sellers. Instead, when a new book comes onto the market, it's merits would be judged relative to all the others available, and shoppers would make the best decision that they could based upon their (sometimes limited) ability to judge. The Pareto principle may not apply in these circumstances, because individual tastes are different, and individual shoppers' limited possession of information may result in them making unexpected, sub-optimal choices. Or in other words, if you don't have recommendations to follow, and must select a book from the entire universe of available books - you may buy a book that is less mainstream and suits you better, or you may buy a dud book, because your judgement was impaired and there was no advise for you to follow. Either way, you're far less likely to follow the herd, by buying the most popular book.

The reason that the Pareto principles applies to book sales (and to so many other products) is because people copy each other's behavior. They choose the books that are on the top ten list, rather than selecting from all the available books. And as a result, a virtuous circle kicks in for some books, which become increasingly popular as a result of what Malcolm Gladwell describes as a *recommendation epidemic*, whilst others languish at the end of a Chris Anderson style *long tail*.

This kind of purchasing behavior is, in fact, another example of leadership bias. Because Harry Potter or the Da Vinci Code may be the most popular book, they are therefore assumed to be the best choices. As a result, some shoppers limit their purchasing exclusively to hits, and some retailers devote the limited shelf space solely to those hits. Sadly, in this instance, leadership bias becomes a self fulfilling prophesy. Payoff (for the author) is allocated in accordance with sales, and sales are distributed along a power curve as a result of leadership bias.

I don't mean to question the merits of young wizards at posh schools, or plucky professors pursuing errant monks. Many hit books are great reads. I only intend to question whether their sales volumes, relative to those of other books, are truly merited based upon their relative quality. The answer, I suspect, is that they're probably not. So, whilst the (financial) payoff for the author will be determined by the Pareto principle, the same is not the case for the reader. By following the crowd, rather than making the effort to find a book that truly suits their individuals tastes, the reader has potentially made a sub-optimal choice for themselves. And this is why it is leadership *bias*, rather than just selecting the leader. In this situation, the choice of the best seller does not represent maximized utility for the reader. Buying best sellers simply because they *are* best sellers is a dysfunctional behavior arising from a cognitive bias, because it results in a suboptimal reading experience.

At the heart of this cognitive process, lies our struggle to reconcile subjective and objective truth. Whilst we may all claim to support the sentiment that "beauty is in the eye of the beholder," our displays of herd mentality, when buying books, or in any context in life, seems to belie this notion. If we truly believe that beauty is in the eye of the beholder, then why do we all so frequently seek the same things? The same books, the same holiday resorts, the same restaurants, the same nose jobs. It is depressing how readily we seem willing to subsume our own personal tastes in favor of the prevailing orthodox wisdom of the day.

This tendency towards doing as our fellow man does is compounded by the canonical view espoused by cultural commentators of both the highbrow and lowbrow variety. Classical music experts love to categorize their music into a complex taxonomy of baroque, romantic, classical and modern, whilst musing over whom may be the "greatest" composer. Cinephiles have heated debates over the top ten movies of all time, or the most influential director. It seems that, whatever the context, we can't resist turning creative endeavor into competitive rankings. On many occasions, I've encountered otherwise perfectly intelligent friends who are prepared to argue dogmatically that such and such a movie is, as a point of fact, superior to another movie. Doubtless they can provide plenty of subjective evidence in order to support their claims. And yet, they rarely pause to consider whether such a ranking of creative endeavors is meaningful. What do we mean when we say that one creative work is better than another? Can this ever be anything more than our own subjective opinion?

I've also observed that we tend to be quite uncertain about our own personal tastes. I know many people who are unwilling to comment on the merits of a movie that they've just seen with their own eyes, until they've read a review by a critic in whom they trust. In other words, they trust the judgement of others more than they trust their own. This at the heart of the reason why individuals herd into groups. Since we are uncertain in our own views, we seek safety in numbers. We're not sure if we *should* like a particular movie, book, piece of music, brand of chocolate bar, or whatever, until we see other people enjoying it too. It's safe to enjoy a movie if we know that it got a five star review in a respected newspaper. Whereas if we leave the movie theatre saying we've enjoyed a movie that it turns out the critics have panned, then others might think less of our judgement.

Every year in London, The Royal College of Art, a prestigious post-graduate art school, runs an highly popular event known as RCA Secret. Each year, some of the best known names in art are invited to submit original pieces of art to the exhibition. These works are then available for sale to the public for a fixed price of $60. Given that prestigious names such as Anish Kapoor, Tracy Emin and Yoko Ono have participated, this price seems a remarkable bargain. But, of course, there's a catch. The big name artists' work is exhibited alongside works by young art students - what you might call "unknown artists", (or more charitably, "emerging talents"). All of the works are in postcard format, and are exhibited anonymously - so if you buy a piece of art, you have no way of knowing if its by a celebrity or an unknown until after you have purchased it.

What's interesting here is that, without any knowledge of the artist's identity, purchasers are forced to make their decision based upon the intrinsic merits they perceive in the work itself. Doubtless some will attempt to game the system by guessing which celebrity artists are participating, and looking out of their characteristic styles. But two can play at that game. The celebrities may, for fun, attempt to disguise their styles, whilst the students may attempt to pass their work off as that of someone famous, by adopting a trademark style. Ultimately, you are presented with the option to buy a piece of art that you like at an affordable price - and it may just turn out to have been made by someone famous. Taking the big names out of the equation is either liberating, or daunting, depending on your point of view.

The success of RCA Secret indicates that many people enjoy the secrecy of the event. And whilst the idea of picking up a priceless work of art for a small sum is surely tempting, that is not really what the event is all about. From the purchaser's perspective, this is essentially a gambling game, and a test of taste. If you buy a piece simply because you like it, and it turns out to be by a famous artist, then you may feel that you have demonstrated superior taste, and flatter yourself with the notion that you posses a special affinity with that particular celebrity. From the artist's perspective, the event is a great leveler, presenting, as it does, the practically worthless art of unknowns on a level with the highly valued work of celebrity artists.

And what happens when these works are presented side by side? Does the work of the "great" artists shine through. Can the critics, or indeed the great unwashed public, tell them apart? The answer is, not really. If it was easy to distinguish between them, then the event would not have been such a success, over so many years. And this difficulty in distinguishing between the work of the great and the unknown indicates that the value of a work of art is not necessarily intrinsic to the work itself. This point would be obvious to anyone involved in the international art market. Of course an artist's reputation has a big impact on the value of his work. The same is true of any creative profession. An unpublished writer will have a much harder job of getting a publishing deal than JK Rowling, regardless of the intrinsic qualities of their work. And rightly so, from a strictly commercial perspective. Even if JK Rowling were (uncharacteristically) to write an exceedingly boring book, the *brand equity* in her name alone would be sufficient to ensure reasonable sales, (albeit expending some of that brand equity in the process).

Concepts such as brand equity, reputation and popularity are all mechanisms that lead to herd behavior, focusing, as they do, on the extrinsic properties of a work, such as what other people think about it, or how well it has sold, rather than on the intrinsic merits of the work itself. For intrinsic merits, we may substitute the term *substance*, whilst for extrinsic properties, we may think of *hype*, or *spin*. These days, everyone seems pretty scornful about spin. But what is a critic's review of a movie, if it is not spin in some form or another? We don't like the idea of spin because it seems false and misleading, encouraging us to frame an event or a work in a particular way, whilst coaxing us into overlooking what may be material to the subject in questions. And yet, this is precisely what a reviewer does. Reviews put a spin on a work - it is a good movie or a bad movie. It's an insightful book, or an obvious book. It's a catchy tune or a tedious dirge. Typically, a review will then focus on the facts that support the argument, and dismiss those that do not.

We should take care, at this point, to qualify the power that spin may have over substance. In the early days of Britain's *New Labour* government, the

LEADERSHIP BIAS

party was extremely effective at managing its message through the media, and steering the news agenda. The government's "spin doctors" were largely tolerated because their message was in tune with the popular sentiment of the time. The country needed a change, and that was exactly what the new government appeared to offer. But as the government's popularity waned, their message became increasingly less communicable, as the public and the media became resistant to spin.

Marketing types also have a tendency to over estimate the importance of hype over substance. Every year, the prestigious marketing group, Interbrand, publishes a ranking of the world's most popular brands. In the eighties, this listing was dominated by fast moving consumer brands such as Coke, Pepsi and Heinz. This was only natural, since these brands represented popular products that consumers interacted with on a daily basis, en mass. In the nineties, IT brands such as Microsoft, IBM and HP began to dominate the rankings. Again, this was a natural result of the emergence of the PC as a mainstream consumer product. Finally, in recent years, Interbrands listing has been dominated by internet savvy brands such as Google and Apple. The important point to note here is that in each case, it is the intrinsic properties of the products themselves that propel the brands into the limelight, and not the other way around.

Google is not one of the world's largest brands because the logo is attractive. Neither is it because they've spent a fortune on "brand building" advertising, (they haven't). The Google brand is popular because it's the moniker for the world's best search engine. To imagine that brands make products is to imagine that tails wag dogs. And putting a popular brand onto a terrible product is nothing more than putting lipstick on a pig.

For years, Interbrand estimated as stratospheric valuation for Microsoft's brand. And yet, whilst Windows retains enduring popularity (essentially because of lock-in, an intrinsic property of the product), Microsoft has largely failed on each occasion when it has attempted to extend its dominance into other product areas outside of its core Windows competency, (with the one notable exception of X-Box, where the Microsoft branding was fairly low-key anyway). The point is that having one of the world's most "valuable" brands didn't deliver any substantial benefit to the company when it entered new sectors with uncompetitive product offerings. A strong brand can help you to attract attention to new product offerings, but it will not deliver long term sales if the product itself does not offer sufficient intrinsic merits. So, whilst our hypothetically bad book from JK Rowling may achieve short-term sales, it will ultimately only serve to undermine confidence the JK Rowling brand.

Products confer meaning upon brands, and never the other way around. A brand is only ever as good as its product - a tough truth for any marketing guru to accept, but true nonetheless. However, where a strong brand is applied to an average product, it can be very effective as a tool to differentiate in an otherwise commoditized market. So, for example, branded pharmaceuticals, such as Advil or Nurofen, may command a price premium over their non-branded equivalent (ibuprofen).

Brands, then, like critics and spin doctors, have their limits. By communicating the extrinsic properties of a product, they may steer the crowd, but their power is limited if insufficient intrinsic value is present. These mechanisms for determining intrinsic value from extrinsic factors nonetheless have a number of distorting factors upon the market that frequently result in leadership bias. As we have seen, people tend to use extrinsic factors such as the opinions of friends, experts or spin doctors or brand popularity as a shortcut to determining intrinsic value. As a result, we often end up going to see the same movie, because we've all read the same review. We buy the same operating system, because we've heard its the best. We support the same sports stars because everyone else seems to like them.

Over time, this herding behavior can lead us to become detached from reality. One can have too much of a good thing. One can tire of a dish which is served to us every day. A lazy monopolist may become complacent, and fail to maintain their early high standards. Suddenly, that leading operating system that everyone thought was the best doesn't seem to measure up to the challenger brand. The latest book is not up to the author's previous standards. A few pioneering sheep break away from the herd to nibble at pastures new (these pioneering sheep are known as bellwethers). The rest of the flock may initially look on with curiosity, but ultimately, their instinct to follow will overcome their resistance to change, and they'll follow along. And so, the value that the herd gleans from its pasture increases for a time, as the intrinsic properties of the new pasture are greater than those of the previous, overgrazed field.

Effectively a value-lag has been introduced into the economy. Since individuals in this context behave as a group, they are less quick to respond to changes in market conditions. They are also likely to overreact to small changes, when they do, finally respond. As a result, the herd will pile in to purchase a leading stock - artificially inflating its price. They'll rush to buying a popular book, further inflating its sales. And it will take them quite some time to notice that the number two choice has just become more attractive than the number one choice.

So, whilst individuals are *frequently* inclined towards leadership bias, groups (or herds) are *always* inclined towards is. Since group-think results in everyone doing the same thing, the group anoints a new leader with each decision that it makes.

Part 7 - Secondomics in practice

Secondomics is a generalized principle, which may be applied to any situation where things are ranked in accordance to their advantages, whilst a different payoff may be discerned when one allows for the associated (and sometimes hidden) disadvantages.

We've explored a variety of examples to illustrate the principles of secondomics, ranging from the founding fathers, to penguins, nuclear bombs and genetics. In this section, we'll see how those principles apply equally well to everyday situations in business and life in general.

We'll start by examining three remarkable *challenger brands*: Avis, Virgin and Apple, that pioneered intelligent new ways to turn their second-rank status to their advantage. We'll also consider how a brand leader, such as Starbucks, may create new growth opportunities by acting as if it was in second place. And finally, we'll consider how secondomics may even offer advantages in academic and social situations.

Of course, coming second is not the answer to all of life's problems. What secondomics can offer is an antidote to today's increasingly competitive and adversarial culture, where victory is frequently valued above and beyond all else, and the merits of "also-rans" are all too often underestimated or even entirely overlooked. By applying the the principles of secondomics in our personal and professional lives, we may effectively redefine what it means to succeed, reappraise our position in life, and find new ways to maximize the value of what we have now, and may achieve in the future.

Chapter 25: Secondomics at work

Example 1: Avis vs Hertz - "We're only No. 2. We try harder."

In 1918, as the First World War was coming to its bloody end, 22 year old entrepreneur, Walter L. Jacobs, opened his first car rental office in Chicago. At the time, cars were still a relatively new innovation. Jacobs' fleet was comprised of a dozen Model-T Fords, the world's first mass-produced car, that put America on wheels. Whilst he was not the first to launch a car rental service,

Jacobs' business proved to be enormously successful. So much so that by 1923, it was generating a million dollars a year, at which point Jacobs decided to sell to John Hertz. The company became known as Hertz Drive-Ur-Self System, and Jacobs stayed on to run the business.

With investment from General Motors, and Jacobs' business acumen, Hertz grew to become the world's largest car rental group. In 1932, Hertz launched its first rental office adjacent to an airport, anticipating the lucrative "fly-drive" market that was soon to dominate the car rental industry. Hertz did not have the airports to themselves for long, however. Others scrutinized their success with jealous eyes. The arrivals hall was about to become crowded with a glut of multi-hued car rental desks.

During the Second World War, Michigan-born Warren Avis served as a pilot in the United States Air Force. When the war came to an end, Avis was struck by the difficulty in procuring ground transport at airports, and resolved to start his own car rental firm, which he did in 1946 at Willow Run Airport, Detroit. Avis Airlines Rent a Car Systems proved to be successful, beginning its international expansion by the early 1950s. But even as Avis grew, it found itself perpetually in second place to the larger and more successful Hertz.

By the 1960s, Avis was struggling. When Robert C. Townsend was appointed president, the company had not returned a profit in over a decade. Townsend knew that big changes were needed in order to turn the business around. And so he took a fateful trip to Madison Avenue, the New York home of America's advertising industry.

Townsend's decision to appoint hip ad agency, Doyle Dane Bernbach (DDB), proved to be an important milestone for both companies. Since its launch in 1949, DDB had developed a reputation for innovation in advertising. The agency was famous for its enormously popular and highly regarded "Think Small" campaign for the VW Beetle. In the 1950s, advertising tended to be a sensible business. Copywriters would draft ads that were informative and factual, but tended to lack flair and emotion. DDB was part of a vanguard that changed this approach, pairing up copywriters with art directors into "creative teams," who were positively encouraged to think the unthinkable, coming up with outlandish, off-the-wall creative ideas. The Think Small campaign was just such an idea.

Whilst, in 1960, other car manufacturers were building ever larger family cars, VW was preparing the launch of the small, odd looking Beetle. It seemed to be exactly the sort of car that Americans did not want to buy. Add to this the fact that the Second World War was still fresh in people's minds, and that the Beetle had been developed in Nazi Germany, and the car's chances in the US did not look promising. DDB's campaign to launch the Beetle, turned this on its head, with the proposition "Think Small" (a line to be echoed almost four decades later by Apple's famous "Think Different" campaign). The campaign challenged conventional wisdom, using clean, single-minded art direction and witty, counter-intuitive propositions, DDB's ads positioned the Beetle as an innovative challenger to the status quo, filled with personality and individualism. And for a country founded upon the pursuit of freedom, this sales pitch proved to resonate with its American audience.

The recent success of the Beetle campaign was probably on Townsend's mind when he walked into DDB's fancy offices. Could they pull off a similar turnaround in fortunes for Avis? Townsend quickly found that DDB's business style was just as challenging as the tone of their ads. The creative team of copywriter Paula Green and art director Helmut Krone wanted to know "why does anybody ever rent a car from you?" It was a reasonable question - after all, Avis was perpetually in the shadow of Hertz, the bigger, smarter, more successful market leader. Hertz had better airport locations, a larger network and a bigger fleet. Why *would* anyone choose Avis over Hertz?

It was not an easy question to answer, and so DDB engaged in a 90 day process with their new clients in order to address it. Ultimately, they did arrive at an answer - one that was to have a greater impact on both the car rental and advertising industry than either company could ever have imagined. DDB had persuaded VW to "think small" when the rest of the car industry was thinking big. They offered a similarly counterintuitive prescription to Townsend: embrace your second-place status.

The creative team of Green and Krone developed one of the most famous campaigns in advertising history. The first ad featured the headline "*Avis is only No.2 in rent a cars, so why go with us?*" The answer was simple, as the ad went on to explain. Because Avis was in second place to Hertz, they had to be better than Hertz in order to stay in business at all. "We can't afford to take you for granted. Go with us next time. The line at our counter is shorter." Or as they put it more succinctly in their strapline, "We try harder." It's a line that the company still uses to this day.

The results of this new campaign were nothing short of remarkable. Townsend had more than delivered the turnaround that his shareholders demanded. After a straight record of losses for the past 13 years, Avis leapt back into profits in the year of the campaign's launch, returning a respectable $1.2 million in profit on revenues of $38 million - an 11% increase in revenues over the previous year.

This success was not the result simply of fancy advertisements. The campaign went far deeper than that. The senior management at Avis toured their entire operation, ensuring that every member of staff understood the campaign, and the "we try harder" ethos that went with it. Avis agents wore iconic "We try harder" pin badges to remind both themselves and their customers of the company's new found ethos. And customers were also involved, with advertisements encouraging them to provide feedback on the performance of agents. Were they greeted with a smile? Could the agents try even harder?

Whether Avis actually "tried harder" before the campaign launched is unclear, but something certainly happened after the campaign was introduced. Perhaps the idea of an underdog organization that had to be the best in order to stay in business was exactly the vision that the staff needed in order to raise their game. The campaign didn't simply change the way in which Avis presented their business - it changed the way in which they conducted their business as well.

Interestingly, before *We Try Harder* was launched, DDB ran focus groups to ascertain how consumers would react to the proposed campaign. This is a standard approach when considering a new campaign strategy. Focus groups are a method of research favored by the advertising industry in which the researcher recruits small groups, each consisting of around 5 individuals, representing a particular type of customer. The researcher then engages the group in a discussion, with the aim of eliciting their frank and honest views of a product, service or advertising campaign.

The *We Try Harder* campaign did no perform well in research. The focus groups did not appreciate the campaign's honesty, and struggled to comprehend the benefits of being second. When asked to evaluate the proposition, they simply could not make sense of it. Why would anyone want to be second, or want to go with the second best service? But, as is so often the case in this type of research, how people thought that they would react was entirely different to how they actually responded in practice. The research subjects were simply comparing the ads to their preconceptions of what an ad should be. The *We Try Harder* campaign didn't correspond to their expectations, and so they rejected it.

Fortunately, Townsend and DDB did not reject it. Undeterred by the unfavorable research feedback, they displayed the leadership and resolve of true innovators and went ahead with the campaign anyway. And the rest is history.

The challenge "why would anyone want to be second?" is one that I frequently encountered when trying to sell the idea of this book to people. This resistance is an intrinsic property of secondomics, since it's integral to the advantage of coming second. If it was easy for people to get past their leadership bias and rationally evaluate the payoff that second place affords, then that payoff would in itself be lessened as a consequence. Just as, in our example of the previous chapter, if all of our commuters decided to wait for the second, less busy train, that the second train would become busier than the first. The same applies to waiting in line at an Avis desk - you have a shorter wait time with the second most popular car rental company. But if everyone were to switch from Hertz to Avis, then that advantage is gone.

Example 2: Virgin Atlantic vs British Airways - "No way BA"

At the beginning of the 20th century, Britain was still the proud owner of an empire, upon which, the sun famously never set. London was the "Imperial Capital" of this mighty empire, and "her imperial majesty the queen-empress" Victoria, reigned supreme. Of course, the seeds of demise were already present - how could a nation of 38 million inhabitants possibly justify the domination of such a large part of the globe, for their own selfish advantage? But if the British empire's days were numbered, the British were, at the time, unaware of it.

By the 1920s, new technology was emerging that was to bring the disparate parts of the empire more closely together. Pioneering aircraft such as the Vickers Vulcan and the Supermarine Sea Eagle offered the potential for commercial passenger air transport. Imperial Airways was founded in 1924, proudly operating routes from the capital to the far-flung extremities of the empire. Over the years, through various mergers, and eventually nationalization by Britain's socialist government, Imperial Airways became part of British Airways (BA) - one of the world's largest "flag carrying" airlines.

BA was big. Very big. And very proud of the scale of its operations. Until the 1990s, it used the strap-line "The World's Favorite Airline," an indication that the organization still retained much of the imperial hubris of its earlier incarnations. Even as Britain's global influence diminished after the second world war, the scale of it's flag carrying airline remained a source of national pride. In the 1970s, BAs advertising employed the slogan "fly the flag".

In all of BA's extensive experience in operating an airline, one area in which the company did not possess much experience was dealing with competition. Effectively a state-owned monopoly, BA was used to having things its own way. And so, when competition finally did emerge, the company struggled to adapt, much like an only child might, upon the birth of a younger sibling. The first rival to challenge BA's dominance of London/Atlantic routes was Freddie Laker's Skytrain service. An early pioneer of the "no frills" concept that was to become hugely popular in the late 1990s, Skytrain offered discounted fares for transatlantic flights between London and New York. By 1980, it had taken a 14% share of the market for transatlantic services.

BA's response was to engage in a ruthless price war with their new rival. A war that proved so costly that Laker ultimately could not win, and in 1982, the airline collapsed, owing £270 million to banks and other creditors. A year later, Laker's liquidators in America took several airlines, including BA, to court, alleging conspiracy and violation of anti-trust laws. The case was settled out of court.

When a new challenger enters an existing market, it inevitably has an impact upon prices. With Laker's arrival, offering deep discounts, it was only natural that other airlines would respond in kind. Price competition is an important aspect of how markets operate - without it, the only limit on prices becomes what the consumer is willing to pay, and for some essential services, such as transport, that may result in very high prices indeed (and huge profits for the lucky monopolist or cartel). But there's a fine line between legitimate price competition and "predatory pricing". This latter is the practice of setting short term prices at such a low level that a smaller competitor may not be able to compete, with the intention of subsequently raising prices again, once that competitor has been driven out of business. Were BA's prices competitive, or anti-competitive? Did Laker's arrival provide precisely the stimulus that BA needed in order to offer a more consumer-friendly approach to pricing, or did the airline instead decide to use all of its post-imperial might to put a smaller competitor out of business? Since this is a legal argument, rather than a philosophical one, it's beyond the scope of this book. Instead, let us simply note that Laker's demise is indicative of one of our disadvantages of coming second: *sometimes the winner does take it all*. This, if you remember, was the ability of a leader to use its leadership position in order to dominate its competitors. In the case of predatory pricing, the market leader's superior financial position enables them to endure reduced revenues from price cutting for longer than their smaller, less well-financed rivals.

Whilst Laker's Skytrain may have been grounded, the company had established the potential for a challenger in the lucrative market for transatlantic aviation. The second pretender to BA's dominance achieved far greater and more sustain success (as we may expect from the *second* challenger). Virgin Atlantic took to the skies in 1984, with a blaze of publicity, and a hint of rock star swagger, flying from London Gatwick to Newark, New Jersey in a rented 747.

Richard Branson's Virgin Group describes itself as a "branded venture capital organization," with more than 200 companies worldwide sporting the familiar red and white Virgin signature logo. The company claims that, in the eyes of their customers, they represent a "sense of competitive challenge." Virgin has repeatedly established businesses in new sectors, to which it is frequently a "virgin," in so far as it has no track record. It challenges incumbent suppliers with price cutting and alternative business models. Some ventures, such as Virgin Perfume, Virgin Vodka and Virgin Cola, are unsuccessful, whilst others, (most notably Virgin Atlantic,) have prove to be very successful indeed.

Of course, Virgin didn't start out as a branded venture capital organization. Back in 1984, when his first flight took to the air, Branson's day job was being the boss of Virgin Records, an independent record label famous for signing big name artists like The Rolling Stones and Janet Jackson. The music industry, much like the airline industry, was dominated by a small number of major record labels. If you weren't one of the majors, you were an independent; and staying in business as an independent meant competing against these gargantuan competitors, requiring a heady mix of entrepreneurial zeal and chutzpah. It was precisely these qualities that had guided Branson to success in the music business, and they were to serve him equally well in aviation.

It's Branson's predilection for competitive challenge that makes Virgin Atlantic so relevant to secondomics. As the company's website memorably expresses it, being competitively challenging is all about "sticking two fingers up to the establishment and fighting the big boys – usually with a bit of humor." Whilst Laker got embroiled in a price war with BA that they could never win, Virgin instead "stuck two fingers up" at the powers that be - and the public loved them for it.

In the spirit of Avis's *We Try Harder* campaign, Virgin Atlantic did not just compete with BA on price, but sought every opportunity to adopt new technologies, customer service methodologies and other innovations in order to differentiate themselves from their larger foe. For example, Virgin Atlantic was an early adopter of seat-back display entertainment systems, allowing their passengers in economy to choose from a variety of entertainment channels, whilst in BA, you had no option but to watch the BBC news followed by a proscribed movie selection on a squint-inducing screen at the end of the aisle.

Rattled by Virgin's success, BA responded with what Branson described as "dirty tricks." These allegedly included poaching Virgin customers, tampering with confidential company files and a negative PR campaign. This case was settled out of court, with an apology and damages proffered by BA.

Whilst Virgin Atlantic may claim to reject the values of BA, and everything it stands for, it's hard to imagine Virgin without their larger nemesis. History provides a context for fledgling entities defining themselves against their imperial foes. Much as it took oppressive taxation and heavy handed treatment from the British red coats for the 13 American colonies to rebel and form a more perfect union, so too Virgin needed its imperial foe to rebel against in order to define its own values. Would Jefferson's fine words in the Declaration of Independence have ever been written if the continental congress had not had something to seek independence from? And on a much more mundane level, would transatlantic passengers have ever got their seat-back displays in economy if Virgin had not sought to differentiate itself from its larger rival?

Challengers in second place tend to define themselves by the negative space in the wake of the leader. Or in other words, being in second place requires that you have someone to beat in first place. The bigger the foe, the harder you'll need to fight. The harder you fight, the more that you'll achieve. And sometimes the momentum you build up in fighting your foe propels you out in front. Today, it is the USA that receives criticism for its imperialistic tendencies, whilst the British (sometimes reluctantly) toe the line of US foreign policy. Although we're yet to see such a reversal in fortunes between Virgin and BA, the airline industry is more volatile than ever, so perhaps anything is possible.

Example 3: Apple vs Microsoft - "Think different"

Apple and Microsoft, two companies that have dominated the IT industry over the past three decades, both launched within a year of each other, in 1976 and 1975 respectively. Back then, Apple made hardware, whilst Microsoft made software. So there was initially no competition between the two companies. Indeed, Microsoft made software that ran on Apple's hardware. Programs like Word and Excel, that became a key part of Microsoft's global business empire, were originally developed for the Apple Macintosh computer.

The history of the two companies is well documented. In the early years, the two company's founders, Steve Jobs and Bill Gates, got along fairly well. Jobs needed software for his new Mac computers, whilst Gates needed computers to develop software on. Indeed, in these early days, it seemed that Microsoft was the underdog - one of several developers working on Apple's platform. But Gate's ambition extended far beyond this, and his desire to own the platform upon which he developed would soon see the two companies entering into conflict.

In 1985, the same year that Steve Jobs was unceremoniously dismissed from the company that he founded, Microsoft released Windows - the first serious competitor to the Macintosh, that Apple had released the year before. Early versions of Windows did not look very promising. As an extension to Microsoft's crude MS-DOS operating system, Windows at the time was severely limited in comparison to the Mac. But during the late eighties and early nineties, Windows just kept getting better and better, whilst the Macintosh... didn't.

By 1994, the tables had already turned. Windows was becoming ubiquitous, whilst the Mac was losing market share. With Jobs at the helm, Apple might have been able to outsmart the competition, but after a decade of weak, ineffectual management, in Jobs's absence, Apple was reduced to attempting to settle its differences is court. Apple argued that Microsoft has infringed its copyright on the Mac user interface, by coping their software's "look and feel". Unfortunately for Apple, the court found that they had already licensed much of the Mac's graphical appearance to Microsoft a decade earlier, when Microsoft had begun developing software for the platform. Apple lost the case.

A year later, Microsoft launched the ground breaking Windows 95, a product that represented such a significant technological leap forward that it left the Mac OS in the dust. Thus began Apple's precipitous decline, which was only halted upon the return of Steve Jobs in 1997.

Whilst Jobs had, at times, struggled with the challenges of leadership in the 1980s, to the extent that he was ultimately ejected from his own company, his second stint at the helm of Apple has proved to be truly remarkable. It seems that Jobs has thrived in the second place position that he inherited upon his return. Jobs has always loved the idea of being an underdog. Back in the early eighties, as he oversaw the development of the Macintosh, he encouraged the Mac team to think of themselves in precisely this way. Their project would be the challenger to the Apple II, the company's market leading product at the time. The group developing the Mac were renegades - outsiders within their own company, whose mission was to challenge the status quo. He even flew a pirate's skull and crossbones flag above the Mac developers building on Apple's campus, to illustrate just how subversive he intended them to be, within his own organization.

In other words, Jobs had contrived to create a second-place status for his

Mac division, within his own (at the time) market-leading business. He saw the value in being the underdog. He lived and breathed the *We Try Harder* motto. Ironically, upon his return to the company in 1997, it truly was the underdog, and he took to the challenge like a duck to water. One of his first acts was to devise a new motto, which would frame the *We Try Harder* sentiment in a new, edgier, counter-culture mode.

So it was, that Steve Jobs, much like Robert Townsend before him, took a trip to his advertising agency. Jobs had history with his agency. He had worked together with Chiat/Day, (now TBWA/Chiat/Day), way back in the eighties. Then, the challenge had been to launch the revolutionary Macintosh personal computer, and the 1984-inspired ad they created became the stuff of advertising legend. Now, the challenge was bigger, and far more pressing. Save the company.

In June 1997, industry bible, Wired Magazine, published a cover with an Apple logo wrapped in thorns, with a single word beneath it: "pray." Back then, Apple seemed incapable of turning a profit, and the market share for its products was diminishing precipitously. Since the company still had cash in the bank, rival Michael Dell suggested Apple should close down and "give the money back to the shareholders." At the time, it didn't seem like an unreasonable suggestion. The received wisdom was that Apple's business model was fundamentally flawed. The success of Windows had lead to the commoditization of PC hardware, driven by cost cutters, such as Dell. It didn't much matter what your PC looked like, as long as it was cheap and ran Windows. Apple's machines were not cheap, and they didn't run Windows.

Whilst other CEOs may have attempted to re-tool Apple's business model to become another Dell, selling cheap, industry standard hardware, Jobs was indulging in a new advertising campaign. It's worth noting that personal involvement between a company's CEO and its advertising agency is not the norm. Typically, marketing directors deal with ad agencies, and marketing directors often don't even get a seat on the board. For regular companies, advertising campaigns are just not regarded as important enough to command the personal attention of the chief executive officer. But for Avis in 1960, and for Apple in 1997, an advertising campaign was considered so important, it was a strategy to bet the company on. Apple was not a regular company, and Jobs had no interest in received wisdom - he was preparing his organization to *Think Different*.

In both Avis's *We Try Harder* campaign and Apple's *Think Different* campaign, the lead competitor's menacing shadow is palpably present. We try harder *than Hertz*, Think differently *to Microsoft*. But these straplines were not messages of challenge to the competitor, they were rather mission statements to inspire staff and customers alike. They were a call to arms to all those who find an underdog irresistible (appealing to the *big taker* in us, if you remember our toilet paper algorithms).

In a very real sense, back in 1997, one of the most important things about Apple was that *Apple wasn't Microsoft*. This was, perhaps, the only justification for rejecting Dell's otherwise sage advice. It didn't matter so much whether the Mac was any good back then. The fact was that it was the *only* alternative to Windows - a product that had become so popular that the Mac was now the only thing that stood between it and total market domination of desktop computing. A fact that Microsoft themselves were keenly aware of. After recently being on the receiving and of punishment from the US Department of Justice for anti-trust violations, Microsoft knew that they needed this tiny competitor to stay in business, or otherwise they could be hit with yet more regulatory interference. Microsoft's decision to provide their old rival with funding to stay afloat in this difficult time was as much pragmatic as it was noble.

Even with this new source of funding, Apple was facing an uphill battle. The Mac OS, the system at the heart of every Macintosh, hadn't received a major update since the early nineties. It was substantially inferior to Windows by this point, with no obvious route forwards. And even supposing that Apple could find a way to leap ahead of Microsoft, it was by no means certain that this would be sufficient to keep the company in business. By this point, Windows was benefitting from Metcalf's Law, that we explored in Chapter 7. People were buying Windows in preference to Mac, not just because it was better, but, even more importantly, because it was what everyone else bought. There was an advantage in using the same system as everyone else - it made it easier to get software and support.

In other words, at this point, Apple's mission was to swim against the current. They would need to swim harder just to stay in the same place, and to gain ground on Microsoft, they'd need not just to try harder, but to try much harder. But how do you persuade a losing team to turn their fortunes around? How do you convince them to pick themselves up off the floor and push themselves harder than they've ever worked in their lives before, for a goal that seems almost unattainable, against impossible odds?

The answer is, that you must provide them with a vision. And vision is precisely what *Think Different* offered. It was, after all, light on actual substance. The campaign seemed to be comparing Apple with some of the greatest figures of the twentieth century, including Albert Einstein, Martin Luther King and Mahatma Gandhi. Big names from entertainment, sports and business were also present (notably, for our purposes, Richard Branson). It seemed pretty presumptuous to utter Apple's name in the same breath as these legends.

But Apple would argue that it was not its intention to position Apple as equal to these luminaries, but rather, that these people possessed the qualities to which the company, its customers and suppliers should aspire. Notably, in their way, each figure had triumphed against challenging odds, "sticking two fingers up to the establishment and fighting the big boys," as Branson would have put it.

The campaign worked, in as far as it captured peoples' imagination and bought the company some time. But the trouble with promising great things, is that people will eventually expect you to deliver upon your promises. And fortunately for Apple's long suffering shareholders, Jobs went on to do precisely that.

Seizing the spirit of his *Think Different* manifesto, Jobs went about redefining Apple, based upon the negative space left by Microsoft. Apple would be the Yang to Microsoft's Yin. Where Microsoft was about cutting costs, Apple would be about adding value. Where Microsoft focused on business customers, Apple would woo consumers. Where Microsoft embraced enterprise, Apple would embrace entertainment. Where Microsoft was sensible, Apple would be cool.

Jobs was a demanding task master, extracting every drop of energy from his team, knowing full well that if Apple paused for a moment to catch its breath, it would be washed away by the current it was swimming against. And as the years passed by, Apple remained in business. It didn't increasing in market share, but its decline had been halted. This achievement alone would have been remarkable, since, by any reasonable measure, Apple should, by this point, have no longer existed. Their vertically integrated business model (selling both the hardware and the software) just didn't make sense in the modern IT industry.

But then, the IT industry changed. The early growth of the industry had come largely from the business sector, where Dell's cost cutting, commoditized business model made perfect sense. But at the beginning of the 21st century, the rapid growth of the business IT sector was flagging, and an entirely new sector of consumer electronics was just beginning to take off. It was a new game, with new rules. Consumers were less interested in commoditization, and more interested in things like ease of use, attractiveness, and an illusive sense of "cool". It would take quite some time for industry giants like Microsoft and Dell to adapt their offering to this new environment. Their entire business model was predicated upon a sector that seemed to offer no further growth potential. In order to keep growing, they would have to unlearn everything that they had learned.

Apple, meanwhile, was a company that had been swimming against the current, and as a result, had been working twice as hard just to stay in the same position. The idea of growth for Apple had seemed like an impossible dream. But now the current was turning in Apple's direction, and all Apple's hard work in learning to swim so hard was about to pay off, big time.

Apple entered into a sustained period of frenetic innovation and remarkable growth that will go down in history as one of the world's most remarkable business turnarounds. Occupying, as it now does, the negative space around Microsoft's mighty empire, Apple had established battlelines upon which it staked its territory, constraining its lead competitor's territory in the process. iPod and iTunes' early lead in personal music players and digital downloads proved impossible for Microsoft to compete against - despite the key strategic importance of this emerging sector to their plans for Windows Media. On other fronts, Apple was also holding its own, from software for creative professionals, to e-commerce and retail.

Even in Microsoft's core territory, its desktop operating system, Apple was finally presenting a serious competitive challenge. Whilst in 1995, Windows leapt ahead, leaving the tired old Mac OS in the dust, a decade later, and the tables had seemingly turned. Microsoft's Vista operating system was dogged with problems, whilst Apple's Mac OS X was highly regarded, and was gaining market share.

Apple's arch enemy, whilst still the larger company, was finally beginning to take the threat seriously, but by this stage, their growth strategy was hamstrung, and somehow the lazy, presumptuous, patrician culture of a market-dominating organization was incapable of competing with the ballsy, entrepreneurial chutzpah of this challenger.

It brings to mind the 1990 hit comedy *Crazy People*, where Dudley Moore plays an advertising executive who starts coming up with ads that tell the truth, such as "Volvo Cars, they're boxy, but they're good," and "AT&T - we're tired of taking your crap." His honesty gets him sent to a psychiatric hospital, but his straight-talking ads turn out to be a huge hit. When his former employers try to capitalize on this success, they struggle to recreate the magic. In one memorable scene, at a team meeting at the ad agency, the boss pounds the table and demands to know why his team can't "*do honest*". Did Microsoft boss Steve Bullmer pound the table (or perhaps throw a chair), and demand to know why his team couldn't "*do different*"?

Interestingly, almost all of the ads in Crazy People followed the secondomics formula. They frankly acknowledged their shortcomings relative to the leader, and then defined themselves by their difference. Finding a unique selling point in the negative space. Like acknowledging that your cars are boxier, but then embracing boxiness as a desirably quirky aspect of your brand personality. It may seem crazy to acknowledge your second place status, as Avis, Virgin and Apple all implicitly did in their advertising, but once you've acknowledged it, the results can be liberating. As Apple's *Think Different* ad puts it, in a line that could be a fair description of Moore's friends in the psychiatric hospital, who help him to write his ads:

> "*Here's to the crazy ones. The misfits. The rebels. The troublemakers. The round pegs in the square hole. The ones who see things differently.*"

What Avis, Virgin Atlantic and Apple all have in common is that they are *challenger brands*. For each company, there's a gorilla in the room. A market leader so dominant that they must work harder, smarter and more creatively in order to stay in the game. Through their vision, management and marketing, they must embrace the advantages of second place. Specifically, these challenger brand employ three of our advantages of second place:

1. Enemy in your sight

Whilst carefully cultivating a likable image, these brands are not above the occasional negative campaign, or dirty trick. Virgin Atlantic happily knocks British Airways and American Airlines at every opportunity it gets. Whether it's slogans like "no way BA/AA" when it's competitors consider a merger, or playing the patriotic card by painting a British flag on its planes when BA removes the flag from its own fleet, Virgin rarely misses an opportunity to gain from the market leader's misfortune.

And whilst Apple sometimes likes to cultivate a counter-culture, Bob Dylan, hippy-esque style, they are also willing to take the fight to the competition when it suits them. The "I'm a Mac and I'm a PC" campaign is a no-holds-barred attack on the shortcomings of Microsoft's market-leading operating system.

Whilst challenger brands can get away with such negative strategies without seeming unsporting, the same approach would not work for the market leaders. Imagine if British Airways started running ads that criticized Virgin

Atlantic, or if Microsoft started attacking the Mac directly with negative campaigning. Such an approach would only serve to make the market leader seem complacent, lazy, out-of-ideas and destined for a fall. Market leaders are thus left with no option but to take the higher ground, and avoid dignifying their competitors' knocking campaigns with a response.

So, when you find yourself in the number two position, seize the opportunity to take a couple of well aimed potshots at the guy in front. They'll resonate with your customers and prospects, and your competitor will struggle to return fire without sustaining self-inflicted damage.

2. Room for growth

The market share for Microsoft's ubiquitous web browser, Internet Explorer, is in a long term decline. Whilst the company had certainly neglected development of the product for many years, this is not the reason for it's problems. The true reason for Internet Explorer's declining user base is quite simply that from a position of such overwhelming dominance (almost 95% market share in 2002), there's really nowhere to go but down. Conversely, a company like Apple need only *release* a web browser, and they can expect to make some inroads into the leader's market share. This market adjustment may be nothing more than regression to the mean.

But, more broadly speaking, the problem for Microsoft these days is that they are a victim of their own success. They employ an enormous global workforce, who grapple with the problem of what they should do next, but whichever avenue they explore, they struggle to find new opportunities and approaches to trump their past achievements. And sometimes, in order to innovate, it's necessary to tear down what came before in order to embrace the new. This is the essential process of *creative destruction* described by economist Joseph Alois Schumpeter, whereby economic growth is achieved by the continual destruction of older systems in favor of newer approaches optimized for current market conditions.

The problem is perfectly epitomized by Microsoft's continual mis-steps in the digital music sector. By attempting to protect their existing Windows Media business, the company was too slow in responding to the new threat from Apple's iPod business.

Conversely, with such a tiny market share, in the late 1990s, Apple really had nothing to lose. Why not bet the company on a radical new business model? It was essentially a do or die moment - they had nothing to lose, and therefore everything to gain from thinking differently.

So, be ready to acknowledge when you have nothing to lose, and be prepared to make big changes and take big risks in order to challenge the leader. This is, after all, one of your key advantages - your competition can't afford to take such big risks.

3. Everyone loves an underdog

Avis's *We Try Harder* campaign was trading on the good will afforded to the underdog. How did the car rental company address DDB's fundamental question of "why does anyone ever rent a car from you?" Quite simply by playing to the fair mindedness of their audience. Remember the story of the toilet paper roles, and our innate desire for balance? When one role gets bigger than the other, we start to take from the larger role in order to even the score. Well the same instinct turns out to be true of queues at car rental desks at airports.

Remember how one Avis ad argued that their number-two status meant that their line at the counter would be shorter? This is the quintessential underdog play, proposing, as it does, that car renters should adjust their behavior in order to even out the length of the lines.

So, don't be shy about your second-place status - be frank about it, take advantage of people's natural fair-mindedness and highlight how doing business with the number-two could prove to be mutually beneficial.

Think like an underdog, before you become one

But what if you're the leader?

With all of these many advantages of second place, we should spare a thought for the plight of the leader. If you're out in front, with your nearest competitors applying the principles of secondomics, occupying your negative space and flanking you an all sides, how do you stay innovative, how to you protect your leadership position, and where do you find new avenues for growth?

Let's take Starbucks as an example, of which I'm very fond. Much of this book has been written in the comfortable confines of its many fine establishments.

When I take the short walk from my office to the shops, I pass by no less than four separate Starbucks coffee shops, in a distance of less than half a mile. One is in the business park. A second is in the local supermarket, a third, is literally just around the corner from the supermarket in a stand-alone shop unit, and a forth, just a few blocks down, right in the center of town. There's nothing unusual about my walk into town. It would be much the same wherever I was in the USA or the other 43 countries around the world in which Starbucks has a presence.

Where McDonalds grew in the 1980s to become an entirely ubiquitous part of urban and suburban life, Starbucks has done much the same today. And like McDonalds, whilst its remarkable growth we fueled by its immense popularity, that growth began to stall as the brand's very ubiquity began to prompt a backlash. For everyone who, like me, enjoys a quiet morning sipping coffee at their local Starbucks, these days you can find as many who are eager to criticize - citing everything from the company's environmental record, its trading with the developing world, its American origins, or simply its homogeneity as reasons to distain the brand.

It doesn't have to be this way, of course. Sweden provides us with an alternative model. It's the first country in the world where a McDonalds restaurant was forced to close. In the northern town of Umeå, the summers are beautiful, benefitting from the warm air of the Gulf Stream, and with such proximity to the north pole, that the sun never quite sets. The winters, however, are dark and bitingly cold. Perhaps it was one such dark winter which drove a local group of militant vegans to wage war against this invading American multinational. Waging a sustained campaign during the 1990s, these protestors eventually had their way, and demonstrated once and for all that global retail brands would have to tread with care if they wish to prosper in Sweden.

Perhaps that's why Starbucks has yet to attempt an entry into this potentially lucrative market. Swedes have certainly acquired a taste for fancy coffee, and there's no shortage of home-brewed chains of coffee shops to prove it, like Wayne's Coffee or Robert's Coffee. Whilst Wayne and Robert both sound like they might be west coast Americans, and the interiors of their stores certainly evokes a sense of Seattle, they're actually both as Scandinavian as Abba.

As a result of Starbuck's absence from Sweden, a far greater variety of coffee establishments have flourished. Not just the big Scandianvian chains, but independents as well. And that may well be just how the sensible Swedes like it. After all, the homogeneity of Starbucks culture is one of the aspects of the company's growth that has piqued the ire of some. And even I, when walking around London or New York, and seeing a Starbucks on almost every street corner, am forced to ponder if it isn't possible to have too much of a good thing. There are over 10,000 stores in the US. They all serve the same coffee, the same sandwiches and the same pastries. Their walls are all painted the same

SECONDOMICS IN PRACTICE

green and beige hues. They all play the same music, and in their windows hang the same odd-looking elliptical glass lamp-shades, spattered randomly with tints of orange and blue. Perhaps the brand has expanded too far. Perhaps it has become a victim of its own success.

Like those nice, independent coffee shops in downtown Stockholm, Starbucks started out nice and small. An independent coffee importer and retailer in Seattle's waterfront Pike Place Market. And in the early days of its growth, most people admired this plucky upstart with the chutzpah to attempt such ambitious expansion. But something happen on the way to success, as early good will gave way to increasing ambivalence. The initial excitement of being thrilled to "discover" a great new coffee, for some, gave way to the contempt that is bred from familiarity.

It can be tough at the top. Whilst Starbucks is far and away the market leader in coffee shops (its closest US rival, Caribou Coffee, doesn't come close), success has not been kind to them, and in 2008, the company has began to rationalize its operations, with the closure of underperforming stores. Critics claimed that the company had grown too far and too fast.

So how can Starbucks get its groove back? How can the leader become the challenger, and start to surprise, delight and innovate again? How can they get a jaded audience to look at them afresh? And how can they engineer substantial change within their business, without damaging it in the process? In order to answer these questions, lets return to Steve Jobs for a moment.

Whilst, for most of his professional life, Steve Jobs has been in the underdog position: Mac vs the mighty Windows; Pixar vs the mighty Disney; it hasn't always been that way. If you recall, back in the early days, Apple was bigger than Microsoft, and Bill Gates had to dance to Jobs' tune. The Apple II was, in its day, the best selling computer in history. But even then, the writing was on the wall for the company. Others watched Apple's success jealously, looking for a way to muscle in on an emerging sector. Some competitors were laughable, and easily brushed away into the trash can of computing history. But others represented a far more serious threat. Jobs knew that Apple had to start thinking like an underdog again, before they became one. That's why he set up the Macintosh division as rebels within the organization. A *skunkworks* project.

A skunkworks is a research and development team which is deliberately set apart from the main organization, and operating with a lot of latitude, often steeped in secrecy. The purpose of such a team is to *think differently* from its parent organization, unhampered by the standard rules and process. In other words, in order to think outside the box, these teams are established outside of the

183

standard corporate campus.

In the typical homogenous environment of the big American corporate, the skunkworks provides an means of inculcating heterogenous ways of working. It offers an alternative view. It offers variety. And isn't that precisely what is lacking within Starbucks? One of the frequent criticisms leveled at Starbucks is the way in which it spreads a homogenous culture, eliminating independent retailers and draining the variety and locality from our communities. This may sound somewhat histrionic and overstated, but it's an argument I've heard many times over, from many different friends, family and colleagues.

So how could the spirit of the skunkworks save Starbucks? Think back to my walk from work to the shops. I literally only need to walk one block in order to pass two Starbucks. How am I to decide which Starbucks to go into? They are pretty much identical. Of course, there are small differences - one is a little more roomy than the other, one has a nicer view from the windows than the other, one may have friendlier staff. But otherwise they're just the same.

Starbucks are not the only coffee shops that I pass on my journey. Many other cafe chains have a presence on the same street. The reason for this concentration is because this is a great place for coffee shops. There are lots of office workers like me walking past. And we office workers are usually willing to pay a premium to have our latte frothed for us. But as great as this spot may be for coffee shops, isn't it overkill to have two shops on the one block? Why did Starbucks do it?

The reason is because Starbucks is, in one sense, a real estate business. They're about buying retail property. They want to get all the good sites, and they know that if they don't get them, their competitors will. Hence their zeal to claim every good spot, even if this means they have two shops in such close proximity. From their property manager's perspective, it hardly matters, providing that both stores turn a good profit.

But the problem, as we have seen, comes in the longer term damage that this kind of over concentration does to the brand. Even fans of Starbucks, like myself, would be frustrated if every store on the street was a Starbucks. There comes a point of concentration at which, not only do you suffer from diminishing returns (there's only so many coffee shops that a neighborhood can support), but you're actively damaging your brand, through overexposure. Like the famous Monty Python sketch about spam.

But if Starbucks were to let some of their properties go, their competitors could muscle in. Secondomics provides an alternative solution. If you're

SECONDOMICS IN PRACTICE

struggling to maintain your success in first place, and don't want to lose ground to the competition, *be in second place as well*. Introduce a second, skunkworks brand. Build a team of rebels and renegades within your own organization, and encourage them to create a new line of coffee shops that thinks different and tries harder. Give them the space and latitude that they need to credibly compete with Starbucks by defining themselves in the negative space that Starbucks leaves behind. And start aggressively rolling out this new concept wherever the Starbucks brand seems overexposed.

It hardly matters that people know both brands are from the same organization, as long are they are entirely different. In the UK, one of the nation's most popular mass-market newspapers (The Sun), and one of its most prestigious (The Times), are both published by the same parent company (News International). The readers of one would be unlikely to read the other, but the fact that they share the same parent company doesn't appear to concern their readers. Likewise, shoppers at the Gap may have no interest in shopping at Banana Republic, and visa versa. It matters little that they're just different brands from the same retail company. So too, a second brand from Starbucks could be genuinely differentiated from its sibling, provided that it offers something genuinely different.

This second brand may do more than solving the company's real estate strategy and overexposure. Incubating an alternative culture within a giant organization provides an essential ingredient for success in any business these days - diversity. Starbucks, much like Microsoft, has got a little bit too good at doing what it does. As a consequence, it struggles to generate new ideas, new approaches and diversity of thinking.

If a big skunk walks into a room crowded with people, its certainly going to shake things up. Likewise, a big skunkworks in the heart of a corporate behemoth will help facilitate adaption to change and adoption of new ways of thinking.

Ironically, in this way, secondomics provides the leader with the tantalizing possibility of staying in first place, by being in second place as well.

Chapter 26: Secondomics in life

Example 1: How I met my partner - "it's not who-you-know, but who who-you-know knows"

Whilst the applications of secondomics in business are pretty clear, it is less obvious how they may apply more broadly, to life in general. After all, secondomics is concerned with rankings, and whilst rankings may be all important in business, when we actively compete with each other for success, the same is not necessarily true in other areas of life. Whilst, from an evolutionary perspective, we may compete in matters of reproduction, we surely don't compete in matters of love.

Love, like happiness and fun, may seem to be an uncountable property. But whilst our love for our partner may be difficult to quantify, our love for opera versus pop is easier to assess, and our love for bananas versus apples, even easier. This is because we can start to measure these things based upon behavior. Rather than relying on the subjective and unreliable accounts of the individuals concerned, we can observe what they actually do in practice. If someone claims to love opera more than pop music, we may look at the number of plays recorded on their iPod for each genre to see if this is true. If we wonder whether Americans love their bananas more than their apples, we simply need to look at which is imported in greater quantity to get a pretty good idea.

And whilst the data generated by human relationships are much harder to count than data on an iPod, or import figures, count them we can.

Web 2.0, the web's much-hyped second coming, is based upon a group of technologies that facilitate the networking of humans, rather than computers. The first phase of the Internet enabled computers in disparate locations to connect with each other on a seamless network. But that's about as far as the technology went. The Internet is concerned with computers on networks, rather than the individuals who use those computers. Over time, however, software emerged that started to build networks of users on top of those networks of computers. Early examples of this *groupware*, such as Lotus Notes and Microsoft Exchange, provided a means for large companies to connect disparate workforces across multiple sites. Users could browse each other, search for specialisms, explore reporting hierarchies and send messages.

More recently, a new class of web-based applications have extended the concepts of groupware into the territory of mere mortals. Now anyone can connect with everyone on *social networks* such as Facebook and MySpace. Users can express their personal relationships with each other by linking. These links, in the case of Facebook, can be categorized by relationship type, differentiating between friends, family, colleagues and partners.

From an economist's perspective, of course, this offers us a whole new category of data to play with, making the mysteries of human relationships suddenly more tangible than they ever have been before. They become countable, since we can start to count the links between profiles, and map out how individual relationships fit within larger communities. These data are usually represented in some form of *social graph*.

What's interesting about the social graph, for our purposes, is where the value lies. We've already explored Metcalfe's law, which provides a means of calculating the overall value of a network, which Metcalfe argued was equal to the square of the number of its nodes. But this assumes that all nodes on the network are connected to all other nodes, which is not the case on a social graph. In this case, our nodes are users - the people who post their profiles and link to their buddies. And this is just the point. They link to their buddies, but not to strangers. In fact, in a very real sense, the value in social networks is as much concerned with who isn't connected as who is. If everyone on Facebook was a friend of everyone else, your list of contacts would become less like your address book, and more like the phone book.

Ironically, however, even as you value the exclusivity that social networks provide - keeping strangers out - on many occasions in life, letting stranger is is precisely what you need and want to do - like when you're looking for a new job, or a date. And on these occasions, you'll be looking to leverage your existing connections in order to build new ones.

At the heart of any graph is where the relationships are strongest. We find clusters of interrelated nodes, indicative of the close bonds of family or school friends. In these clusters, everyone knows everyone else, and the potential for introductions is therefore limited. It's at the periphery of the graph where the true value lies. This is where the links in our own graph come to an end, and so this is where the new links - to strangers - may be forged.

As counterintuitive as it may seem, it is the nodes at the periphery of our social graph that offer us the greatest value. Put simply, it's not so much our friends, but our friends-of-friends that truly count. If you're looking for a new boyfriend or girlfriend, you're unlikely to find them in your close group of personal friends (unless you live in the bizarrely insular world of the TV sitcom

"Friends"). Your new partner is more likely to be someone new. And you're not likely be introduced to someone new by a friend, because you probably know the same people that they do already. You have a far better chance of being introduced to someone new by a friend of a friend - or in other words - a second-tier friend. And so it turns out that secondomics applies in human relationships after all.

Websites like Facebook may have supplied us with new sources of data to mine, but there's nothing new about the data themselves. Our networks of relationships were always there, they just weren't so easy to map out. When I met my partner, almost a decade ago, I found him exactly where I should have expected - right there on the edge of my social map, via a friend of a friend. I didn't discover him on a social networking website, but in the old fashioned way - at a party. It wasn't the regular kind of party that I would normally attend. It was the party of a couple who were friends of friends, and I was still getting to know them. At this point, I'd been long-term single, and I guess I'd been holding out to meet the right person. Since I'd been to lots of my friend's parties, there wasn't anyone new to meet there, but at the party of a friend of a friend, I had the opportunity to meet a whole new group of people. As it turns out, he was from Sweden, having only recently moved to London, and had it not been for that friends-of-friends party, it's unlikely that we would ever have met.

Example 2: How I chose my college - "second choice isn't necessarily second best"

In 1989, as a mixed up art student, studying a foundation course in art and design at Kingston Polytechnic, I had a decision to make. It was the time in the academic year when foundation students chose which art schools they wished to apply to. Then, as now, there was a clearing house system, where every student had the opportunity to select a first and second choice. The idea was that this allowed everyone to apply for a prestigious college, but also apply to a safe bet if they didn't get into their favorite.

I was shy, insecure and ambivalent about my abilities. Some days I would think that I was a genius, who would one day rule the world, and on other days I felt that nothing I did was ever right. And as much as I tried to take on board criticism from others, I always struggled to accept it as the constructive feedback that it was intended to be, and instead I would take it as a personal insult. Underneath it all, I was struggling with deep-seated rejection anxieties.

In fact, you might say that I was the typical art student.

Sitting in the studio, listening to my fellow students discussing their options, it was clear that there was only one choice to be made. Everyone wanted to go to Central St Martins, a prestigious college in the heart of London's hip Covent Garden shopping district (it *was* hip back in the eighties). St Martin's alumni included some of the biggest names in art, design and fashion, and the best and brightest travelled from all over the world to study there. In fact, it was so darn prestigious that you had to be pretty good yourself to even consider applying.

Our tutor at Kingston, Alan, was as hard as nails. He'd seen many kids from his course apply to St Martins over the years. Frequently, they would be rejected, and as a result, he wasn't short on opinions regarding who should and should not apply. He wasn't particularly diplomatic in the way he delivered his frank and honest assessment to his students. In the weeks leading up to the deadline for applications, many a student would be seen walking away from his office in tears, after Alan had unceremoniously shattered their dreams.

What should I do? I mused over this question as I sat at my desk, looking at the blank application form in front of me. I could put St Martins down as my first choice. After all, it seemed to be what everyone else wanted to do. But what would I tell Alan when he asked me which colleges I was applying to? I wasn't sure that my fragile ego could take the pummeling that he would give me for my presumption. It wasn't much of a secret that Alan did not particularly rate my work. Each year, he'd pick out a couple of star students that he'd groom as his St Martins applicants, and I was not one of them. I imagined that he would be furious if I applied, since I'd bring down the reputation of excellence that he'd been nurturing over the years for Kingston applications with the admissions panel at St Martins.

The truth is, I wasn't ever seriously considering applying to St Martins at this point. We'd all had it drummed into us by Alan that putting St Martins as our first choice if we didn't stand a chance of getting in was a waste. We'd be better of putting a middle-ranking college down as our first choice, and then we'd still have a second choice as a backup if that fell through. These middle-ranking colleges were pretty good in their own right, even if they weren't St Martins, and they didn't like to see themselves put down as a second choice, interpreting this as some kind of sleight on the part of the applicant.

In other words, the standardized admissions process of first and second choice applications had resulted in the colleges themselves speciating into first choice and second choice colleges. First choice colleges would only consider applicants that had put them down as first choice. Those colleges who were more flexible were rewarded by only being put down as second choice.

It was at this point that I rebelled. Uncertain about which choice was best for me, frustrated that I wasn't considered good enough for St Martins, and fearful that I may be rejected by everyone, I elected to do the unthinkable - putting a second choice college down as my first choice. I'd visited Maidstone College and been impressed by what I'd seen. It might not have been as hip and challenging as St Martins, but the students seemed to be producing good work there, and I could see myself fitting in. I thought it was a smart move, and I felt pretty smug about the idea that I could be confident that I would be accepted by my first choice art college. How many of my fellow applicants could make such as claim?

Ironically, I later found out that I only got into Maidstone College by the skin of my teeth. The tutors there didn't like the idea of someone putting them first. Evidently they knew their station in the pecking order. St Martins set an extremely high standard in terms of their applications. Maidstone knew that they were lucky to get to pick and choose from St Martins rejects, many of whom would have certainly been accepted by a lesser first choice art college, but since they betted their future on an application to St Martins which did not pay off, they were now forced to settle for Maidstone, a second choice art college instead. With this in mind, it seemed positively suspect to the admissions panel at Maidstone that I had put them first. What was wrong with me, they pondered? Ultimately, they decided to make me an offer, but it was a a close run thing.

I thoroughly enjoyed my first year at Maidstone, making many great friends, who I'm still in touch with today. But there was something niggling away at the back of my mind. What if I had applied to St Martins? Would I have got in? Had I allowed my insecurities to cloud my judgement, and my academic development was suffering as a result?

Whilst my social life at Maidstone was terrific, I felt that the course work was not particularly challenging. With the kind of egotism that only an eighteen year old can muster, I couldn't help feeling that I stood out amongst my peers as being exceptionally gifted, and that it was time for me to move on. It turned out that there were a limited number of places for transfers to St Martins at the beginning of the sophomore year, and I decided to apply. With similar ambivalence to the way I'd approached the admissions process a year earlier, I'm not sure that I had ever seriously intended to transfer to St Martins. Really, I just wanted to know if they'd let me in, and since I already had my place at Maidstone, I now had nothing to lose.

When my offer letter from St Martins arrived, I was thrilled, and accepted without hesitation. It seemed the obvious thing to do. It was only after I'd put my letter of acceptance in the mail, and met up with my friends on campus that my doubts began to emerge. I realized what I great year I'd had at Maidstone. How much I'd developed, despite myself. And how much I was going to miss this place, and all of my friends when I left. Suddenly, I could see that I'd been stumbling forwards blindly, making decisions based upon prejudice and impulse, rather than giving any thought to what I actually wanted in life, and what would make me happy.

But the die was cast, and I was on my way to one of the world's hippest art colleges, in one of the world's hippest capitals.

I'd like to say that St Martins turned out not to be what I had expected, but since I hadn't given any serious consideration to the possibility of me being accepted, this would not be entirely true. Nonetheless, despite my lack of preconceptions, it still came as a surprise. Where life at Maidstone had been studious, serious minded and career focussed, St Martins was, by contrast, frivolous, laid back and experimental. Much like Avis's *We Try Harder* campaign, the Maidstone students worked hard because they knew they had to. Whereas the St Martins students were budding patricians. Their very acceptance at the country's most prestigious art college was sufficient indication of their destiny. They had nothing to declare but their brilliance, and their brilliance was so self evident, that they didn't have to work very hard in order for it to shine through.

Most of the students at St Martins actually were brilliant. Their wit, imagination and charisma stood in stark contrast to the honest, earnestness of the typical Maidstone student, who tended to make up for what they lacked in talent through sheer hard work. I was like a roundhead amongst cavaliers. Descended, as I was, from a long line of middle class methodists, who had a blind faith in the godly virtues of hard work. It was a philosophy that I had never previously challenged.

The atmosphere of idle presumption at St Martins in the nineties was intoxicating, and I soon fell in with the crowd. Abandoning my studious ways, I mooched through my final two undergraduate years, killing time by sitting in the school's coffee bar, sagely discussing which pop stars were hot or not.

Despite my lethargy, I graduated with a reasonable degree, and I got my first job, in no small part due to the prestige of being a St Martin's alumnus. In fact, had I stayed at Maidstone, whilst I would have certainly worked a lot harder, and would have truly earned my qualifications, rather than claiming them as a patrician birthright in the St Martins way, I would doubtless have struggled far more to get my first job, for want of the bauble of a prestigious school on my resumé.

So what does this sorry tale of youthful naiveté tell us about secondomics? If I had been following the principles that I've set out in this book, what should my actions have been, and how may the outcome have differed? To answer that, we need to reappraise the admissions process.

The system essentially comprises of three tiers of art schools, with St Martins in Tier 1, at the apex, and Maidstone Tier 3, at the bottom. (Whilst there were certainly other art schools with equivalent prestige to St Martins, it really was the stand out first choice for budding designers in the late 1980's). Tier 2 was occupied by those other art schools that were good enough to only consider first choice applicants, but were not as good as St Martins.

What made the admissions process tricky, however, was that whilst there were three tiers to choose from, applicants were only allowed two ranked choices. Logically, your first choice would not be from a lower tier than your second choice. And as we've already established, Tier 1 and 2 schools do not consider second choice applicants, so your second choice must always be from Tier 3. Which leaves us with the following three options:

```
C=Choice
T=Tier

Option 1:  C₁=T₁,  C₂=T₃
Option 2:  C₁=T₂,  C₂=T₃
Option 3:  C₁=T₃,  C₂=T₃
```

Option 1 is essentially for the grade-A students only. The risk in applying to a Tier 1 school is that you get rejected, in which case you can't resort to Tier 2, and are thrown back into Tier 3. Option 3 is for the bottom of the class - those who don't even have a chance of getting into a Tier 2 school. Leaving Option 2 for everyone else - the vast majority.

So why did I choose Option 3, when it later transpired that I was good enough to transfer to a Tier 1 school in the second year? The answer is that I was so frustrated that Alan did not believe I was good enough for Tier 1 that I petulantly picked Option 3 instead - cutting off my nose, despite my face, as the saying goes. In other words, I was suffering from leadership bias. Had Option 1 not existed, I may very well have chosen Option 2, but instead, I made the irrational choice of Option 3.

So, what might have happened if I had selected Option 2? Let's take a closer look at how this system works. Let's simplify things and say that there are three types of students, good, average and poor, and that good ones apply to Tier 1, average to Tier 2, and bad to Tier 3. Let's also say that there is a 25% chance of getting into your first choice. If we have 100 students of each category, this would give us student bodies comprising of the following:

```
Tier 1: 100% Good
Tier 2: 100% Average
Tier 3: 30% Good, 30% Average, 40% Bad
```

Significantly, Tier 3 actually has more good students that Tier 2. And this is before we allow for the fact that Tier 3 colleges can filter out bad students during the selection process (the figures above assume that Tier 3 colleges have accepted everyone). Once you allow for this, it becomes probable that there are more talented students at Tier 3 colleges than at Tier 2. This begs the question of whether Tier 2 colleges are *really* better than Tier 3. It rather depends upon the relative importance of the quality of the teaching, versus the quality of one's fellow students. My personal view is that you learn as much from your cohorts as you do from your teachers, and on this basis, with secondomics in mind, if I was that petulant eighteen year old with a decision to make, my reasoning would be as follows. Apply to you first choice (St Martins), but don't be too disappointed if you don't get it. Your second choice may be far better than you realize, and will doubtless be better than the mediocrity of a tier 2 college. Or in other words, don't let your fear of failure, (accepting second choice,) put you off going for what you really want.

Example 3: How I choose where to meet my friends - "the stupidity of crowds"

It's easy to think of secondomics as an argument for following the crowd - like our birds in a v-formation, or our cyclists in a peloton, where those in second place are positioned behind a leader. But this needn't be the case. In fact, secondomics may also be read as a manifesto for the radical instigation of change. And I like to think that, in my small way, I assist in the radical instigation of change every time I decide where to meet my friends for a coffee on a Saturday morning.

London, where I live, is a very big city. It's not densely populated, like New York. It sprawls across miles and miles of suburbia. And every Saturday morning, a large proportion of its population, of almost 8 million, congregates in a relatively small centre to go shopping and meet up for a coffee. Despite London's generous space, this concentration in the centre can make the place feel claustrophobically crowded. The simple task of meeting for coffee becomes a complex logistical operation, involving waiting in line to be served, and aggressive maneuvering in order to secure a seat. By the time I'm finally seated with my friends in a coffee shop, my coffee has usually got cold, and I'll probably struggle to hear what my friends are saying over the elevated noises of those around us.

The whole processes is not unlike our wildebeest in chapter 1, who herd from one watering hole to the next, and then vie to get a space to drink at the water's edge before the group moves on again.

The solution is, of course, to try not to move with the herd. And to do this, we need to find a watering hole that the other wildebeest don't know about, and hope that they won't follow us there. This is, of course, a secondomics strategy, since it involves ranking all of the available drinking establishments, and then opting for the second best, in the hope that you'll avoid the crowds that are all piling into the more popular establishment. The trouble is, of course, that just as wildebeest herd from one watering hole to another, so London's crowds can be quite fickle in terms of which drinking establishment that they tend to frequent.

As we've seen, in every herd, there tend to be the bellwethers - those who are prepared to break from the herd in order to seek out pastures new - frequently (and usually inadvertently) leading the crowd in the process. Our entire culture is built upon the idea of leaders as people with a vision, who, like Moses, lead their followers boldly to the promised land. In practice, reluctant leaders are far more common. They experiment with something new. On occasion they get lucky, and find something worthwhile - like a patch of clover in a meadow. The rest of the herd eyes their spoils with jealous eyes, and descends en mass, usually trampling the remaining clover in the process.

And so it is with coffee shops in central London. You can take your choice between good and busy, or bad and empty. At times, it can seem as is there's nothing in between. But that's not true. With an adventurous spirit, and an inquisitive mindset, there are usually better alternatives, if one strays a little from the beaten track. Maybe it's a café tucked away on the top floor of a bookshop, a small bar on a hard-to-find back street, or a coffee shop attached to a photography gallery. These are places for those in the know, where great coffee and a convivial atmosphere are readily available, without the nuisance of sharing it with an excessively large crowd.

But, of course, it rarely lasts for long. When you're on to something good, word soon gets around, and eventually, the crowd descends, leaving one with no option but to seek out a new social sanctuary. Frequently the previously number one drinking spot, which the crowd has just abandoned. Finding the right establishment is like an eternal game of hide and seek.

And so it is that the serious coffee drinker must always be on the move, never settling on one spot for very long. Always staying ahead of the herd, always prepared to go the extra mile in order to find a coffee drinking experience that is just that little bit better - thanks to the absence of excessive crowds. Such a coffee drinker is the avant-garde - in the vanguard of coffee shop selection. A leader, albeit a reluctant one. And certainly not a follower.

OK, so I'm a self proclaimed coffee drinking trend setter. But how is my pattern of selecting coffee shops indicative of secondomics? The answer lies back in chapter 20, when we considered how secondomics operates over time. There, we saw much the same trend taking place in the Manhattan real estate market, where areas such as SoHo were cheap, and so became popular with an artistic crowd, who made the area fashionable, which in turn attracted wealthy professionals, who pushed up prices, forcing the artists to move on to a new neighborhood. And so the process repeats. For neighborhoods, substitute coffee shops, for artists, substitute me and my fellow vanguard of coffee drinkers, and for the young professionals, substitute the herd.

In secondomic terms, if we rank coffee shops in terms of advantages, such as the quality of the location, the quality of the coffee, the ability of the baristas to make a smooth foam, the tastiness of the pastries, and so on, then the one at the top of the list is the one that will usually attract the herd. The main disadvantage is obviously overcrowding, and when you factor this in, you get the overall payoff, which is essentially how much you will enjoy your visit. Whilst the advantages will remain fairly constant, the disadvantages can change rapidly, as the fickle loyalties of coffee drinkers switch from one establishment to another.

In choosing my coffee shop, I am merely maximizing my potential payoff by taking into account how crowded the coffee shop will be. I'm not choosing to be a leader in coffee fashion. Indeed, that's exactly what I don't want to happen, since I don't want my choice of coffee shop to become too crowded.

When we apply secondomics to our own ranking, this will often result in us preferring to follow, rather than to leader, like a wheel sucker in a peloton. But when we apply secondomics to the rankings of things that we are selecting, such as coffee shops, we will often turn out to be leaders - albeit reluctantly - since secondomics leads us to make a more accurate assessment of payoff, and others will likely notice this and start to copy our successful behavior over time.

An alternative method of decision making

Average outcomes are all that you can expect to come from average choices. If you follow the crowd when choosing where to go for a coffee, you can expect to find somewhere popular, but don't expect to find somewhere to sit down. If you choose your college based entirely upon your confidence of getting in, you can expect to find yourself surrounded by average fellow students.

Secondomics provides us with an alternative method of decision making, one where we must actively seek out the less popular choices, rather than going with the flow. One which may very well turn us into leaders - not like moses, but like a bellwether sheep, whose appetite for clover leads the entire flock to pastures new.

We learn that primacy isn't everything in life. If we always consult the leading specialist, we'll always get the an orthodox perspective on a situation. Seeking out the second-tier expert, like cultivating relationships with friends of friends, can provider a broader perspective, and greater diversity of experience, which can enrich our lives in any number of ways.

Conclusion

Attitudes to risk - America vs Britain

Whilst I was writing this book, a number of my British friends said, "oh they won't like that in America." When I asked why, the explanation would usually be that Americans are so fixated on leadership and coming first that they wouldn't ever be willing to accept that there are advantages to coming second.

When you consider what an extraordinary world power America has become today, in cultural, political and economic fields, its easy to forget the nation's origins as a collection of thirteen rebellious British colonies. In the 18th century, America was forced to enduring the indignity of the British redcoats burning down their towns, and paying native americans to butcher entire families of colonists. It was by no means certain that America would win the war for independence, and they probably would not have done so without financial and military support from the French. General Washington lead a half-starved, half-naked army to victory against all odds.

Of course, the America of today is very different from those thirteen colonies which founded its constitution. Nonetheless, something of the revolutionary spirit of 1776 endures in the nation's psyche today. American culture tends to favor the underdog, since Americans were once underdogs themselves. This is best exemplified by the popularity of the children's book "The Little Engine That Could," where a small engine manages to pull a long train up a mountain, where larger engines refused to try. As the plucky little train pulls its heavy load, it recites the mantra "I-think-I-can," over and over again.

It's the same "I-think-I-can" spirit of the founding fathers in 1776, or of President Barack Obama's "Audacity of Hope." Not only does American culture overtly favor the underdog, but it also elevates the importance of trying over succeeding, which is perfectly exemplified by the nation's entrepreneurial zeal. In Silicon Valley, having a dotcom flop on your resumé is sometimes seen a badge of honor.

In 1776, as brand new nation, America found herself in a secondary position to the British - economically, militarily and in political influence. The founding fathers skillfully took advantage of the benefits of secondomics: they struck a deal with Britain's enemy, France (*disproportionate share of payoff*); they benefitted from the weakening of British forces resulting from other European and naval engagements (*cover from threats ahead*); and they elicited a broad base of international support, including an increasing number in Britain (*support for the underdog*).

Today, the tables are turned. America is the world's most powerful nation. As a result, she comes in for a great deal of unwanted attention - whether it's terrorist attacks, illegal immigration or jealous rival nations. Meanwhile, Britain, once the subjugators of a vast empire, has since presided over the indignity of the breakup of her colonies, and the relegation of her global influence to that of a second tier power, that frequently follows a foreign policy set by her former American colonies. Nonetheless, the British enjoy an exceptionally high standard of living, and benefit from a powerful ally across the Atlantic to protect her when the going gets tough.

As a consequence of these contrasting histories, American culture tends to encourage risk-taking, whilst British culture tends to discourage it. These attitudes to risk have an enormous impact upon our approach to competition: if we have an exaggerated perception of the risk of failure, we may become reluctant to compete altogether; whilst if we're too willing to gamble on victory, we may miss the benefits that second place affords.

Secondomics is not an argument against participating in competition. Far from it. Instead, it is an argument in favor of determining well formed outcomes. Rather than fixating on winning at all costs, secomdomics should remind us to be goal focussed in everything that we do, whilst taking care to assess the payoff of possible outcomes carefully. Britain's risk-averse culture tends to discourage engaging in competitive behavior, for fear of failure. I hope that this book has served to illustrate that the fact that we can't always come first does not mean that we shouldn't compete.

Rather than a manifesto for losers, Secondomics is intended as a call to action to compete, but with a healthy and balanced view of what success and failure in competition may look like. Whilst America has the Little Engine That Could, Britain has Thomas the Tank Engine. Like his American cousin, Thomas is smaller than the average engine, and is frustrated that he doesn't get to pull trains like the bigger engines. Eventually, however, his merits are recognized by the Fat Controller, who gives him his own branch line. So whilst he's never recognized as equivalent to the bigger engines, he at least gets his own second tier line to play on. Not such a bad analogy for where Britain finds herself in international relations today, and whilst she may lack the glory (or ignominy) of her imperial past, Britain can quietly get on with things on her branch line, whilst avoiding many of the pitfalls that are encountered by the larger engines on the main line.

Second class - a word by any other name would spell as sweet

"Gay used to be such a nice word," is a phrase that was very popular in the 1970s, as an older generation struggled to come to terms with the idea that such a jolly term was now being used to refer to such a shocking behavior. Once used a a pejorative term, "gay" has been claimed as a badge of honor by homosexual men, and increasingly women, around the world, as an expression of pride in their sexual orientation. Similarly, other terms of abuse have been adopted by counter cultural or rights movements to demonstrate pride in a minority identity.

This is the way in which our language evolves, and our society's thinking evolves along with it. So, for example, terms like "colored" or "negro" are replaced over time with words like "African-American" or "Black," which are less tainted by negative associates of past prejudice.

I would argue that "second" is another word that has become deprecated as a result of society's shared leadership bias, and that the time has now come for it to be rehabilitated.

Whilst it's hardly as important an issue as the civil rights implications associated with the use of words to describe minority groups, the analogy is still relevant.

We have become fearful of using the term second, since it may hurt people's delicate sensitivities. Take the example of airlines and train companies. Whilst no one has any qualms about promoting a "first class" service, there is a great deal of reluctance in using the term "second class" to refer to the service for everyone else. Travel companies go to great lengths to avoid using this term, for example:

- "World Traveller Class" (British Airways)
- "Tempo Class" (Air France)
- "Comfort Class" (Via Rail)
- "Coach Class" (Amtrak)

It is as if these companies are fearful of offending us by implying that we are regarded in any way as of secondary importance to their first class customers. Of course, in some respects, such as safety, we second class passengers should be regarded as of equal importance to those in first class. But in other respects, it's quite proper that we receive a second class service. Smaller seats, less fancy food, less fancy waiting lounges at the airport. There is no problem with receiving this second class of service. I'm proud to travel second class, every time I see how much cheaper my ticket is, relative to a first class fare.

Traveling second class allows me to go to many more places than would be possible if only first class fares were available. It's a choice that I freely make, and its an option that I am grateful to have. I feel no shame in traveling second class. It doesn't mean I'm a "second class citizen," it simply means I get to maximize my utility by making my travel budget take me further.

This book has the word "second" proudly emblazoned on the cover, and I hope that, over time, others will have the confidence to let this word come back out from the closet, with pride.

The undercover seconomist

I was inspired to write this book after enjoying a meal with friends. When one of our group, Chris, ordered wine, he selected the second cheapest bottle on the menu. I commented on his choice, asking if he always went with the second cheapest, to which he agreed that he did. Joking, at first, I asked Chris if there was a pattern in his behavior. Did he always pick the second choice in life? Was he the kind of guy that took the magazine that was second from top of the stack? Did he find that he always graduated second from top of his class at school?

I only intended this as a joke. One which, upon reflection, might be regarded as thoughtless or cruel. It's not uncommon for me to let my words run away with me, and in doing so to commit such minor transgressions. However, Chris did not seem put out by my joke. Instead, he ran with it, agreeing that this was a fair characterization of his behavior, and offering analogies of similar behavior exhibited by animals, such as the way in which penguins never want to be first into the water, for fear of being caught by leopard seals. Chris was, of course, also joking, but as he continued, it struck me that there was more than a grain of truth to what he was saying.

Chris *was* the kind of person who would favor second over first. He's intellectually brilliant, but there's not a hint of egotism about him. He's very self

CONCLUSION

assured and happy in his own skin. As such, he acts as if he has nothing to prove. Perhaps its this inner strength that helps to inoculate him from the leadership bias that so often serves to occlude our vision. He's also a natural introvert, with a strong sense of ethics, which he draws from his internal resources. As such, his behavior is more likely to be influenced by his own internal reasoning than by the actions of others. In other words, he's unlikely to "rise to the bait" of others, and will not be distracted by their heckling or taunting.

This rare combination of internal strength, introversion and analytic flare makes him one of life's natural seconomists. The reason that Chris did not take offense to me asking if he preferred second to first was because it was true, and he was perfectly comfortable about it. People like Chris may be rare, but they are far from unique.

As you become increasingly aware of the way so much of life can be explained in terms of secondomics, you start to notice seconomists wherever you turn. It's nothing to do with these people having read this book (although hopefully some of them have), but rather, these are people to whom the principles of secodnomics just come naturally. It's in their nature to quietly get on with things and make the best of a situation. They often go unnoticed precisely because seconomists don't stand out from the crowd. They don't come first in a race, you won't find them in a popular café and they're usually behind your field of vision, rather than out in front. And yet, they're immensely successful. Not in an ostentatious way. They're unlikely to parade their success and wealth in your face. They've not been successful in a big, showy way, such as writing a best selling book, or landing a huge contract for their business. It's just that they do pretty well in all the small things, and this steady, modest, incremental success all adds up over time.

The other thing that you'll tend to notice about seconomists is that they tend to be very happy. They've found a balance in their life that works for them, and they like things just the way that they are.

But what comes naturally to some, is not always so easy for others. I'm certainly not a seconomist myself, as much as I admire them. The trouble is that I can't resist getting drawn into competitive behavior, and as my partner will tell you, I can be both a bad winner and a bad loser. An unpleasant combination. So what can we learn from seconomists?

Simply this. Winning in life is not always about coming first, and to pursue true happiness, we should aim to be our best, not the best.

Appendix I

Philosophy, ethics, economics of secondomics

Mathematicians have a way of making simple ideas sound complicated. "Regression to the mean," for example, is a mathematician's way of saying that "you can't win them all". Of course, mathematics encompasses areas of genuine complexity, for which no amount of home spun truisms can provide an adequate account. There is no layman's explanation for the solution to Fermat's last theorem, for example, and so for the vast majority of us, in some situations, we'll just have to take the mathematicians' word for it.

The scope of applications for mathematics is incredibly broad - from the simple, earthly and mundane, to the abstract and etherial. So, where ideas can be expressed in plain English, why resort to mathematics at all? Why not save math for the really difficult stuff, like Fermat, and his theorems? The answer is that mathematics provides us with an alternative perspective on our world. One that can be less skewed by the biases that otherwise tend to occlude our view.

As we look at our world from a mathematical perspective, we start to raise questions about the values that we associate with things, and explore their meanings in comparative terms. Why do we prefer one thing to another? Are we investing too much time in things that don't make us happy? Could we allocated our resources more efficiently, in order to achieve a better result?

The beauty of mathematics is that it may provide us with certainty. We may be confident that two plus two equals four. There are precious few assumptions required in mathematics. As a result, mathematicians enjoy the luxury of being able to prove their theories. A mathematical proof is undeniable - there can be no doubt about its veracity.

Sadly, these absolute certainties do not translate into the real world. In reality, we can never be absolutely certain about anything. Scientist have theories, which are supported by scientific evidence. These theories are what we believe to be true to the best of our knowledge, but they are not true in the sense that a mathematical theorem is true. They could, at any point, be disproved if some evidence to the contrary came to light. Hence Isaac Newton's Principia Mathematica gave us theories that were held to be true of how all matter in the universe behaved, and they proved to be very useful indeed. But later scientific advances, such as relativity and quantum physics, were to disproved the universal veracity of Newton's ideas.

So we can never be certain about the real world in quite the way in which we can be certain about the abstract world of mathematics. When we are applying math to the real world, then, where does this certainty go? If two plus two always equals four in theory, don't you always get four apples when you add two apples together with another two? Well, not exactly. In simple arithmetic, like 2+2=4, we have these wonderful things called rational numbers. We know that one two is always exactly the same quantity as another two. Apples are not like numbers in this respect. No two apples are identical in the real world. There are different sizes, different colors, different flavors, different prices, in different locations... It seems impossible for two things to be identical in the real world. And here we encounter our first shortcoming in the use of math to describe the world around us. A mathematical model of the real world will always be just that. A model. A model of a thing is not the thing itself. It is a simplified representation of that thing.

If the simplification does not result in the loss of anything that is material to the subject of the model, then we may expect to elicit useful results. But the model breaks down if it misses salient points, or misapplies values. For example, if we're attempting to calculate the *value* of the our two plus two apples, this may not be four if I don't have the appetite to eat them all before one of them rots.

And so we must introduce more complexity into our model in order to factor in the value of apples rather than their quantity. We need to allow for how many apples I can eat over what period of time, and how perishable the apples are. If I have different varieties of apple, then some may be more perishable than others, and I may prefer the taste of some to others. Suddenly, our two plus two model looks simplistic in the extreme.

The truth is that in the real world, nothing is as simple as two plus two equals four. And even as we attempt to fine-tune our models, we can never make them perfect. Why? Because mathematics assumes rationality and consistency. And yet human behavior, like so many things in the real world, may be inconsistent and irrational. Maybe one day I fancy Golden Delicious apples, and the next day I fancy Pippins. The factors influencing my changes in taste from moment to moment are so complex, subtle and inconsistent that they defy mathematical modeling.

So whilst abstract mathematics may deal in absolute proofs, and scientists deal in evidence - disprovable, certainly, but reliable nonetheless, those of us who choose instead to focus on human behavior find ourselves at the at the bottom of the heap in terms of reliability. Since we can't mathematically model my taste in apples, we're neither mathematicians nor scientists. What does this leave us with? Economics.

Economists use mathematics in order to model human behavior. An ambitious undertaking, and one which may cause many a pure mathematician or scientist to scoff. Classical economics offers useful tools such as supply and demand, which are proven in the mathematical sense. With this tool, we have a model for how supply and demand are brought into balance through the price mechanism. More buyers than sellers, and the price goes up. More sellers than buyers, the price goes down. Simple and provable, as far as it goes. But not always how things happen in practice.

In practice, people don't always act rationally. What they are prepared to pay for an item is potentially influenced by any number for factors. Surely too many to feed into an economic model. Nonetheless, this does not stop economists from trying. An entire breed, dedicated to this mission - econometricians - attempt to do just this. Building ever more complicated models in an attempt to anticipate what the economy will do next - typically with very little success.

So is this just is a fools errand? Is human behavior too random to ever be successfully modeled? Of course not. The fact that supply and demand is a theoretical model, which never occurs perfectly in the real world does not mean that there isn't some truth to it. It can still help us to understand some aspects of how markets operate. The discipline of applying mathematical models to real life scenarios can also help us to solve problems by abstracting them in such a way as to enable us to find unexpected parallels to the ways in which things operate.

A common criticism applied to economics is that it is a cynical philosophy. These days, Oscar Wilde's much quoted line "the cynic knows the price of everything and the value of nothing" is frequently misattributed to economists. I say misattributed because economics is in fact very much concerned with the value of things, and the non-linear relationship that value has with price. But whilst the economists' approach may not conform to Wilde's definition of cynicism, a better case may be made for it resembling that of the New Oxford American Dictionary, which describes cynicism as "believing that people are motivated purely by self interest". Classical economics is predicated on just such a notion.

In this book, I have predominantly favored scientific accounts of the various subjects that I cover, believing that there is a rational explanation for everything, even if we can't always discern what it may be. As such, whilst I frequently discuss examples of altruism, I haven't blushed or shied away from asking the question "why?" Why does this person behave in an altruistic manner, and what are they getting out of it?

Is it therefore cynical to study human behavior in economic terms? I would argue that it is not, for two reasons. Firstly, because the emerging field of behavioral economics provides us with a framework to study "irrational" behavior, which is economic parlance for acts that are apparently not motivated by self interest. And secondly, because I do not accept that an act of generosity is rendered less meaningful if the actor derives benefit from their own actions. After all, this book is largely concerned with non-zero sum games, which, as we have seen, allow for the possibility of a win-win outcome. Economists have a term for this: "enlightened self interest," whereby, whilst we act in our own self interest, we may also be helping others. For example, people derive considerable feel-good factor by donating money to good causes. This feel-good factor surely doesn't diminish the value of this generosity. Philosophy provides some support for this view. Whilst St Paul wrote that "love seeks not its own interests," arguing that for an act to be deemed virtuous, it must not be motivated by self interest, Thomas Aquinas, in the 13th century, took a different view, arguing that we should love ourselves more than our neighbors, since self-love was an example which we might follow in loving others.

So, whilst I've tried to avoid making moral judgements about the various competitive strategies that this book covers, I would argue that there is nothing intrinsically immoral in applying a skeptical, analytical eye to the motivations that underly human behavior. The fact that an individual derives benefit from his actions need not impact upon his virtuosity, either positively or negatively.

Appendix II

The formula of secondomics

The idea for secondomics came to me one day whilst I was at a restaurant, ordering the second cheapest bottle of wine on the menu. Suddenly, it struck me that there were parallels between what I was doing, and the way in which migratory birds fly in a v-formation. This unlikely realization led to a number of other unexpected parallels, which constitute the main subject matter of the book.

Whilst I've stuck to plain English, rather than math for much of this book, it is also worth exploring the formula that underlies most of the examples. Considering the subject in these abstract terms allows us to provide a tighter definition of our subject, and draw clearer parallels.

What most of these examples have in common is the following principle: *in a ranking system where advantages are allocated relative to rank (or visa versa), the actor in second place may get the highest payoff where there are unique disadvantages associated with first place that are greater than the difference in advantages between first and second place.* Or in other words, how big a prize you get is determined by your rank, so first gets the biggest prize. But sometimes there are also big disadvantages to coming first, in which case, you may be better off coming second.

Essentially, Secondomics is concerned with the difference between rank and payoff. Whilst ranking systems tend to focus exclusively on advantages, payoff is the difference between advantages and disadvantages.

Let's start with our definitions:

```
f = payoff
r = rank
a = advantages
b = disadvantages

f(r) = a(r) - b(r)
```

APPENDIX II

Or in other words, the payoff for r is the difference between the advantages of r and the disadvantages for r.

a(r) > a(r+1)

In most cases there are more advantages of being in a higher rank. Secondomics is concerned with situations where the following is true:

f(2) > f(1)

The payoff for second rank is greater than for first. And since we know the following:

f(1) = a(1) - b(1)
f(2) = a(2) - b(2)

f(2) > f(1) gives us:
a(2) - b(2) > a(1) - b(1)

And since we know that a(1) > a(2), or the advantages of first rank are greater than those of second, then:

b(1) > b(2)

The disadvantages of first rank are greater than those of second.

So in our motoring example in the introduction, the advantage of driving fast (a) is getting home sooner. The disadvantage (b) is the risk of getting caught by the police. Calculating the payoff (f) is tricky, since this involved deducting one type of thing from another. Economists solve this problem by talking in terms of utility - a numeric representation of value that the individual derives from a thing, rather than the quantity of the thing itself. And this utility value allows us to deduct disadvantages from advantages.

The reason that the second fastest car has the highest payoff is because the risk of getting caught (b) is far greater for the fastest car, whilst the difference in terms of getting home sooner (a) is not as great.

With our penguins, the advantage of going first is having the best chance of catching fish (a), the disadvantage is the greater risk of getting eaten by a leopard seal (b). For the second penguin (r(2)), the disadvantages are substantially reduced, but the advantages are only slightly reduced, resulting in the following payoff matrix:

207

SECONDOMICS

	1st Penguin r(1)	2nd Penguin r(2)	3rd Penguin r(3)	4th Penguin r(4)
Chance of catching fish (a)	50	40	30	25
Chance of getting caught by seal (b)	50	25	20	15
Payoff (f)	0	15	10	10

These figures are made-up for the purposes of illustration, since I couldn't make it to Antarctica to ask the penguins personally

This perfectly exemplifies the kind of scenarios that I have sought out in this book - where we see a steady decline in a across r, but a precipitous decline in b from first to second, followed by a subsequent steady decline. Of course, this will not always be the case, but our leadership bias often causes us to miss it when it does happen. And this is a great shame, since it is usually much easier to come second rather than first.

Appendix III

End Game

In the Appendix II, I illustrated how we might express secondomics as a formula. In many situations, targeting second place is a part of a mixed strategy, with the ultimate aim of placing first. We should therefore evaluate the impact that a switch in strategy from targeting second to first place at the end of the game will have upon our formula.

To do this, we must first make a distinction between position and rank. Let's take our peloton of cyclists as an example. Rank (r), in this context, describes where a cyclist is during the race, relative to others in the group. Position (p) is where the participants place at the end of the race. Since, as we've discussed, a cyclist may prefer to spend much of the race in second place, with the intention of coming first at the end, rank and position are two very different values. So this gives us the following:

```
p position
f payoff
r rank during race
a advantage
b disadvantage
```

Position is the payoff for a given rank:

```
p = f(r)
```

And we've already established that payoff is the advantages less the disadvantages for that rank:

```
f(r) = a(r) - b(r)
```

We can consider the race as determined at a certain distance before the finish line. For the sake of example, let's say that at 500 meters before the finish line, we can measure all parameters to determine who's going to win. So $a(r)$ means the advantages of being rank r 500m before the goal post.

$$a(r) = d_r + e_r$$

d = distance ahead of 2nd place (if you're in the lead!)
e = energy left to spend in the final rush

$$a(1) = d_1 + e_1$$
$$a(2) = d_2 + e_2$$

What about disadvantages? Well there's a mental disadvantage to being second - it's hard to push yourself ahead if someone has a lead, so:

$$b(r) = m_r$$

So if second is going to win $f(2) > f(1)$ then:

$$a(2) - b(2) > a(1) - b(1)$$

which gives us:

$$d_2 + e_2 - m_2 > d_1 + e_1 - m_1$$

Since the cyclist in second place has no "distance ahead of second," $d_2 = 0$. Equally, there's no mental disadvantage of being leader so $m_1 = 0$. So:

$$e_2 - m_2 > d_1 + e_1$$

In this example, when we reach 500 meters before the finish line, we're comparing the energy levels of the two cyclists, whilst adjusting for psychological disadvantages, and relative distance from the finish line. We should expect the energy levels of the cyclist in second place to be greater, since he's benefited from the energy efficiency of wheel sucking. Then, at our arbitrary tipping point, our cyclist will abandon his energy efficiency strategy, in favor of the pursuit of victory.

Glossary

Actor: the person who acts in a system or experiment. So, for example, in the context of a game, an actor would be a player; in an economic model, actors may be consumers; in a psychological experiment, an actor would be a test subject; in zoology, an actor would be an organism.

Anchor: a piece of information that biases an actor's judgement. In behavioral economics, an anchor is likely to be an initial price offered for a good, from which an actor will then adjust to determine the good's value.

Allele: one of a number of genes occupying a given position on a chromosome. Humans, and other diploid species, have alleles in pairs, one from each parent. See also: *dominance*.

Altruism: an action that benefits a recipient at the *actor's* expense.

> **Reciprocal altruism**: a group of *actors* behaving altruistically towards each other. The actors must be able to identify and punish individual actors who do not do their fair share of altruistic acts.

> **Kin altruism**: an action that benefits the genetic relatives of an *actor*, at the actor's expense. For example, a parent risking its life to save the life of its offspring.

Attribution: the cognitive process of determining a causal relationships between things.

> **Fundamental attribution error**: a *cognitive bias* where the observer infers an exaggerated causal relationship between two things, without sufficiently allowing for other causal factors and/or baseline data. So for example, concluding that someone has a short temper, because they appear angry, without sufficiently allowing for the circumstances that caused them to become angry.

Availability heuristic: the cognitive process of determining the frequency or likelihood of a thing based upon the ease with which we can recall similar things having occurred in the past.

Axiom: something that we take as a given, assuming that it is a fact because it is useful, even though we may have no means of proving its veracity.

Behavioral economics: the introduction of psychological principles into economics in order to allow for the fact that humans do not always behave rationally to *maximize their utility*.

Classical economics: assumes that markets are self-correcting and that free markets can regulate themselves. Underlying this school of thought are various assumptions, including the *axiom* that *actors* are rational, and will therefore act to *maximize their utility*.

Cognitive bias: a thought process that consistently results in expectations or inferences that differ from empirical data, usually as a result of reliance upon *heuristics*.

Diploid: see *allele*.

Dicta Boelcke: Eight rules for air-to-air combat written by Oswald Boelcke, flying instructor to the Red Baron.

Dominance: the process by which conflict between *alleles* is resolved in *phenotypic expression*. For example, a person with alleles for both blue and brown eyes will have brown eyes, where the brown-eye gene dominates the blue-eye gene.

> **incomplete dominance**: conflicting *alleles* result in a blended outcome. For example, where alleles for red and white petals result in a pink rose.

> **co-dominance**: conflicting *alleles* both are expressed *phenotypically*. For example, in the AB blood type.

Dualism: a philosophy that characterizes things in polarized terms. For example, Descate's mind-body dualism. In secondomics, dualism is concerned with the tendency to frame competition in terms of win-lose outcomes, or *zero-sum games*.

Equilibrium point: a *game theory* concept, where each *actor* has arrived at his optimal *strategy*, assuming that the other actors will not change their strategy.

Fitness: in evolutionary biology, a relative measure of an organism's capacity to effectively reproduce, hence "survival of the fittest."

Game theory: an area of mathematics invented in the 20th century to model the interaction between *actors* in a system as they compete with each other to *maximize their utility*. Game theory has a variety of applications, including economics and evolutionary biology.

GLOSSARY

Gini coefficient: a measure of income distribution in an economy, expressed as a value between 0 and 1. At one extreme 0 represents total equality, where everyone earns the same amount, whilst 1 indicates total inequality, where one *actor* earns all the money, and the others earn nothing.

Hamilton's rule: the principle of kin selection originally observed by W. D. Hamilton, which states that organisms may behave altruistically towards their kin if the cost to the giver is outweighed by the benefit to the recipient, and only in proportion to their genetic relatedness.

Heterozygous: a pair of different *alleles* of a particular gene.

Homozygous: a pair of identical *alleles* of a particular gene.

Heuristic: a rule of thumb used in making a judgement, observation or prediction. Whilst not always accurate, and sometimes resulting in *cognitive bias*, heuristics can be an efficient method of decision making. Heuristics may be used unconsciously, and may be *selected* through evolution.

Kin selection: see *Hamilton's rule*.

Leadership bias: my term for our tendency overestimate the *utility* afforded by first place, typically by mischaracterizing situations as *zero-sum games*, or thinking in excessively *dualistic* terms.

Limbic hijacking: a mental state triggered by a sense of an imminent danger, whereby the parts of the brain associated with conscious rational thought temporarily ceded control to the limbic system, associated with processing emotions, in order to arrive at a rapid fight-or-flight response.

Maximizing utility: see *Utility*.

Metcalfe's law: states that the value of a network is proportional to the square of the number of connected users of the system. This is based upon the assumption that there is a direct correlation between the value of a network and the number of potential connections between nodes on that network.

Mixed strategy: see *strategy*

Negative utility: see *utility*

News stand owner's curse: where browsers at a news stand will take the copy of a magazine that is second-from the top, rather than the top copy, because they prefer to have a magazine that has not been previously browsed. This results in the top copy become quickly dog-eared

Neuro-Linguistic Programming: a school of psychotherapy, coaching and self-help training, encompassing a variety of tools and techniques, with a focus on modeling excellence.

Non-zero-sum game: a category of game in *game theory* whereby the value of the game is not fixed, and therefore one *actor's* gain does not necessarily come at the expense of the other actor/s.

Pareto principle: also known as the 80/20 rule, is a *heuristic* that suggests that in many situations, 80% of a resource is associated with 20% of actors. So, for example, in business, 80% of your income may come from 20% of your clients, or in economics, 80% of a country's wealth may be controlled by 20% of its population.

Payoff: refers to the value of a game in *game theory*. In other words, it's the prize at stake.

Peleton: a grouping of cyclists, cycling on close formation in order to optimize efficiency by riding in each others slipstream.

Peter principle: describes bureaucratic hierarchies, where each *actor* is eventually promoted to his own unique level of incompetence.

Phenotype: a characteristic of an organism that is determined by its genetic makeup.

> **Phenotypic expression**: where an *allele dominates* (or co-dominates), and consequently determines a phenotype in its host organism.

Prisoner's dilemma: a two-player *non-zero-sum* game, whereby two *actors* must collaborate in order to achieve the maximum overall *payoff*, but if one defects, the defecting actor will get a greater individual *payoff*, whilst the other actor will get a substantially lower *payoff*, unless both players defect, in which case, both will get a lower payoff.

Pure strategy: see strategy

Recursive secondomics: a situation where the principles of secondomics are compounded, resulting in the selection of ranks that are lower than second. This is primarily concerned with resource depletion, such as the *News stand owner's curse* and the *SoHo effect*.

Regression to the mean: the tendency of a data series to return to typical values after an exceptional value (either high or low) is recorded.

GLOSSARY

Sales promotion: a marketing discipline concerned with driving short term sales through promotional means such as competitions, free prize draws, or value-add offers.

Secondomic generosity: the behavior of attempting to appear as generous as possible, whilst ensuring that no one ever takes you up on your generosity, because there's always another, more generous alternative offer available.

Secondomics: the study of (competitive) situations where the rank of second offers a greater overall *payoff* than all other ranks.

Selection: the process whereby those genes that are *fittest* replicate more than less fit genes, and as a consequence, fitter *alleles* will replace less fit *alleles* entirely in a population over time. Also referred to as "natural selection".

Strategy: describes the behavior of an actor in a game. A pure strategy would remain the same, regardless of the situation, for example, always betting heads on the flip of a coin; whilst a mixed strategy would combine multiple different strategies, either determined by randomized probability, or based upon the strategy of other actors.

Theory of forms: also known as "theory of ideas". Plato argued that our universe contains imperfect representations of ideal forms that exist in a more perfect universe. This provides a philosophical basis for grouping things into sets sharing similar properties, and then ranking them in accordance to their relative similarity to the idealized form. Whilst Plato's theory of ideas may be at odds with modern scientific empiricism, it continues to influence the way in which we think about rankings, and therefore competition.

Utility: a term used in economics to describe in very general terms, the relative desirability, value or benefit of goods, services, situations or (in the case of secondomics) ranks. In *classical economics*, it is assumed that *actors* will seek to maximize their utility, meaning they will choose the goods and services that suit them best. Current thinking in *behavioral economics* argues that this is not always the case. Actors may not always act rationally. In secondomics, negative utility (or "disutility") refers to the disadvantages of coming first that are frequently overlooked.

Utils: a relative measurement of utility. A good is assigned a higher number of utils than another good if it affords greater utility.

V-formation: describes a flock of migratory birds, who position themselves in flight to form a shape resembling the letter V. The gene for this behavior may have been *selected* because it is aerodynamically efficient.

Winner's curse: the tendency of the winner in an auction to have over-estimated the value of the asset for which they have successfully bid.

Zero-sum: a category of game in *game theory* whereby the value of the game is fixed, and therefore one *actor's* gain always represents a loss to the other actor/s.

Bibliography

Levick, Dr G Murray (1914), Penguins, A study of their social habitat, McBride, Nast & Company, New York

Dawkins, Richard (1976), The Selfish Gene. London: Oxford University Press

Smith, Adam (1776), An Inquiry into the Nature and Causes of the Wealth of Nations. London: W Strahan and T Cadell

James Buchan (2006), Adam Smith and the Pursuit of Perfect Liberty. Profile Books Ltd.

Kelly, Kevin (1999) New Rules for the New Economy: 10 Radical Strategies for a Connected World. Penguin

Duke University (2008, April 17). Why Parents Are Stricter With Older Children. ScienceDaily.

Hamilton, WD. (1964). The Genetical Evolution of Social Behavior

University of Manchester (2008, January 2). Parents Show Bias In Sibling Rivalry. ScienceDaily

Peter, Dr J Lawence; Hull, Raymond (1969). The Peter Principle: Why things always go wrong. New York: William Morrow & Company, Inc.

Adams, Scott (1996). The Dilbert Principle. Harper Business

Ellis, Joseph (2000). Founding Brothers: The Revolutionary Generation. Alfred A. Knopf

Sullivan, Brian K (1983). Sexual Selection in the Great Plains Toad (Bufo cognatus). Behavior

Berard, John D. et al (1994). Alternative Reproductive Tactics and Reproductive Success in Male Rhesus Macaques. Behaviour

Taleb, Nassim Nicholas (2007). The Black Swan, The Impact of the Highly Improbably. New York: Random House Publishing Group

Anderson, Chris (2006). The Long Tail: Why the Future of Business Is Selling Less of More. New York: Hyperion.

Gladwell, Malcolm (2000). The Tipping Point: How little things can make a big difference . Little Brown

Sun Tzu translated by Dr Han Hiong Tan (2001). Sun Zi's The Art of War. H H Tan Medical P/L

Andersson, Malte and Wallander, Johan (2004). Kin selection and reciprocity in flight formation? Behavioral Ecology Vol. 15 No. 1: 158-162

Hockman, Paul (2006). Pack Mentality. Fortune June 1, 2006

Tracy, Jessica L, and Matsumoto, David (2008) The spontaneous expression of pride and shame: Evidence for biologically innate nonverbal displays PNAS
http://www.pnas.org/content/105/33/11655

English, Dave (2003). The Air Up There, 62

http://news.cnet.com/8301-10784_3-9926476-7.html

Tversky, Amos and Kahneman, Daniel (1974). Judgment Under Uncertainty: Heuristics and Biases. Science

Swisher, Kara (2008). Google's PR Head Elliot Schrage Heads to Facebook. AllThingsD. http://kara.allthingsd.com/20080505/googles-pr-head-elliot-schrage-heads-to-facebook/

Brooks, Fred (1975) The Mythical Man-Month. Addison-Wesley

Ventour, Lorrayne (2008) The food we waste. WRAP

Goleman, David (1995) Emotional Intelligence. Bantam Books

Knuth, Donald E (1984). The Toilet Paper Problem. The American Mathematical Monthly, Vol. 91, No. 8

Vandello, Joseph A., et al. (2007) The Appeal of the Underdog. Personality and Social Psychology Bulletin

http://www.telegraph.co.uk/news/uknews/1572972/Wine-list-'a-mystery-to-millions'.html

Westin, Drew (2007) The Political Brain: The Role of Emotion in Deciding the Fate of the Nation. PublicAffairs

Ariely, Dan (2008) Predictably Irrational: The Hidden Forces That Shape Our Decisions. Harper Collins

Andersson, Malte and Wallander, Johan (2004). Kin selection and reciprocity in flight formation? Behavioral Ecology Vol. 15 No. 1: 158-162

Hayek, Fredrich August von (1944) The Road to Serfdom. Routledge

Dawkins, Richard (1982) The Extended Phenotype

http://www.mailonsunday.co.uk/legacygallery/gallery-5490/Superstitious-sportsmen.html?selectedImage=46926

Knight, Sue (2002), NLP At Work: The difference that makes a difference in business Nicholas Brealey Publishing Ltd

Diamond, Jared M (1997) Guns, Germs and Steel. W W Norton

http://www.guardian.co.uk/sport/2004/jul/24/tourdefrance2004.tourdefrance1

Holmgren Henri; Eriksson, Peer (2003) The Classic Avis Advertising Campaign of the 60s. Dakini Books Ltd

http://www.telegraph.co.uk/news/obituaries/1510173/Sir-Freddie-Laker.html

http://news.bbc.co.uk/onthisday/hi/dates/stories/february/5/newsid_2535000/2535297.stm

http://www.virgin.com/AboutVirgin/WhatWeAreAbout/WhatWeAreAbout.aspx

http://news.bbc.co.uk/onthisday/hi/dates/stories/january/11/newsid_2520000/2520189.stm

Watty, Piper (1930) The Little Engine that Could. Platt & Monk

Acknowledgements

I've had a great time researching Secondomics. It has prompted many stimulating conversations with colleagues, friends and family, and I'd like to thank everyone who gave me their input and suggestions.

Special thanks to Martin, my partner, for reading through multiple drafts and helping me to make the science parts more scientific. Thanks to Chris and Sally for supplying the original inspiration; to Justin and Wallis for believing in the project; to Justin for providing robust and honest feedback on the first draft; to Danny & Piotr for their unstinting support; to Danny for such thorough feedback on draft one; to Costas, Justine, Thomas, Vicky, Simon, Ian, Diana, Mum and Dad for reading my flaky first draft; to Ben, Jennie, Thomas and Birgit, for listening to me indulgently; to Will for telling me about toads and baboons; to Shannon for her excellent advice; to Leander for his support; and to all the partners at Starbucks on Earls Court Road, Old Brompton Road and Chiswick Park for serving me great coffee whilst I was writing.

A big thank you to all my friends and family in London, Cumbria, Devon and Sweden.

Graham Bower is the founder and Managing Director of Taglab (www.taglab.com), a digital strategy and web design agency in London, UK. With a fourteen year background in business strategy for creative industries, Graham's work has appeared in a wide range of publications. In 2008, Graham underwent successful surgery and chemotherapy for cancer, whilst continuing to manage his business. He's now enjoying his own second chance in life.